THE NEW BATTLE OF BRITAIN

A Conservation Handbook and Directory

1-6-72

THE NEW BATTLE OF BRITAIN

A Conservation Handbook and Directory

H. F. Wallis

CHARLES KNIGHT & CO. LTD.
LONDON
1972

Charles Knight & Co. Ltd.
11/12 Bury Street, London, EC3A 5AP

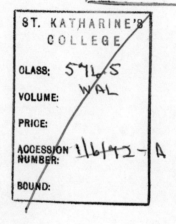
Copyright © 1972
H. F. Wallis

Set and printed in Great Britain by Staples Printers Limited
at their Rochester, Kent, establishment

SBN 85314 124 X (hard cover)
SBN 85314 125 8 (soft cover)

To my wife, Elizabeth

Contents

Preface

They are calling 1970 'European *Conversation* Year' – and not without reason. There has indeed been too much talk and too little action on this front. So let me say at once that I have written this book as a guide to action, and that if it does not inspire or provoke someone somewhere to do something, I shall deem it to have failed.

Not only do I feel that much of the talk has led nowhere, but that some of it has actually been counter-productive. Those doom-laden publications and television programmes – designed perhaps to shock people into a realisation of the gravity of the 'Eco-Crisis' – may produce a feeling of helplessness before such vast and menacing problems; an inclination to 'switch off' and let tomorrow go hang—precisely the kind of reaction calculated to ensure that the threatened catastrophe takes place.

Thus I thought it necessary to try and redress the balance, as it were, by showing that there had been some considerable achievements in the environmental field already and that more were in prospect, so we need not despair.

There has also, to my mind, been too much emphasis on the problems and too little on how they can be and are being tackled, and by whom, and in particular what part the ordinary citizen can play.

I felt that the role of local government in regard to the environment had not been sufficiently stressed. As one concerned in this field as a journalist for many years, I thought I had something to contribute here, not only in relating what I had learnt that was relevant, but in trying to win some belated recognition for those men and women in local authorities who have been working on these problems for decades before European Conservation Year, and whose efforts have been largely disregarded by a previously uncaring public.

The main problem for anyone trying to produce a book of this kind is to know where to draw the line. The environment is a very big subject indeed. It really ought to include something on housing, for instance, which for millions of people is far more important than other matters which occupy the attention of environmental writers.

But if one is to cover the field adequately, one cannot perforce give as much space as one would like to individual aspects, many of which warrant a book in themselves. This imposes severe limitations at the outset, so I must stress that the book can do no more than provide introductory or background material on all these matters. For this reason 'further reading' lists are included.

I hope the book will prove especially useful to new councillors and MPs, who

ix

cannot afford to go 'naked into the debating chambers', where environmental questions are sure to be discussed to an ever-widening extent in the coming years. I also hope members of amenity societies will find it useful in helping to tackle problems arising in their areas, and that it might contribute to public enlightenment, without which we cannot hope to win this battle.

Finally, my thanks are due to a number of people who have helped in the production of this book. Those who read the manuscripts have included Professor David Donnison, of the Centre for Environmental Studies, Mr Ian Christie, of the Civic Trust for the North-West, Mr J. Skitt, transport and cleansing manager, Stoke-on-Trent. Mr J. C. Holliday, of the Dept of Town Planning, Lanchester Polytechnic, Coventry, and Mrs Dily Cossey, secretary of the Birth Control Campaign.

May I also thank Pergamon Press for permission to reproduce material on common land and rights of way first published in their *Take Home Books* series and David Peschek, editor of *Municipal Review* for permission to use extracts from an article on pollution which first appeared in that journal.

I am also indebted to my wife, Elizabeth, who was, and is, a constant source of inspiration and who also happens to be a qualified librarian – she produced the index and compiled the directory. Mrs June Neale typed the manuscript with her customary skill.

Note: *Where appropriate, details of the most important legislation, and bodies responsible for administering it or giving advice, are noted in the ensuing pages. It should be borne in mind, where local authorities are mentioned, that the local government system is in process of radical change and that new councils are due to come into being by April 1, 1974.*

1. A Question of priorities

From time to time nations, as well as individuals, should take stock of where they are heading. This not only means assessing how much progress has been made towards predetermined goals, but questioning the goals themselves.

For generations Britain, along with most other states, has been wedded to the idea that everything will come right so long as the gross national product continues to expand. While this has never been sufficient in itself – surely of equal importance is how the 'cake' is distributed? – it is even less valid today, as other factors have come more and more into the picture.

Governments of all political persuasions have constantly maintained that only through increased growth can the needs of the under-privileged in our society be met. If this were so, one would have expected poverty in Britain to have been virtually wiped out by now. This is far from being the case. After decades of growth, there are still more than one-third of a million adults and a million children in this country in old-standard initial poverty, and less than one-half of this is being removed by the social security provisions.*

The inequalities are still striking, with the top 5 per cent of income earners taking about one-quarter of the national income, and there are signs that the gap between rich and poor could be widening. One of the reasons for this is that machines are replacing men at an increasingly rapid rate. There has also been a big rise in unemployment, with some forecasters suggesting that it could reach well over the million mark by the end of 1972.

A similar pattern has emerged elsewhere. In America, which has been more firmly committed to the growth concept than we have, the inequalities are even more blatant. A milestone in the history of mankind was passed by the United States towards the end of the 'sixties when surveys showed that the average American family was spending more on luxuries than necessities.

Robert and Leona Rienow say in their book, *Moment in the Sun*, that lavishness has become commonplace. 'The vast, almost endless assortment of baubles – usually for Christmas-giving – such as gold golf tees at 35 dollars each and a sable lipstick brush in a gold case for 27 dollars, comes somewhat closer to distinguishing the United States as an economic wonderland. But mostly it is the mahogany-cased colour television, the dryers, movie cameras and such appurtenances of middle-class living that establish our pace. And celebrity homes throughout the nation, with their seven or eight baths, numerous fireplaces and 900-square foot S-shaped swimming pools are common enough to characterise our affluent society.'

* Circumstances of Families, Ministry of Social Security (HMSO 1967).

This is the country where obesity is such a constant threat that millions of dollars a year are spent on reducing pills – 30 per cent of women from the poorest levels of American society are said to be grossly overweight, and we have heard about the poor health of a high proportion of army draftees.

On the other hand, it is the country where nearly one in four children – 15 million – now lives in poverty. Nearly half of all the children in families of five or more are listed among the poor.

This preoccupation with growth and relative disregard for distribution of the fruits thereof has important international consequences, too. The advanced countries, and especially the USA, are collaring so many of the world's natural resources that to continue along these lines could produce an explosive situation in the years ahead. If present trends continue, the United States, with $9\frac{1}{2}$ per cent of the world's population, could within 15 years be consuming some 83 per cent of all the raw materials produced by the entire world. What a grim prospect for the rest of us, especially those countries which already have a desperate struggle to feed their existing populations! The United Nations Food & Agricultural Organisation has estimated that around 10,000 people could already be dying from malnutrition throughout the world every day. Already shortages of important raw materials are occurring and we have been warned that others on which we rely cannot last for ever. Unless the advanced nations change course and conserve stocks, we could be heading for catastrophe. (see section 2, 'The Price of People'.)

Let us not become bemused by our technological achievements. Even if we could be kept alive as suggested by a diet of pills and a kind of bread made from algae – the green slime on stagnant pools – how many of us would want to?

Apart from this supremely important conservation problem, there are other sound reasons for questioning the worship of growth. Although a fantastic volume of consumer goods have poured off Britain's assembly lines in recent times, it has not led the inhabitants of these islands to revel in the good life. There have been considerable benefits, it is true. People are indisputably better fed, clothed and housed than they were at the turn of the century, and welfare services have improved out of all recognition. Millions now have money to spare for a car, colour television, Continental holidays and the like. Yet far from producing a happy, contented people, discontent is widespread.

Dr Roger Tredgold, physician-in-charge of the department of psychological medicine at University College Hospital, London, told the Royal Society of Health congress in 1971 that millions of people, bored with their jobs or surroundings in this 'sick' society, were finding outlets for their frustrations which could destroy us. After referring to widespread aggression, especially on the roads, sex obsession and drug worship, he declared: 'The dangers of destructive action are far greater than ever before and could exterminate the human race as neither the barbarian invasions of the Dark Ages, nor the Black Death, ever really threatened.'

Many other expert observers are voicing similar fears. The gross national product may be rising – although too slowly for some people – but this is clearly doing little or nothing to remove these discontents. Indeed, by increasing the inequalities between the haves and have-nots, it could be perpetuating them.

Nor is it even satisfying those who have. Gordon Rattray Taylor, in *The*

Doomsday Book, points out that 'one of the best-established principles in economics is the one which says the more you have of everything the less satisfaction you get from having some more (the law of diminishing returns). One car may make a great difference to your life; the fourth car just gives you the choice of whether you will go there in the sedan or the convertible. One crust may save a man from starvation; a thousand crusts would simply be a litter problem.'

Standards of living may have risen, but what about the quality of life? Who can deny that our cities, in which most people live, have become uglier, noisier and generally more oppressive, and that our countryside and coast have been wracked by the urban invasion? Or that one consumer product, the motor car, has created the most formidable environmental challenge of our times? With road space limited not only by the extent of our land but by other more pressing demands on it, how much longer can we tolerate unrestricted production for the home market? Dare we go on passively accepting the annual loss of 50,000 acres of farmland and open spaces to urban purposes, which include the building of more roads for cars and factories for other consumer goods?

Some people say there is no need to worry unduly as we shall still have plenty of open space left by the end of the century. Do they suggest that the process should then come to a halt? And if not, when is some government going to say 'enough'? Or must we wait until the whole of Britain is built up? There is a case for scaling down this development now, before priceless assets are lost forever. Food is one consumer product we are likely to need more and more of, and everyone is agreed that recreational demands will go on rising.

Do we really need the mountain of packaging foisted on us by industry and for which, as Mr Peter Walker, Secretary of the Environment, has pointed out, the housewife pays twice – for the packaging itself and again for its disposal? There is a further cost to the community in the effect on our countryside and coast of all those plastic cups and bottles, and other paraphernalia which lie around for years because they are not broken down by natural processes.

Production of this packaging, incidentally, forms part of the GNP. So does that part of our consumption of petrol which has gone up as a result of traffic jams. And the more bombs we produce, the higher our GNP. How can we measure progress in such a fashion?

Wouldn't we all be better off if manufacturers devoted their resources to improving the quality of the product or cutting down pollution? One of the most deplorable examples of a warped sense of values is the attention paid to motor car styling and performance, and the relative disregard for safety. Basic safety measures, as Ralph Nader has pointed out, would cost no more than £50 for the average car. And what justification can there be for subjecting millions to yet another intrusion into their privacy in the form of supersonic aircraft, so that a few businessmen can get there an hour or two earlier?

Values elsewhere are even more lopsided. America has prospered economically to a much greater extent than we have, but the environmental consequences have been shattering. Conditions in New York, for instance, are so unbearable that the city is fast becoming a 'ghetto' for the under-privileged, and this situation is reflected to some degree in other American cities. The problems of pollution and desecration of natural beauty are far worse than ours.

But the country which has easily topped the 'growth league', with an annual average increase of 12.4 per cent from 1958–68, is Japan. It also has the worst pollution problem in the world. So grave is it, in fact, that the question is being seriously asked as to whether the country will be habitable by the 1980s.

For many Japanese citizens it would seem barely habitable now. Tokyo's rivers are open sewers and the city air so toxic that parents dare not allow their children to play in the streets at certain times of day – while policemen on point duty have to be given periodical supplies of oxygen to enable them to continue. Pollution is causing widespread illness and even death. Forty-five people have died from eating mercury-contaminated fish and 71 have had their central nervous system impaired, resulting in numbed hands and legs, defective speech and loss of sight. Certain riverside dwellers have developed fragile bones which fracture easily due to the release of cadmium from a mine. Tokyo is four times noisier than New York, which is not a quiet city by any means (see also 'Crisis in the City').

Here is the ultimate absurdity of boarding the technological chariot with no real consideration of where it is going. Japan may have succeeded in raising family incomes – but what is the purpose of that if living conditions in the widest sense are so intolerable?

We in Britain owe our relatively civilised surroundings to the extent to which people have successfully resisted the blandishments of governments to raise the growth rate without proper regard for the consequences. We have had to be content with a modest rate of around 2.7 per cent. But, as Mr H. V. Hodson, former Editor of *The Sunday Times*, wrote in that paper (Jan. 10, 1971): 'It has long been apparent that the British people do not really care about economic growth; that is to say, they do not care enough to make the sacrifices and efforts necessary to get it. But', he added, 'despite this it is one of the most agreeable countries of the world to live in, for any class of people. Maybe the British have a better sense of values than their economic rivals.'

The planning system we have created, which more and more nations are seeking to emulate, and the positive conservation measures taken in this country have helped to preserve qualities in the British scene which are of inestimable value. James Reston wrote in the *New York Times* that 'while they (i.e. the British) are no longer showing us how to run the modern world, they may just teach us how to live in it.'

This could explain why a growing number of Americans are making their homes in Britain and why the 'brain drain', by all accounts, would seem to have gone into reverse. In the May, 1971, issue of *The Ecologist*, Brian Johnson, who is a Fellow of the Institute for the Study of International Organisation and the Institute of Development Studies at Sussex University, stated that the 'astonishing flood' of American applications for British academic, scientific and business posts confirms that many Americans have grasped the difference between 'standard of living' and 'quality of life'. The British Embassy in Washington, he said, recently had to double its staff dealing with work permit applications of Americans wanting to move to Britain. His own university was deluged by American applicants. The ratio of American to British applications for scientific appointments was running as high as 10 : 1. Many of these applicants held astonishingly senior positions and were prepared to accept salary cuts of 50–60 per cent to come here.

Britain's tourist trade has increased dramatically in recent years, too, and is now running at record levels. No fewer than 6,730,000 overseas visitors came here in 1970–1, 16 per cent more than the previous years, and spent £572 million The target for 1975 is 10 million.

Despite the enormous strain of a rising population with rising demands of all kinds, we have somehow managed to keep this country sufficiently sane and attractive for others to want to come here. The British people have recognised that the 'good life' does not consist merely of piling up consumer goods, but that intangibles like beauty, peace, rest and relaxation, and clean surroundings have an indispensable place.

Nor is it the case, as Mr Anthony Crosland alleged in a Fabian Society pamphlet (*A Social Democratic Britain*) that concern with the environment is largely a middle-class matter. Mr Crosland, who was the Minister with responsibility for the environment in the last Labour Government, berated conservationists for what he called their 'class hypocrisy'.

'Their approach is hostile to growth in principle and indifferent to the needs of ordinary people', he declared. 'It has a manifest class bias and reflects a set of middle- and upper-class value judgments. Its champions are often kindly and dedicated people. But they are affluent and fundamentally, though of course not consciously, they want to kick the ladder down behind them.'

In the first place, conservationists are not some peculiar homogeneous sect, but ordinary human beings with a wide range of attitudes. Certainly they are not opposed to all economic growth; this would be absurd. What they are saying is that if we want to keep this country reasonably green and pleasant in future, when the pressures will be unprecedented, we shall have to give more attention to protecting the environment and hence less to development as such.

His inference that the needy will be helped by increased growth has already been revealed as arguable. In his book, *The Costs of Economic Growth*, Dr E. J. Mishan shows that this is really a matter of reallocating what we already have. To make a dent in this problem, he writes, a sum of about half a billion pounds a year would have to be transferred to the under-privileged group – about 2 per cent of our national income. A reduction of our defence budget to about three-quarters of the present estimate would suffice to provide it.

Do those who live near the runways or beside the motorways and other main roads come from the middle classes? Do they enjoy the scream of the jets and the perpetual roar of traffic? Were not most of those who took part in the angry demonstrations over the Westway motorway in London working-class folk? And what about that notable protest by the inhabitants of Port Tennant, Swansea, who picketed a factory in an anti-pollution campaign? A government survey into life in high blocks of flats showed that working-class tenants were more concerned about the 'appearance of the estate' than almost anything else.

Mr Crosland should not assume that because the voice of the middle classes is heard more often on such matters, only they are concerned about them. They just happen to be more articulate. Throughout history middle-class speakers and writers have voiced working-class aspirations.

The matters with which I shall be dealing in this book are not the concern of this or that section of the community alone, but of the whole of society. And since nothing less than our survival is involved, it seems sensible that we should be prepared to devote more of our resources to these purposes. If this means accepting a lower rate of economic growth, it need not worry us unduly. The essential thing is to get our priorities right.

Should we continue to pursue policies which mean further indulging the whims and fancies of the better-off at the expense of their less fortunate brethren – and which really satisfy no-one – or should we seek to transfer more of our energies towards ensuring a fairer distribution of our national resources and improving the quality of life? Does space exploration offer the kind of rewards for humanity which, say, reclamation of the deserts or studies of the relatively undiscovered oceans would be likely to produce? Should we go for bigger and faster aircraft or safer and quieter ones? Is it more important to be able to travel freely by car about our towns and countryside or that town and country should be enjoyable to live in and to visit?

These are the sort of questions we shall need to ask in future. And it follows that we shall have to ensure that such alternatives are examined *by the whole nation* as a matter of course, not resolved by politicians wedded to technical advance at all costs and foisted on an unwilling community.

This means using our collective strength as a people to see that our representatives in parliament and local government are made fully aware of our concern with the environment, so that they place the proper degree of emphasis on conserving and enhancing the beauty, character and natural resources of these islands.

That securing such radical changes of approach will be no easy task seems self-evident. We shall not only face deeply ingrained traditions, attitudes and prejudices, but we shall be seeking to do no less than persuade or cajole a profit-orientated society into forsaking its natural inclinations for short-term gain in favour of broader objectives – and at a time when world competition is growing fiercer.

Professor Barry Commoner, the American biologist, has shown that one of the main reasons why pollution has increased so sharply in the United States since the war is that the captains of the technical-industrial complex have adopted production patterns which do more damage to the environment – plastics have replaced wood and glass; detergents have replaced soap, fertilisers have replaced land and so on – and that these determiners of our collective fate have done so because they saw the prospect of more markets, more possibilities for growth and more profit.

But something is stirring from which we can take heart. Charles Reich, in an article in the *New Yorker* (Sept. 26, 1970) – later reproduced by Penguin – gave vivid expression to the new environmental awakening thus . . .

'There is a revolution under way. It is not like revolutions of the past. It has originated with the individual and with culture, and if it succeeds it will change the political structure only as its final act. It will not require violence to succeed and it cannot be successfully resisted by violence. It is now spreading with amazing rapidity and already our laws, institutions and social structure are changing in consequence. Its ultimate creation could be a higher reason, a more human community and a new and more liberated individual.'

Further reading

Arvill, Robert, *Man and Environment*, Penguin, 1967.
Barr, John (ed.), *The Environmental Handbook*, Pan Books, 1971.
Barr, John, *The Assault on our Senses*, Methuen, 1970.
Rienow, Robert, and Leona Train, *Moment in the Sun*, Ballantine, 1st pr. 1969.
Mishan, E. J., *The Costs of Economic Growth*, Penguin, 1969.
Holman, Lafitte, Spencer, Wilson, *Socially Deprived Families in Britain*, Nat. Ccl of Social Service, 1970.
Galbraith, J. E., *The Affluent Society*, Hamish Hamilton.
Galbraith, J. E., *The New Industrial Estate*, Penguin, 1969.
McConnell, Brian, *Britain in the Year 2000*, Times Mirror, 1970.
Taylor, G. Rattray, *The Doomsday Book*, Thames and Hudson, 1970.
Nicholson, Max, *The Environmental Revolution*, Hodder and Stoughton, 1970.
Gresswell, Peter, *Environment: An alphabetical handbook*, John Murray.
Protection of the Environment, HMSO, Cmnd 4373, 1970.

2. The price of people

Is not a country over-populated when its standards are lower than they would be if its numbers were less? – J. Maynard Keynes

Among the long-established beliefs now being challenged is the idea, cleverly nurtured by successive governments and commercial interests, that more people means more growth and higher living standards. That this challenge has been so long delayed seems inexplicable when one appreciates that all the matters to be discussed in this book are influenced by the number of people inhabiting these islands. On the other hand, it is only quite recently that the scale of environmental disaster we could be faced with has been appreciated, and thus only recently that the causes have been looked at by a wider public and the experts listened to.

There are also, it is true, religious and ethical reasons why the subject has so far been taboo and why, even when some odd individual has asked an awkward question, people have been ready to accept the answer, shrug their shoulders and turn to other things.

One of the answers given is that Malthus, who predicted that population would outstrip food supply, had been proved wrong in the past and there was every likelihood that, with another 'green revolution' ahead, he would be proved wrong in the future.

There would also seem to be a feeling that there is some kind of natural law regulating population growth with which it would be disastrous to tamper; that we have to accept people in the numbers so determined much as we accept the weather. Closely allied to this, and largely influenced by religious teaching, is the belief that there exists a sacred right to bear children in numbers which are purely a matter of family choice, and that no government or community has any

7

right to interfere in this. Here, as in the previous case, the doctrine of acceptance prevails.

However, the 'permissive society' is not likely to countenance such taboos and restraints for long and the barriers are, indeed, being broken down. A milestone in this process was the debate in the House of Lords in February, 1971, when Lord Snow predicted a black future unless action was taken to reduce world population, and Lord Beaumont of Whitley called for a population policy for Britain and advocated free contraceptives on the National Health Service. Events moved very fast since then and in the following May a Select Committee on Science & Technology called for immediate government action 'to prevent the consequences of population growth becoming intolerable for the everyday conditions of life'.* The report recommended the setting up of a special government office to tackle the problem.

This would have been unthinkable a year or two back. The discussion has been taken up by economists, who have been arguing about the contention that population growth leads to economic growth and higher living standards. This, too, is significant, because economists have not been noted for their concern with the environment – I suspect, for instance, that their definition of standards of living would omit most of the matters with which we are concerned in this book. If they cannot agree within their restricted definitions, therefore, this is quite remarkable.

It used to be thought that, with machines taking over more and more of the jobs formerly done by men, the demand for human labour would tend to decline. Like the Malthusian theory, however, this did not seem to be the case for a long time. Such was the world demand for the products of the machine that more human labour was called for, not less. We would now seem to be reaching a point, however, where to feed more labour into the production machine will only lead to widespread unemployment or under-employment.

One is seeing in America particularly, where automation has been carried further than anywhere else, the emergence of a substantial and widening pool of unemployment, much of it long-term and defying all attempts to reduce it. Millions of unfortunate folk are being succoured at a meagre subsistence level by state benefits.

In Britain, too, increased growth still leaves substantial numbers by the wayside. Unemployment or under-employment is leading to poverty on a rapidly rising scale – the Child Poverty Action Group estimated that this had doubled in the four years up to 1971. Hard to imagine this happening in such an affluent society.

It may be possible by determined action to alleviate such effects, but these trends should certainly make us pause to question our assumptions about population. Elsewhere the situation is only too starkly clear. India increased food production from 55 million tons on the granting of independence to 72 million tons in 1965, yet with 140 million more mouths to feed, consumption actually went down on a per capita basis from 12·8 ounces a day to 12·4.

Japan, too, has seen its economic advance wiped out by population increase and Egypt's population has risen so fast since the Aswan Dam was embarked upon that the benefits it will bring could be largely offset. At present rates Egypt will have twice as many people in 15 years' time. Nobody gains if twice as many

8
          * House of Commons Paper 379 (HMSO £2.40).

goods have to be shared among twice as many people. And even if the advanced countries can achieve rates of production which are higher than the rates of population increase, are the benefits likely to be more than marginal?

Just as there would seem to be a need to re-examine this particular argument, so it would appear we should take another look at Malthus. Despite the technological advances, it remains true that world resources are not unlimited and rising populations and living standards are bound to exert more and more pressure on these resources. We are told, for instance, that if British and American plane-makers sell their planned total of supersonic airliners, the world could face a critical oil shortage within 15 years, and that even at present levels the world's forests could not supply everyone with a small daily paper.

The pressures being placed on these resources are unprecedented. Two-thirds of the people who have ever lived in the world have been born in this century.

The outlook for Britain

Britain's population is expected to rise by the end of the century from the present 56 million to around the 70 million mark. To feed this number the Agricultural Research Council has estimated that the country will need at least twice the existing net production of home-grown food. Can this be achieved on a rapidly shrinking land area? – some 50,000 acres a year of agricultural land and open space are being surrendered to other purposes. By the year 2000 an area the size of Devon and Cornwall combined is expected to be buried under concrete and asphalt.

Dr Paul Ehrlich, Professor of Biology, Stanford University, California, prophesied at a symposium on population called by the Institute of Biology in September, 1969, that Britain would be extremely hard-pressed to feed her population by the end of the century. He referred to the decline of world fisheries due to over-exploitation and pollution, and to the impossibility of expanding terrestrial agriculture because of the danger of soil erosion. 'If current trends continue,' he said, 'by the year 2000 the United Kingdom will simply be a small group of impoverished islands, inhabited by some 70 million hungry people, of little or no concern to the other 5–7 billion people of a sick world.'

Exaggerated? Cheap sensationalism? Turn to your newspapers of August, 1970, and you will find there the report of an official inquiry into the health of farmland soils, which found that in parts of England and Wales the fertility and structure of the soil had broken down to 'dangerous proportions'. This is happening here and now, not at some far-distant date.

But even if British agriculture could accept the challenge, will the whole country become a mass-production factory for human life? This was the question asked by L. R. Taylor (Rothamsted Experimental Station, Harpenden) in a brilliant introduction to the symposium proceedings.

If 'natural' population control by war, famine and disease were rejected, he added, man must find his own acceptable controls – there was no third alternative.

More than 90 per cent of biological and social scientists attending the symposium felt that the optimum population for Britain had already been exceeded – Dr Ehrlich thought it should be well under 20 million. One hopeful sign he saw was that population control should be easier to achieve in the developed countries where it posed the biggest threat in relation to mankind, because these countries were the major wasters of protein and non-renewable resources and the source of the most threatening environmental decay. We in Britain consume in a lifetime 10 to 20 times as much of the earth's resources as the average Indian and pollute on a similar scale, so that our population of 56 million could be more of a global disaster than India's 500 million.

America's consumption of world resources is fantastic. Hugo Fisher, administrator of the Resources Agency of California, has estimated that the U.S., with about $9\frac{1}{2}$ per cent of the world's population, will by 1980 be consuming some 83 per cent of all the raw materials and resources produced by the entire world. What will the situation be like elsewhere? According to a statement issued by 38 Nobel Prize winners led by Sir Julian Huxley, unless a favourable balance of resources and population is achieved without delay, 'there is in prospect a Dark Age of human misery, famine, under-education and unrest which could generate growing panic, exploding into wars fought to appropriate the dwindling means of survival.'

Back in 1965 the United Nations Food and Agricultural Organisation estimated that 10,000 people were dying every day from malnutrition throughout the world.

Even if food needs could be met, however, could we also provide all these people with decent housing and educational opportunities, bearing in mind that we seem to be constantly struggling to catch up with existing pressures in these fields? Could we in Britain cope with triple the number of cars on the roads and meet the needs for more recreation and leisure facilities on land which will by then be far more built up than it is at the moment? Will not our towns become more congested still and will our remaining unspoilt countryside and coast survive the pressures?

Much of Britain – central Wales and the Highlands of Scotland – is thinly populated, but England, with 910 persons to the square mile, has a density well above that of what we are accustomed to regard as the teeming State of Madras. Certainly London and the south-east of England, with over 17 million people, has one of the biggest concentrations of people to be found anywhere and the Highlands of Scotland and depopulated Central Wales, which make the total picture look less alarming, might be on the moon so far as the everyday lives of these inhabitants are concerned.

Effects of overcrowding

In his *Doomsday Book*, Gordon Rattray Taylor points to some of the apparent effects of high-density living, quoting a 'classic study' in Chicago in the 1930s which showed that crime, mental sickness, suicide and drug-taking rates were high at the centre and declined steadily as one moved farther away.

'Under natural conditions', wrote Desmond Morris in *The Human Zoo*, wild animals do not mutilate themselves, masturbate, attack their offspring, develop stomach ulcers, become fetishists, suffer from obesity, form homosexual pair-bonds. Yet confined in the unnatural conditions of captivity, they exhibit just such neurotic behaviour patterns common to man caged in his crowded cities.'

In this frenetic jostling and elbowing scramble, human beings are depersonalised; made to feel small and insignificant, mere bubbles on a torrent of humanity. And the featureless concrete towers which confine them as they struggle for room to breathe bear witness to the dominance of the machine.

Attempts to thin out the numbers of people by redistribution have not been conspicuously successful. Most of the movement has been away from the cities into the greener, more spacious areas beyond. The population of the South-East is actually expected to rise still further – from 3 to 4 million by the end of the century. The consequent decline of the world's great cities has been one of the sadder aspects of 20th-century life. Are we ready to face the probability of further decline leading, perhaps, to urban anarchy, by doing nothing about the population problem?

Time is most definitely not on our side. Any change of approach is bound to take a long while to produce results. We had a chance to do something way back in 1949, when the Royal Commission on Population recommended that our numbers should be stabilised, but nothing was done. Since then the population has gone up by seven million.

People seem to think that having a population policy means telling women how many babies they should have. This would, of course, be quite unacceptable. What it does mean is establishing certain aims and considering how best these might be achieved within the framework of a society such as ours, with its traditional respect for individual liberty.

The alternative is tantamount to conniving at the increases taking place, which would certainly lead to gross interference with individual liberties in the long run. But governments have gone even further than turning a blind eye. Family allowances, social benefits and tax reliefs all favour the large family. Politicians of all parties, unwittingly or not, have also played their part in developing social attitudes which put child-bearing on a pedestal and frequently lead to women having more children than they can properly support. In this they have been aided and abetted by women's magazines, the communications media and so on.

How else can we have arrived at a situation where the mother of a large family is treated as some kind of heroine, while a childless couple are subject to a social stigma, however slight; to a thinly veiled charge of not doing their duty to society? Strange how society can be brought into a situation which is supposed to be purely personal and private when it suits certain interests.

Why should failure to adopt a population policy be any more justifiable than failure to tackle any other social problem? Like those other problems, it won't melt away if nothing is done.

We would not be doing anything unprecedented in human history. Far from it. Thirty developing countries have national programmes aimed at cutting the birth rate. Nearly all Asia, representing 58 per cent of the world population, has adopted official policies.

Japan belatedly introduced state-supported legal abortion and birth control in the late forties and succeeded in halving the birth rate in ten years. In India there is a national birth control and sterilisation programme, and abortion is being legalised. And despite Marxist reservations about Malthus, even the Communist countries have acted to check population growth. China is reported to be the only developing nation currently making all population-control methods, including abortion, freely available. It is said that the Pill has become available in a little red envelope with a picture of Chairman Mao on it.

In 1966 the United Nations General Assembly called upon the various branches of the system to assist in developing and strengthening national and regional facilities for training, research information and advisory services in the population field.

Britain's task looks, on the face of it, nothing like so formidable. To achieve zero growth, which is probably the best we can hope for, we would have to reduce the average number of children per family from 2·4 to 2·1. This seems eminently attainable, until one realises that only during the 1930s depression did the figure sink to 2·1 in this country.

Later, and fewer, marriages held down the population in the earlier decades of this century. Thirty years ago one out of four women in the 20–24 age group married; nowadays well over one-half in this group do so. In 1931 only 10 per cent of women married under the age of 20; now it is about 30 per cent. The present recovery in fertility has also been influenced by a marginal but very important increase in the average number of children per couple (Evidence to the Select Committee on Science and Technology, HMSO, May 13, 1970).

Another important factor contributing to population pressure is that people are living longer and fewer children are dying in infancy. For example, in 1901 a newly-born boy could expect to live to about 48; in 1966 this had risen to 68. A newly-born girl could expect to live to 52 in 1901; in 1966 this had risen to nearly 75. Death rates in boys under four years in 1901 were 57 per 1,000; in 1969 this had fallen to 5 per 1,000. Death rates in girls under four years was 48 per 1,000 in 1901 and 4 per 1,000 in 1969 (*Social Trends*, HMSO, May 13, 1970). The latest available figures show a slower rise in the birth rate of 4-5 per cent. One factor throught to have contributed to this was the scare concerning side-effects of the pill.

The unwanted and unloved

One laudable aim from all points of view would be to ensure that only wanted children were born. While it is undoubtedly true that unwanted children later become accepted and loved, it is also true that the casebook of the NSPCC is full of tragic examples of the unwanted and unloved.

Caspar Brook, director of the Family Planning Association, reckons that there are 200–300,000 unwanted pregnancies each year. Though more and more children are being deliberately conceived out of wedlock, the signs are that a high proportion of the 150,000 unmarried women who become pregnant each year do not want their babies – some have put the figure as high as 100,000. Mrs Helene Graham, assistant director of the Family Planning Association, has stated that around three million women of child-bearing age in Britain do not practise birth control, mainly through ignorance.

A really comprehensive education programme in the schools should have top priority in any population policy. It is not only a matter of giving sex instruction, but of encouraging responsible attitudes and making sure that the consequences of irresponsible behaviour are appreciated. A programme of this kind could not only result in fewer unwanted children being born, but less distress for young girls and their families, lower social costs when children have to be taken into care and so on. Ignorance on this subject is still profound. It should not be assumed that because sex is more freely discussed these days, all young people are aware of the facts of life. *Daily Mirror* columnist Marjorie Proops told a Royal Society of Health conference that teenagers still believed old wives' tales about sex. Girls of 14 and over thought that holding their breath during intercourse was a protection against pregnancy and others thought that standing up meant they would not conceive. A survey carried out by Hertfordshire County Council revealed that one in five girls aged 14 believed that only women could use contraceptives.

What young people are getting is a super-abundance of titillation and commercialised eroticism and all too little genuine instruction.

Those backwoodsmen – and women – who thunder on about sin and retribution might bear in mind that the result in many cases is that an unwanted child becomes yet another burden for the local authority to bear, paid for by you and I.

To support the educational drive, birth-control facilities should be freely available in the schools, universities, through the National Health Service and so on. This is not, as some would have it, licensing promiscuity but recognising a situation that exists and trying to do something about it.

What about unwanted children within marriage? Caspar Brook estimates that there are from 500–600,000 unplanned pregnancies every year. Mrs Madeleine Simms, of the Abortion Law Reform Association, and Lady Jean Medawar, of the Family Planning Association, have quoted a survey showing that after five years of marriage 10 per cent of those questioned already had more children than they could manage without excessive strain. Nearly two-thirds of first and second pregnancies were unintended, four-fifths of third pregnancies and all the fourth or later pregnancies occurring in the first five years. Professor Norman Morris found at Charing Cross Hospital that only a quarter to one-third of all babies were planned and in another study in London and Hertfordshire, about half the pregnancies were said to be unplanned.

There would seem to be a good deal of scope here for better family-planning advice and this could undoubtedly be made more freely available. Out of 204 local health authorities in England and Wales who could provide a full family planning service, only about a quarter were doing so at the time of writing, either by themselves or, more usually, by using the Family Planning Association as agent. By a full service is meant that examination and advice are made freely available to all women, whether married or not, of child-bearing age, and that charges for supplies are made in accordance with circumstances. But two London boroughs – Lambeth and Islington – deserve special mention for their decision to give free contraceptive advice and supplies to all women over 16 years of age. They are the first in the country to do so.

It took this country until 1967 to have a Family Planning Act on the statue book and then only as a Private Member's measure. Furthermore, the Act did not make it mandatory for local authorities to provide such services. I suppose we should be thankful that as many as 870 local health authority clinics have been set up, even if most of them only provide a restricted service.

The bill we as taxpayers have to meet annually for unwanted children has been estimated at £100 million. This includes abortion costs, maternity facilities cost of children in care and ordinary schooling – in other words, we are paying out more than four times the cost of a full family planning service.

And all because we failed to make the provision of a full service mandatory. Sometimes the typical British compromise is little more than a mealy-mouthed exercise belonging to the 19th rather than the 20th century. Caspar Brook states that it would cost less than £40 million a year to provide effective birth control for every woman at risk; under £5 each for the 8-million 15–44 year olds who are not pregnant, not infertile and not trying to have a pregnancy. Spending this sum would, he asserts, release £150–400 million of public expenditure on the results of unwanted pregnancies.

A domiciliary service?

Few authorities have taken birth-control into the homes of people who might for various reasons be reluctant to visit a clinic – these, incidentally, are often the kinds of women who go on to have large families, chiefly through ignorance. London, Newcastle, York and Southampton have pioneered schemes and the FPA has sent details to every county Medical Officer of Health with hardly any real response. Simms and Medawar point out that much of the trouble arises because budgets are departmentally designed, so that it cannot be shown that £1 spent on birth control by the General Purposes Committee would show a saving of £10 in the Child Care Department.

However, a welcome stimulus to the domiciliary approach will be provided by grants of more than £100,000 promised by the Government in 1972-73 to implement such a service.

Simms and Medawar urge the adoption by all authorities of enlightened programmes on the lines of the one sponsored by Aberdeen which has made birth control services fully available and secured a drop in the birth of unwanted babies by methods 'which need worry no one'.

The liberalisation of abortion law effected by the 1967 Act should reduce 'back-street' abortions and the risks associated therewith and, generally speaking, make abortion much easier. It marks a step further towards the integration of abortion with normal gynaecological procedures. Research into quick, safe methods is proceeding apace – prostaglandins and the 'lunch-hour' abortion by vacuum curette are the most popular.

All such measures, coupled with direct propaganda drives, can help to create a climate of opinion in which it will no longer be regarded as heroic or clever to have large families and where the two- or three-child family will be regarded as the desirable 'norm'.

The whole question is also, to my mind, very closely linked with the status of women. If women are encouraged more and more to follow careers and to enjoy a truly equal partnership with men, I don't think that babies will figure so largely in their thinking. Such encouragement should be practical as well as spiritual, involving the provision of more day nurseries and creches for the children they do have.

There is some evidence to support this view by the experience of Sweden, where women are to a large extent emancipated, and also in China where the attempt to give women equality is reported to have encouraged later marriages and smaller families.

Whether purely fiscal measures are truly effective or not is doubtful, but probably rate a trial. There certainly seems little justification for weighting family allowances and taxes in such a way that larger families may be encouraged.

Nobody should under-rate the problem of securing acceptance of a population policy. It is sure to be opposed by powerful interests, often on the grounds of morality, but what is moral about attitudes which condemn millions to mean and miserable existences?

The aim of population control is to ensure that our available resources in the widest sense of the term are not overtaxed and that as many of our species as possible, in the under-developed as well as the advanced countries, are able to enjoy a reasonable share of what is available. There is nothing eccentric or revolutionary about this – it is merely common-sense.

Legislation:
Family Planning Act 1967.
Abortion Act 1967.

Mainly responsible (family planning clinics): Local authorities, Family Planning Association.

Further reading

On Population: Three Essays by Thomas Malthus, Julian Huxley and Frederick Osborn, Mentor, 1960

Ehrlich, Dr Paul, *The Population Bomb*, Pan, 1971.

Taylor. L. R. (ed.), *The Optimum Population for Britain. Inst. of Biology symposium*, Academic Press, 1970.

Taylor, G. Rattray, *The Biological Time Bomb*, Panther Science, 1969.

Population of the UK, House of Commons Paper 379, HMSO, 1971.

Why Britain Needs a Population Policy, The Conservation Society (address in directory), 1969.

Town and Country Planning

3. Planners hold the key

We hear a great deal about the shortcomings of planners. Some of this criticism is justified; much of it ill-conceived and damaging to the environmental cause. For planners are the potential allies of conservationists.

They can exert a big influence on the quality of life in town and country, through powers over the shape, size and character of towns and over development and recreational opportunities in the countryside. The route to be taken by new roads, the weight of traffic they shall bear, the location and development of new towns, airports and industry, the level of noise or pollution to which people are exposed and the preservation of the fine buildings we have inherited all come within the planners' province to a greater or lesser degree.

The extent of their involvement with us, and ours with them, is not fully appreciated. They can affect the kind of homes we live in, the layout of our street, the location of the schools our children attend, the length of our journey to work and our opportunities for rest and recreation.

All this needs qualifying, however. Planners have to work within the social and political framework and their actions are circumscribed by politicians and developers. This means that not only what they do is subject to controls but how they do it, especially by the financial budgets – some would term them 'straitjackets' – within which they have to operate. Futhermore, as we shall see later, all sorts of public safeguards have been built into planning law, and the whole operation is now seen, in theory at any rate, as a joint exercise between planners and people.

This is to use the term 'planner' in its broadest sense. It is important to be clear about who does what in the planning field, not only to be able to apportion praise or blame to the right quarter, but to avoid investing any particular planner or group of planners with power to do almost anything, from providing seats in the park to controlling the national economy. It is also important to appreciate that planning is becoming more and more a professional team job, involving specialists like architects, economists, geographers and sociologists as well as town planners in their own right.

Indiscriminate use of the term by popular press, radio and TV has been largely responsible for the poor image planners have with the public. All planning failures are attributed to all planners, and since the very nature of planning makes failure more obvious than success, it would seem the planners cannot win.

So let us, in the interest of justice, try to define our terms. The planners with whom we shall mostly be concerned are those serving on the 173 county and county borough councils in England and Wales, and 57 in Scotland, which were designated as planning authorities under the principal measure, the 1947 Town and Country Planning Act. They are responsible for land use at the local level.

At regional level there are the economic planning councils and boards set up in 1964 following the creation of the Department of Economic Affairs to look specifically at economic prospects and the pattern of employment in the regions, and to advise the Government accordingly. The schism thus created between what is known as physical or land use planning and economic planning has been much criticised, because in practice it is impossible to draw a clear line between them. There is some hope of bridging the gap through the preparation of regional plans, taking a comprehensive look at development within the region, of which the regional plan for the south-east is one example. Eventually, by completing all the regional plans, we may have a picture of the whole country which could help in formulating some kind of national plan.

The Government is, of course, deeply involved in both physical and economic planning, through having the final say in the preparation of local and regional plans and through the system of financial incentives to development areas, inducements to industry to move into these areas and so on.

One of the main motives for the formation of the new Department of the Environment in the autumn of 1970 was to provide closer links between Ministries responsible for land use – Housing and Local Government, Transport (routeing of motorways and trunk roads) and Public Building and Works.

An important part in planning is played by the Department of Trade and Industry through the issue of industrial development certificates. The aim has

16

been to secure a better balance of employment throughout the country. The Location of Offices Bureau also exercises a planning function. The bureau was set up by the Government in 1963 to encourage firms to move out of central London into the provinces. It has had some success – although few concerns seem prepared to go farther out than the Home Counties.

But we have not exhausted the list of planners yet. The development corporations set up under the 1946 New Towns Act are another kind of planning authority. In the countryside there are the National Park planning boards established under the National Parks and Access to the Countryside Act of 1949. This Act also created the National Parks Commission which was later succeeded by the Countryside Commission. Add to this list the Nature Conservancy, which designates and manages nature reserves, the Forestry Commission, responsible for national forest parks and the Water Resources Board, which advises on water conservation, and you will get some idea of the scope of planning in this country.

The officers and members of all these bodies may justly be termed 'planners' as they are all charged in some respect or other with planning the use of land. It would help us all to comprehend this complex system and to avoid unjustly maligning those not concerned if the critics would specify what particular set of 'planners' they are referring to when launching one of their broadsides.

However, it would be foolish to ignore the public hostility to planning which provides such fertile soil on which the critics may cast their seeds of doubt. That a society founded on laissez-faire should have to submit to controls of this kind is intensely irksome to many, so it is not surprising that from time to time some particular planning 'outrage' should provoke demands for a return to the free-for-all of the past. Even some who ought to know better have drawn up schemes which, however cleverly disguised, amount to a call to throw away most of these controls and let the call of the market have priority.

THE PLANNING APPARATUS*
Department of the Environment

(incorporating former Ministries of Housing and Local Government, Transport and Public Building and Works)

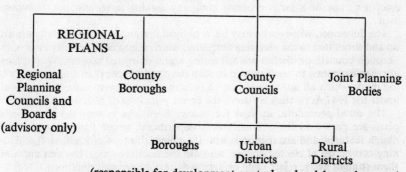

* This pattern will be changed by the new local government system due to come into being on April 1, 1974.

They should think again; better still, they should read the works of such eminent American writers on conservation as Robert and Leona Rienow (*Moment in the Sun* is a real eye-opener for instance). Throughout there is evidence of the disasters which have befallen this great nation through lack of planning. Just imagine, for instance, what would happen over here if some developer wanted to build a road across Ullswater or chop down Epping Forest? Similar things and worse, have actually happened in America, on a scale to make any lover of beauty despair.

Consequences of laissez-faire

If those who want a return to laissez-faire were more aware of the background to the development of planning legislation in this country, they might indeed think again. Our modern system sprang, in fact, out of public health regulations designed to curb a truly desperate situation in the 19th century where whole streets floated in sewage, where something like one-third of urban homes were without water, where thousands of families lived in cold, dank cellars and where disease was rife. Some idea of the way whole communities were demoralised is contained in figures showing that in 568 streets surveyed in Leeds in the 1830s, there were 451 public houses and 98 brothels!

On the other hand, one might point out to the cynics that planning itself goes back much further than this; that it is a very ancient art and that the world's finest cities were, in fact, planned – they include Rome, Venice, Paris, Vienna and, in our own country, Bath, Cheltenham, Newcastle and a host of seaside resorts like Brighton, Weymouth and Tenby.

London's splendid squares were laid out to a plan and the great estates of the 17th and 18th centuries were examples of landscape planning which have never been excelled.

However, the modern system does suffer from its antecedents. It originated from a desire to stop something happening and the emphasis has continued to be placed on negative rather than positive aspects. The apparatus of development control which forms the 'grass roots' of the system is bound to prove irritating to any private developer, whether an individual wishing to extend his house or erect a garage or a large property company seeking to reconstruct the whole area.

The developer, whoever he may be, is obliged first to get plans properly drawn up and submitted to the planning authority, which might be his county or county borough council, or district council acting under delegated powers. These plans are then examined to see if they fit in with the development plan and its supporting maps which all authorities had to present to the Government for approval under the 1947 Act – they lay down the broad principles of land use in the area.*

The usual procedure, at least for county boroughs, is that the developer's plans are passed to the city architect's department, where they are vetted for design features, and are then sent with the observations of officials, to the planning committee of elected laymen who are the final arbiters. They can approve them straight away, reject them or approve them on certain conditions.

People likely to be affected by the proposed development may lodge objections

---

* A new system referred to later, is gradually being introduced under the 1968 Planning Act.

to it before it goes to the planning committee. But how do they hear about it? All too often in the past the first notification that anything was under way was the arrival of the bulldozer on the site. The planning authority now has to see that neighbours are informed of any proposals affecting them, and they in turn may examine the plans of the project if they wish. A register of applications must also be kept available for public inspection.

If an application is rejected, the developer can modify his plans and submit them again or appeal to the Minister, who may order a public inquiry at which interested members of the public may appear in support of either side.

This process can take a great deal of time. About 450,000 planning applications have to be dealt with each year and although four-fifths are approved, the sheer volume of work involved is bound to cause delays. Also, if an appeal is involved this can take from six to nine months to settle.

Planning control can thus be extremely frustrating for the developer. But it brings few bouquets for the planners either. It is not very easy to convince people that if it weren't for these controls things might have been much worse. Even when planners are successful, their success may appear to be a failure. All too often the end-result is the choice of a site which represents the lesser of two evils – but an evil for all that. Instead of being congratulated on preventing the greater abuse, planners are more likely to be reviled for permitting the development at all.

This negative approach has also brought disillusionment to planning staffs, many of whom entered the profession in the spirit of idealism which led to the passing of the 1947 Act. Instead of building a new Britain, they all too often found themselves bogged down in long and petty wrangles with architects, builders or developers, culminating in a thin-blooded compromise which pleased no-one. So they began to drift away into private practice where they hoped to find more outlets for their creative skills, making the shortage of qualified planners in local government worse than it was, and creating more training problems for the Royal Town Planning Institute.

Green belt fears

Planning controls do not always produce such an unfavourable public reaction, however. Those having a preservationist purpose are often widely appreciated. They include the protection of buildings of architectural or historic merit, the placing of 'preservation orders' on trees and the control of outdoor advertisements which, as any traveller to the USA or Italy will testify, can have a hideous effect on the landscape if allowed to run riot.

But the outstanding example of controls valued by the public are the green belts. The fact that they are readily understood and appreciated may be deemed reason enough for seeing that the policy remains unchanged.

However, there are many, including some planners, who would like to see changes. They object to the green belts as they are at the moment because, they say, it is not sound planning to erect a kind of wall around a city for all time. Planning should be flexible and responsive to change. Also, the green belts have had the undesirable effect of transferring the sprawl to areas beyond them and so increasing the journey to work. Furthermore, the sporadic building which has taken place and the consequent increase in traffic has ruined scores of villages.

While accepting the truth of this, others suggest that this is a small price to pay for ensuring that the countryside does not retreat too far from city dwellers – especially when it might be reduced by adopting more positive planning policies for areas beyond the green belts.

A proposed alternative is to allow a certain amount of building in the green belts and to create 'wedges' of open country penetrating the built-up areas – sounds very fine until one examines the idea more closely. How, for instance, will these green 'wedges' be maintained? If they are going to be farmed, could they be the right size and shape for economical agriculture? And would farmers welcome being so close to thousands of townsfolk whose behaviour in the countryside can leave much to be desired? As Nan Fairbrother said in *New Lives New Landscapes*: 'The farming countryside is not a decorative land-surface which can be used to break up and beautify urban areas for the benefit of urban dwellers, but is a working landscape which can only survive in suitable conditions, and these we need to understand clearly.'

If farming in the 'green wedges' weren't possible, as it often is in the more extensive green belts, what we could get as a result would be an even more depressing 'litter' of eyesores such as refuse dumps, petrol stations, bungalows, wire netting and gravel pits among the greenery which so often passes for green belt on the immediate verge of towns.

But the biggest fear must be that adoption of such a policy would indeed be the thin end of the 'wedge', if you'll pardon the pun; that once housing were allowed in one part of the belt it would be doubly difficult to prevent it from spreading to adjoining parts, and pretty soon the whole area would be over-run. The pressures could be too great to permit sophisticated policies of this kind to be pursued. Better in this situation to be safe than sorry and to devise more constructive uses for green belt land, such as the establishment of the country parks envisaged by the Countryside Act of 1968.

Questions of taste

One form of planning control over which there has been much argument is the attempt to adjudicate on matters of taste. Many of you must have asked yourselves, on coming across some particularly obnoxious development, how on earth the planners could have allowed it. You may also pause to reflect at that stage how few really imaginative and attractive schemes there are, especially in the housing field. What we seem to get, by and large, is a low-key mediocrity, a repetition of the mixture-as-before, with the addition, here and there, of a few sales 'gimmicks' designed to catch the eye of the undiscriminating buyer – tile-hanging and canopied porches, pseudo-Tudor and neo-Georgian, and so on.

You may feel that our architects can do better than this and that they would be greatly encouraged to do so if planners would be more decisive in throwing out the mediocre packages.

The first point to note is that only about one-half the total of privately commissioned housing and less than half the total of industrial buildings are designed by architects. Figures for the public sector are much higher, but it has been estimated that £1,000 million worth of development is completed each year without an architect.

Secondly, so far as the schemes designed by architects are concerned, these have to go before the planning committee. Don't ask architects what they think of planning committees unless you have a sadistic streak and enjoy seeing a soul in torment.

Said the Royal Institute of British Architects: 'It would be hard to exaggerate the damage done to local environments, and the frustrations, delays and expense suffered by talented and conscientious architects, as a result of the administration and unintelligent application of planning and building controls by mediocre calibre local authority committees and staff. . .'

The RIBA has a bulky file of complaints by architects about their treatment at the hands of lay committees. For instance, an architect whose design for a house was rejected by the planning committee asked what he should do to secure its acceptance. On being told that the house must be in keeping with its neighbours, he pointed out that it was in the garden of a large Victorian property; did this mean the design should be Victorian? 'Not as far back as that,' came the reply, 'about 1938 will do.'

A house at Epsom was refused planning permission because the outside staircase made it look like a block of flats. Flat roofs tend to be frowned upon by the committees, terraces disliked and copper roofs cause absolute consternation.

Sir Basil Spence had his design for a chapel at Sussex University rejected on the grounds that it was 'out of keeping with the neighbourhood' – his own buildings in fact. 'The planning committee', Sir Basil exploded, 'represents the lowest common denominator of ignorance and bad architecture.' Every young architect, he added, knew that the best way to get over the committee hurdle was to do a mediocre design that was commonplace and therefore up to the average committee's level of appreciation. This had not only failed to produce good architecture but had also destroyed the architect's integrity.

Architects' fury at their plans being thrown out by people who in many cases couldn't even read them was appreciated and a typical British compromise devised to overcome the difficulty. It took the form of the establishment of architectural panels to provide committees with expert advice on aesthetic matters. The first panel was sponsored by the Council for the Protection of Rural England as long ago as 1928 and there has been a steady growth in their number since. There are around 70 in England and Wales, with more than 600 members, of whom the majority are qualified architects and the remainder builders or persons with some knowledge of design, and they advise on some 12–14,000 applications a year.

However, the panels do vary greatly in the way they operate and the extent to which they are used. Some see all applications and some very few. The planning authority decides which schemes shall be passed on.

This is a largely voluntary service by busy people and deserves wider recognition, I feel. General policy for the panels is formulated by the Central Committee of Architectural Advisory Panels, sponsored by the RIBA, the CPRE and the Institute of Building, and supported by about a dozen interested bodies, including the Royal Town Planning Institute.

It seems to be agreed that the system works well enough for it to be extended to the whole of Britain – there are very few panels in the north of England, for instance, where the needs are greatest. There have also been demands that they be placed on a proper footing, with provisions for regular meetings, reference to them of a reasonable number of applications and payment of fees to panel members.

While arrangements of this kind are helpful in raising the general level of design, their scope is strictly limited. You can't produce a silk purse from a sow's ear – if the original scheme is hopelessly bad, nothing you do is likely to make it more than mediocre. There is a limit to the number of times you can throw it out. Perhaps the best you can hope for is that, if an architect has not been employed, the developer may be induced to engage one.

The delegation of decision-making to planning officers rather than committees could be a step forward, though there is a temptation for an officer who doesn't wish to upset his architect colleagues to decide only those schemes which are acceptable and refer the rest to the committee.

Another way of raising standards, it has been suggested, is to make it obligatory here as in some other countries, for all major housing schemes to be designed by architects. The trouble is that many architects are no better than the planning committees who control them and some do not properly consider the environmental implications of their builidngs.

Meanwhile, we stagger on with this rather unsatisfactory compromise.

New town pros and cons
It would be most misleading to suggest, by this emphasis on control, that there have been no opportunities for comprehensive development. Indeed, some of the biggest planning successes, like Coventry's pedestrian precinct, Plymouth's central area projects and various housing schemes carried out by the old London County Council have been of this nature. In some cases such projects have been undertaken by the local authority itself and in others through partnership arrangements with private enterprise, with varying results.

The outstanding planning achievement, of course, has been the creation of the new towns, which have provided a convincing demonstration of what planners can do when given the right opportunities. About 30 new towns have been designated at the time of writing and by the end of the century they are expected to have a combined population of around three million. Their purpose has been primarily to ease congestion in the cities – 11 of the first 20 to be established were designed mainly to relieve Greater London. Others, like Corby, Newton, Aycliffe and Peterlee, were to serve established industries.

One may discern three periods of new-town construction – the first within four years after the Act was passed in 1946, when 11 English ones were started including eight around London; nothing happened after that until 1958, when Cumbernauld (intended to take Glasgow's 'overspill') started the second wave and we had Skelmersdale to relieve Liverpool, Dawley (later renamed Telford) and Redditch for Birmingham, then another one for Liverpool – Runcorn – and in 1964, Washington to relieve Sunderland and Tyneside.

Milton Keynes, more a new city than new town, with an eventual population envisaged at a quarter of a million, saw the start of a third wave in 1967, as it was soon followed by Peterborough, Northampton and Warrington, though these were really expansions of sizeable existing towns.

The location of new towns is the responsibility of the geographical planning division of the Department of the Environment, but the New Towns Division has the task of designating the area and setting up the development corporation.

Once the site has been designated, objections can be invited and an inquiry held. The legal effect of final designation is to make the land liable for compulsory purchase and to enable owners to dispose of their land to the corporation, after seven years, if they so desire. Development corporations must not have more than nine members, who are paid, (but not very much), to build the town.

It was envisaged in the Act that when new towns were completed they would be handed over to local authorities on terms to be decided, but legislation was passed in 1959 establishing a Commission for the New Towns and they, in fact, have taken over the new towns of Crawley, Hemel Hempstead, Welwyn and Hatfield.

Another decentralisation measure which has proved effective to a degree is the Town Development Act of 1952, under which agreements can be made between 'exporting' and 'receiving' local authorities to take people from an overcrowded town. The most notable projects under the Act have been those carried out by the LCC and, later, the GLC at Basingstoke, Andover, Haverhill, Thetford and so on. Swindon is a special case, because although the development has been planned and executed in collaboration with the GLC, the local authority has chosen to go it alone to a remarkable extent, and with quite striking results. The town is at last beginning to realise its enormous potential.

Town development is something of a gamble for the receiving council, whose resources will be limited at the outset but who could end up by owning most of the land, houses and perhaps some of the factories with a greatly increased ratable value. Grants from the Ministry and help with professional advice as well as money from the exporting authority may still fall far short of what is required. Much will depend on the success of efforts to persuade industry to go to the receiving area.

The contribution made by the new and expanded towns towards limiting congestion in the big cities has not been remarkable in terms of the number of houses built, and there is a good deal of commuting between London and its 'satellites', for instance. However, few can deny that in financial and environmental respects they have been a huge success. They have given a new life to thousands of adults and children from overcrowded cities.

Those who disparage the chances of changing human behaviour by changing the physical environment should reflect, for instance, on some comments quoted by Frank Schaffer in his book, *The New Town Story*. First, a teacher describing his early days at an old, tough and overcrowded school in London . . .

'I soon acquired the technique. You walk into a classroom, where the noise is unbelievable and clout the first three children you see. Then, and only then, do you get some sort of order. You can't teach them much, but if you manage to keep them quiet you're a success.'

Now from a headmaster in a new town school with many children from similar areas . . .

'When I first came here, soon after the town started, there were less than 200 children in this school, all from the overcrowded parts of London, and it was as much as I could do to keep any control. Now I have nearly a thousand children but I can get silence in a second.

23

'The change in the children is unbelievable. I put it down entirely to the change in environment. They live in new homes, of which they, no less than their parents, are very house-proud; they have the country on their doorsep, open spaces and sports facilities, a school of which they are justly proud, and a general atmosphere in the town so different from the parts of London they came from.'

And the author added that the children were well-dressed, well-behaved and the scholastic record impressive. They were being taught in one of many excellent new schools, fully equipped and surrounded by spacious playing fields, and the children had built their own swimming pool. The school building itself was well looked after – there wasn't a mark on the walls.

One can criticise many facets of the design and layout of the new towns, especially the earliest ones, where land was employed in the most profligate way, with vast unused and relatively useless green areas. One can also complain, as Ray Thomas did in his booklet on *London's new towns* (published by Political and Economic Planning), that they are largely one-class communities; meaning that all of them, except Welwyn, have a higher proportion of high-income manual workers than London and nearly all have a higher proportion than Great Britain; that they also contain a preponderance of people in the same age group; and that, with one or two exceptions, like Cumbernauld, they haven't been very imaginative in planning for the motor car.

Against this one weighs their high individual housing standards, then prosperity, the vitality of their traffic-free town centres, the growing number of social and recreational facilities – Harlow, for instance, is noted for its achievements in health and music, and for its fine sports centre – and the variety of planning concepts. A whole era of planning and architectural thought is encompassed by Stevenage, Cumbernauld and Milton Keynes.

If we were to go back into big cities with the same kind of resolution and perhaps the same sort of machinery for truly comprehensive development which created the new towns we might be able to halt the decline and ultimate death of these great population centres.

Speeding things up

Planning is all too rarely a subtle art; more often a painstaking chore. To swing the emphasis towards the former, it is essential to do something about the latter – to remove much of the hard graft and speed things up generally. Here there are grounds for hope. A new system slowly being introduced could improve matters considerably. It divides development plans into two main parts – structure plans setting out the broad strategy and identifying 'action areas' to be tackled comprehensively within ten years and 'local plans to meet local needs, in which the main proposals in the structure plan are worked out in detail. Structure plans require Ministerial approval; local plans normally do not. This in itself should save a lot of time.

The 1968 Planning Act which gave force to these arrangements was described by Sir Desmond Heap, Comptroller and City Solicitor to the Corporation of London, as 'an exercise in load-shedding from central to local government'. Among other burdens being shed is one for deciding all appeals centrally – the Minister may transfer responsibility for settling the more straightforward ones to inspectors. The authority itself may also delegate power to planning officers to make decisions instead of applications always having to go before the committee.

The system is only being introduced as and when the Department is satisfied that planning authorities can cope – and this might well in many cases have to await the reform of local government. Building is no respecter of boundaries and the existing boundaries of planning authorities have been over-run to such an extent that all kinds of *ad hoc* links between them have had to be established. Also strategic planning – employment, communications and land use in the widest sense – can only be properly exercised over wide areas.

Local government reform will result in bigger and fewer authorities and make planning more coherent, but it will not come into being for some time. Meanwhile planners, like other local government personnel, have to live with the uncertainty.

The problem of 'betterment'

There are some outstanding gaps in the system which are sure to raise many problems in the years to come. First, the one which has so far defied all efforts at a solution – what to do about land costs? The building of roads and the provision of transport and sewerage services can increase the value of land without any effort on the part of the owner. When the Government placed restrictions on office building in central London, this put thousands of pounds on the price of property because of the increased rents which could be commanded – fortunes were made overnight without lifting a finger. If any part of the green belt were released for building, the value of land held would soar astronomically.

There is strong feeling that the increased value produced by community action – or at least some proportion thereof – should be returned to the community. What are known as the 'compensation and betterment' provisions of the 1947 Act were an attempt to deal with this which eventually had to be abandoned. The Land Commission, set up to do more or less the same job, was very short-lived and few people seem to regret its departure.

Still, the land problem remains unsolved. It has been argued that increased land values might be reaped by the community through an extension of capital gains tax, but nothing further has been heard of this so far.

And although the principle of compensating owners at a fair market price for properties compulsorily purchased has been accepted, no-one can pretend that this concession solves the problem of planning blight – the slump in land and property values which sometimes results from a planning project. To compensate everyone whose property goes down in value as a result of a motorway scheme would be vastly expensive, but anything short of this is bound to cause much discontent. If the community could acquire betterment from those people whose properties had been raised in value as a result of the development, however, it might be possible to find a solution through redistributing such increases.

Involving the public

Whatever steps are taken to make planning more acceptable to the public, there are bound to be matters which require the fullest possible explanation. Planners in future will have to be much more publicity-conscious. By operating so often behind closed doors in the past they have lent support to the idea that they are soulless bureaucrats engaged in some mysterious and complex activity. They become 'sitting ducks' for their detractors. The press is particularly – and I think rightly – sensitive about apparent attempts at concealment. In their own interests, planners should be much more prepared to enter the hurly-burly of public controversy, to respond to attacks made on them and generally to carry out the recommendations of the Skeffington report on public participation.

Enough has been said here, I feel, to show that planning is essentially a *public* activity, affecting all sections of the population and, as such, it should be openly seen to be done. Nor should planners believe that the public have little to contribute. Time after time only public intervention has prevented some planning disaster or other. Piccadilly Circus and Stansted are prime examples. True, we have yet to see the outcome in both these cases, but the really important factor is that for the first time the public have had access to the information on which planning decisions are based and have been able to see the machinery actually working. No commission has ever had the spotlight thrown on its activities as Roskill had and one feels it will not be so easy in future for developers to get away with large schemes which are felt to be detrimental to the community.

Exercises in public participation are bound to take more time, money and effort, and many planners are by no means convinced of their value, though it is contended that far greater savings might eventually be made through securing wider public acceptance of projects at the outset. As for the complaint that many people lack knowledge of the planning system and are only interested in grinding their own particular axes, this is undeniable, but nearly always there are one or two ideas put forward which make the dialogue eminently worthwhile.

Planners are also able to sense the mood of the public and the public, for their part, can feel involved in a community activity. More important still is that planners and planned are brought together. Without such contacts planning is likely to be guided by paternalism and a set of middle-class values which we know are not shared by the community as a whole.

Even so, the consultations must be meaningful and not mere window dressing. Public participation, as Mr Derek Senior, dissenting member of the Redcliffe-Maud Commission, has pointed out, does not mean presenting people with plans to which they can only say yea or nay, but drawing up alternatives with full explanations of what could be involved in each, so that people could state their preference for a particular course of action.

Steps must also be taken to ensure that the dialogue is a continuous one by co-opting suitable people on to planning committees, establishing close links with amenity societies and so on.

What can no longer be contended is that people don't care about planning. When their interests are affected they will turn up to meetings in droves, as experience in Coventry, Liverpool and London has shown. They bring to such gatherings not only curiosity, but a wealth of local knowledge and useful expertise – not to mention that oft-neglected attribute, common-sense.

The world we shall be looking at in this book will be largely the planners' world and many of the problems we shall be discussing will be their problems. It is a world in which the incredibly rapid development of science and technology will present planners with new and improved tools and techniques for tackling their manifold tasks. Sophisticated machines like the computer can relieve them of much tiresome routine and leave them freer to devote attention to more creative tasks.

What technology cannot do, however, is to free planners from the need to make value judgments which will determine the shape of our future environment. These are essentially human decisions and cannot be surrendered to the machine. Such value judgments will be even more important in future. If planning is to retain any credibility in the years to come, planners will have to call on every ounce of moral courage they possess to speak out for a saner environment and not to surrender to market forces or expediency.

They will continue to make mistakes, but how many they make and how often they are right will, I am sure, depend upon how far they are prepared to find out what people want rather than what they (the planners) think they want.

Legislation:

Town and Country Planning Acts 1947, 1962, 1968
New Towns Acts 1946, 1965, 1968
Town Development Act 1952
National Parks and Access to the Countryside Act 1949
Countryside Act 1968
Local Employment Acts 1960, 1963, 1970
Control of Office & Industrial Development Act 1965

Mainly responsible:

Greater London Council, London boroughs, county councils, county boroughs, development corporations, Commission for the New Towns, Countryside Commission, Department of the Environment, Department of Trade and Industry, Ministry of Agriculture, Fisheries and Food

Further reading

Cullingworth, J. B., *Town and Country Planning in England and Wales*, Allen and Unwin, 1964.
Fairbrother, Nan, *New Lives New Landscapes*, Architectural Press, 1970.
Schaffer, Frank, *The New Town Story*, MacGibbon & Kee, 1970.
Thomas, Ray, *London's New Towns*, PEP, 1969.
Thomas, Ray, *Aycliffe to Cumbernauld: A study of seven new towns*, PEP, 1969.
Heap, Sir Desmond, *An Outline of Planning Law*, Sweet & Maxwell, 1969, 5th edn.
Brett, Lionel, *Landscape in Distress*, Architectural Press, 1965.
Howard, Ebenezer, *Garden Cities of Tomorrow*, Faber, 1945.
Riley, D. W., *The Citizen's Guide to Town and Country Planning*, Town & Country Planning Association, 1966.
People and Planning, The Skeffington Report, HMSO, 1969.
Town and Country Planning in Britain, COI reference pamphlet, HMSO, 1968.

BUILT UP BRITAIN

Crisis in the City

Nowhere are the troubles which beset societies wedded to growth at all costs more apparent than in their exploding cities. Cities receive the full weight of such pressures and reveal the consequences in so many ways – in streets of handsome houses torn down to make way for dismally uninteresting office blocks, vying with each other for dominance; in parks and pleasant residential areas uprooted for high-speed roads; in tall blocks of flats built not for people but for 'family units', with carefully clipped grass and 'Keep Off' notices; in acres of decaying housing for 'urban nomads' and other 'second-class citizens'; and, above all, in a restless, seething, elbowing humanity, struggling to breathe in the confined space left by the buildings and the motor cars, and dreaming all the time of getting away.

These, and worse, are the kind of conditions created in the most affluent country in the world, the United States. Those unfortunate enough to live or work in the centre of New York may well ask themselves precisely what is meant by a high standard of living as they breathe air so polluted that it is estimated to be equivalent to smoking 38 cigarettes a day, and as they smell the rotting garbage piling up in the foetid heat from the latest strike of refuse disposal workers.

According to Jeremy Campbell, in the *Evening Standard*, if they live in the suburb of Brownsville, they may well feel that it is breakdown, and not growth, they are witnessing.

'Brownsville is a bubonic outrage, a communicable disease, a terminal case of urban leprosy', he wrote. 'The Mayor of Boston came to inspect its crumbling hovels and remarked: "This may be the first tangible sign of the collapse of our civilisation."

'I walked the streets for two days in a state of incredulity', said Mr Campbell. 'The gutted houses, the naked acres of rubble, the looted shops, the store-front churches bricked up like machine-gun bunkers reminded me of Berlin, bombed into surrender at the end of the war.'

The car-torn city of Los Angeles, with its drive-in everything (even a drive-in mortuary, I hear), and where one is liable to be picked up for vagrancy if found actually walking, is now pleading to be rescued from the smog, the noise and the policies of surrender to the motor car which have created the longest and largest building sprawl in the world.

Italians are still in their honeymoon period with the motor car, and this land of Renaissance culture is now plastered with hoardings bearing witness to the obsession, while the ancient city of Rome groans and creaks under the burden of traffic and noise. The motor car still has Paris, too, in its grip, according to Patrick Brogan, correspondent of *The Times*, who wrote in that paper (June 10, 1971) about plans to demolish the Halles – the old vegetable market and one of the most picturesque parts of the city – declaring: 'The worst of it all is that the demolition of the Halles is not exceptional. Paris is being relentlessly destroyed and in a decade will be recognisable only by the few large monuments washed by M. Malraux, which are getting grubby again.' Virtually all the parks in the city were being dug up for motorways or underground parking, he added.

The Japanese have some remarkable technological achievements to their credit, and they have raised family incomes, but what about day-to-day living conditions? Surely one must question the values of a society which floods the western world with its products but which fails to employ any substantial part of the proceeds on improving the environment? So dreadful has air pollution become, for instance, that we are reliably informed gas masks may have to be issued to the inhabitants if it gets any worse. Children have been warned not to play outside at certain times of the day, and policemen on point duty have to be given oxygen at regular intervals. The city's waterways are also in a lethal state. (See 'A Question of Priorities'.)

Moving farther out

Britain is largely an urban community. The built-up area of England and Wales doubled in the first 60 years of this century and represents about 11 per cent of the total surface area. It is expected to double again by the end of the century.

How do our cities rate against the background described? Not so badly, perhaps, and planners and local government can take much of the credit for this. But can anyone truly maintain that London, Birmingham, Manchester, Glasgow and Cardiff are more pleasant places to live in than they were? If so, why is it that their populations, like those of so many of the world's great cities, are declining as people move farther and farther out? Why do our great cities evince signs of the same sickness afflicting New York, Chicago, Tokyo and elsewhere?

Violence is so prevalent in the United States that the nation is said to be moving towards fortified residential compounds and inner cities which would be sealed off by the police after dark. In 1969, more than twice as many people were murdered in Dallas, Texas (population 836,000) as in the whole of Great Britain (population 55,500,000). Gangs of youths frequently run amok on the New York subway, beating up and seriously injuring many passengers, and the trains have to carry police escorts. Tokyo erupts from time to time in violent demonstrations and Japanese films contain so much violence that a large part ends up on the cutting-room floor when submitted for showing in this country.

But violent crime is steadily increasing in Britain, too, especially in the big cities. Can it be divorced from urban conditions? It is not a symptom of the city dweller's desire for freedom, his wish to escape from the urban straitjacket and worship of the machine?

Biologist Dr W. M. S. Russell told the 127th annual meeting of the British Association for the Advancement of Science that the most probable explanation for these rising crime rates was the natural reaction of any living creature towards overcrowding. 'Crowded monkeys, muskrats, meadow mice and wild rats attack and even kill their young', he stated. In the most congested section of

British cities there had been a tremendous increase in the number of infants and children beaten by their parents. An American commission attributed the growth of violence similarly to mass migration to urban areas and the decay of inner cities.

What, after all, are the complaints which British citizens make about cities? – that they are too big, too crowded, too noisy and dirty, too burdened with traffic and, generally, too inhumane. In other words, many city dwellers feel they do not matter; that they are mere ciphers, herded into buses and trains, factories, offices and restaurants and, when their day's work is done, shepherded off to some lonely bed-sitter or dingy hovel in twilight territory. Even the better-off in their leafy suburbs are frequently disappointed by the anonymity of their sur-roundings and the lack of neighbourhood feeling.

They are mostly too well-bred to indulge in any form of vandalism. Others have no such inhibitions. Manchester Corporation alone has to pay out around £150,000 a year on making good the damage done to schools, houses and parks.

Ripping out telephone equipment has grown rapidly in popularity. The ultimate irony for the harassed commuter who finds himself stranded due to an overstrained public transport system and who wishes to inform his wife or colleagues of the fact is to find that the one telephone box which happens to be unoccupied is out of order; another of those mundane irritations which raise the blood pressure and jangle the nerves.

At times like this we probably feel a little destructive ourselves, but being responsible citizens we suppress the feeling and so add to the constraints imposed on us by city life. Most people can find outlets for their frustrations which enable them to come through all right, but some cannot, and breakdowns occur. About three million people in this country are suffering from some mental disorder. Mr Christopher Mayhew, in an address to the National Association for Mental Health, of which he is chairman, denoted rootlessness, noise, overcrowding, urbanisation, isolation and the rat race as the main causes. The characteristics of contemporary society, he added, constituted a form of psychological pollution dangerous to mental health 'just as open sewers were once dangerous to the health of our bodies'.

A child born in Britain today, it is stated, has a greater chance of entering a mental hospital than of going to university. One girl in six and one boy in nine must expect to receive treatment in an institution for mental disorder at least once in their lifetime.

Is the city worth saving?

Even this necessarily brief outline of the present situation shows how desperate it has become. Huge efforts will clearly be required from all concerned if the city, as we know it, is to be saved.

But first we must ask ourselves whether the city, in its present form, is really worth saving? Are not these compact, high-density urban settlements outdated in this age of the motor vehicle? Shouldn't we start to plan new towns of a more spread-out nature to take into account the greater mobility of the town dweller? There is an influential school of thought among planners which earnestly believes this and which advocates the construction of 'linear' cities on Los Angeles lines (albeit greatly modified). The new city of Milton Keynes, which will ultimately have about a quarter of a million inhabitants, is one product of this thinking.

Against them, however, are ranged those who feel that we must make the compact city work, because a small and crowded country like Britain cannot afford these sprawling communities, eating up still more of our countryside and open space. Some feel, too, that it is the motor car which is out of place in cities and not vice versa, and that other forms of getting about, including a much improved public transport system, must be developed.

There is also the fact, of course, that compact cities are already here and contain much of our heritage of fine buildings, besides representing enormous capital investment. Tearing them down to make way for the motor car is likely to be too big and costly an undertaking. Changes must take place, including a good deal of redevelopment, but the bulldozer mentality which has laid waste to so much of America and which appears to be spreading to beautiful cities like Paris, does not find great favour in this country. The fact that there has been so much public opposition to the GLC's motorway plans is some evidence of the feeling which exists against tearing down established cities to make travelling by road more convenient.

An 'immense laboratory'

However, there has not yet emerged in this country a city 'philosopher' of the stature of, say, the American, Lewis Mumford. Nor have we a Jane Jacobs to stimulate our thinking. In her book, *The Death and Life of Great American Cities*, she describes the city as 'an immense laboratory of trial and error, failure and success, building and design'. Here she says, is where theories can be formed and tested.

One significant finding from recent studies which might help to guide the city planners is that produced by researchers for the Maud Commission on Local Government. They discovered that home to most people is a very small place, no more than a few streets, in fact. When citizens complain about cities being too big, don't they really mean that they can no longer identify themselves with small communities as they did in the past?

London, for instance, has been a huge city for a very long time. Way back in 1719 Daniel Defoe described it as a 'monster'. It was then little more than one-hundredth of its present size. Now it extends over a 40-mile radius of Charing Cross. Some 12½ million people live in this area, one-quarter of the population of the whole country. In fact, one-sixteenth of the population of England and Wales live in one-sixtieth of the land area.

My own experience may be relevant here. I can remember feeling very much at home in the London suburb in which I spent my childhood. I think my parents would agree that here was a genuine community. We weren't aware of living in a huge metropolis, only that we liked our little part of it very much indeed. It was a fascinating corner of London. There was a common opposite and a stable down the road where horses were kept. And lots of yards and alleyways.

I am told that modern building regulations don't allow for alleyways, which just shows what an ass the law can be sometimes. The cars didn't trouble us much; indeed, it used to be quite fun dodging them as they came around the corner.

Now the cars are everywhere, the houses look run-down, the little shops where you could hear all the gossip of the neighbourhood have been replaced by glossy chain stores and supermarkets. The district has become noisier and less convenient, and has lost most of its individuality.

Street games have gone

This has happened to countless small places in London and other big cities. As the better-off have moved out, so areas have been left to crumble away, largely because those who remain cannot afford to maintain their houses properly. Sometimes whole districts have been flattened and homes replaced by tall blocks of flats which, with few exceptions, merely add to the feeling of anonymity and fail to provide for children's play. Even the much-prized (by architects and planners) Roehampton Estate, it seems, is woefully short of proper recreational opportunities.

Children are, I think, especially victimised in modern cities. Traffic has swept away most of the old street games – hopscotch, marbles in the gutter, bowling hoops, spinning tops – and has made cycling a hazardous activity. So should we wonder that so many of the kids of today find outlets in violence or vandalism? We haven't yet appreciated the need to replace these lost facilities.

Closing streets to traffic is useful, but when you get older you need something more adventurous. Miss Audrey Lees, director of environmental health and protection for Liverpool, told a conference organised by the Council for Children's Welfare that city children do not play in playgrounds for more than a tiny proportion – say 5 per cent – of their waking hours even if such places are provided. The rest of the time they are in the streets, the shops, at home or a hundred and one other places.

All children are to some extent rebels against order and organisation, and like to feel they are making their own fun, not having it made for them. There is a world of difference between chancing upon an old derelict house with lots of rooms to explore and having one put there for the purpose.

Money spent on providing adequate playing facilities is not only an investment in the future, but an insurance against the abundant energies of the young being used in less constructive ways. Some measures would cost very little – making school gymnasia and playing fields available outside school hours and during the holidays, for instance.

The way forward

Removing traffic and creating 'environmental areas' on the lines of the Buchanan report on *Traffic in Towns* could be an essential first step in any rehabilitation project – something like this is being attempted in the Barnsbury district of North London. Part of these cities could be set aside for children.

Jane Jacobs has laid down four indispensable conditions for generating 'exuberant diversity' in a city's streets and districts . . .

1. The district, and indeed as many of its internal parts as possible, must serve more than one primary function, preferably more than two. These must ensure the presence of people who go outdoors on different schedules and are in the place for different purposes, but who are able to use many facilities in common.

2. Most blocks must be short; that is, streets and opportunities to turn corners must be frequent.

3. The district must mingle buildings that vary in age and conditions, including a good proportion of old ones so that they vary in the economic yield they must produce. The mingling must be fairly close-grained.

4. There must be a sufficiently dense concentration of people, for whatever purposes they may be there. This includes dense concentration in the case of people who are there because of residence.

This last condition may seem surprising at first, but it is recognising that city vitality is dependent on sufficiently large numbers of people using the streets. People are naturally gregarious and they should be able to mix easily and informally – all colours, classes and ages, that is; not the kind of segregation we find has developed in our cities, with the very rich living at the centre – where 'it is all happening' – the poor and the immigrants in the twilight inner suburbs and the middle classes and more affluent working classes on the outskirts and beyond the green belts.

Thomas Sharp, one of our leading town planners, has described the social effects of such segregation as 'deplorable' and has spoken of an artificial hardening and stiffening of attitudes when people of one social group rarely meet people of another group. How many of our social and industrial troubles are rooted in such causes?

There are some signs of change in the way in which local authorities are now providing homes for the higher income groups, in the attempts to secure more owner-occupation in the new towns and so on – but much more will be required if cities and their inhabitants are not to go under, through being divided among themselves.

Everyone is agreed on the need for policies to reduce city populations, but nobody has yet found a method which really works. Most of the movement away from the centres has taken place voluntarily, to the greener areas on the outskirts, and could lead ultimately merely to an extension of city boundaries. Much real progress has in any case been offset by the overall growth of population and by higher individual expectations in terms of space, housing and general amenities.

Decentralisation policies ought, therefore, to be accompanied by some form of overall population control. They must also be accompanied, and even preceded, by local studies, or there is a danger of the human factor being overlooked. It is at local level, at the place which people call 'home', where the work of planners and architects will be finally judged. And it is precisely this 'grass roots' examination which is jeopardised by the trend towards bigger and bigger planning bodies. The Maud Commission on Local Government recognised the need for some kind of representation at local level to make people feel they could play a part in decision-making. Let us hope it is not overlooked in any future system of local government.

While we must expect planners and architects to play a major part in improving city environments in future, they will be required to work much more closely with the inhabitants. Planning schemes must be advertised in advance and widely discussed.

Citizens, for their part, can help by taking an active and creative interest in their neighbourhoods and establishing civic and amenity societies to promote improvements. Only through a fruitful partnership between planners and planned – coupled with a policy on population – can our cities be saved from anarchy.

4. Cutting down the cars

In the autumn of 1963 I was stuck in a traffic jam. It was no ordinary jam or it would not be worth the telling. Nothing could move at all, in any direction. The traffic lights changed, and changed again; there was no response. We were completely snarled up. As far as the eye could see, cars had come to a halt, leaving their occupants stranded, like starfish on the shore.

Drivers switched off their engines, got out and walked aimlessly about. Explanations were sought, but none offered. It was strangely quiet. Somewhere or other we presumed someone was doing something. Meanwhile all we could do was wait. And the waiting seemed endless. Then, about one hour and forty-five minutes later, a movement began. We gratefully got into our cars and escaped.

This did not happen in the centre of a great city during the rush hour. It happened in Kingston, Surrey, on a Saturday afternoon. And for no apparent reason. There was no football match or race meeting or parade through the streets to account for it. The roads were not being repaired and there had been no accident.

On this particular occasion, it seems, the shoppers, day-outers and visitors to the town for all sorts of odd purposes had become inextricably intertwined with each other; something we had been warned by traffic experts was bound to happen one day, but which we never thought could happen to us.

There have been many similar, if less dramatic, events since then in many parts of the country, but the incident is worth recalling, I feel, because it shows that there is no single traffic problem; that although attention is focused on city centre snarl-ups during the week, the congestion caused by cross-town journeys in the outer suburbs may be just as great or even greater, and more difficult to relieve.

Just as there is no single problem, so there can be no single solution. A motorway may be perfectly acceptable between towns and even around towns, but not into the centre of towns, especially when thousands of families are displaced. A few areas can take more traffic, most already have far too much. Britain has more vehicles per mile of road (70) than any other country and (roads lobby please note) more roads per square mile, too. There are 14 million motor cars now and this number is expected to double by 1986. The planners admit that it would be impossible to accommodate this number of cars on any conceiveable road network.

Already far too many vehicles are roaring and spluttering and belching fumes through places where people want to shop in safety and comfort, and through others where they wish to live undisturbed. At the same time, it is clear

34

that people also want to go on using their cars, because no other method of transport offers such convenience and flexibility. How to resolve this dilemma has been the subject of innumerable plans, projects and propositions.

The most widely publicised was the Buchanan report on *Traffic in Towns* issued in 1963. It came out to the accompaniment of an almost embarrassing chorus of praise. Rarely has a document been so effectively killed by kindness as this one. Even the team's conclusion that costly town reconstructions would be necessary in many cases to provide pedestrian/vehicle segregation was loudly applauded – then quietly forgotten.

Nevertheless, the report set people talking and thinking about the subject to a remarkable degree. It clearly sowed quite a few seeds and if they mostly failed to flourish officially, they found fruitful soil amid some common pastures; notably at Barnsbury, in North London, where the residents got together to produce a scheme for a traffic-free 'environmental area' on Buchanan lines. This, in modified form, was ultimately accepted by Islington Borough Council and the GLC.

The 'safest town'

There is not much else to be seen on the ground as a result of Buchanan, however. Actual achievements have sprung from other sources. While the Buchanan group were theorising, for instance, Hugh Wilson and his team of architects and planners at Cumbernauld New Town were creating traffic/pedestrian segregation to the *n*th degree. This was only possible by making the new town a compact settlement, so that people did not have to walk too far to shops, friends and so on. Now they can do so without having to cross main roads by means of a separate footpath system.

Cumbernauld, in fact, is said to be the safest town in Britain, with road accidents per head of population only one-fifth of the national average. For once, children can play in safety on the abundant open space, which is not only fine for them but a great relief to their parents. Mr Ferdynand Zweig, one of Cumbernauld's critics, sourly complains that 'children run wild all over the town', but he nevertheless quotes comments from residents such as 'The children, they have a marvellous time here. They can run and play, safe from the traffic', and 'The children are happy and, looking at them, we too are happy.'

In his report on the new town (*The Cumbernauld Study*, Wates Ltd.) he does make one disturbing observation, however – that children who are not used to traffic, when they come into contact with it in Glasgow and elsewhere, are frightened and cling to their parents' hands. Can you shelter them from such influences too much?, he asks.

Whatever the defects of Cumbernauld – and they are many – I would suggest that this kind of planning is more far-sighted in regard to traffic than the approach to the new city of Milton Keynes, where the demands of the motor car have been conceded to the extent that the new city will consume 100 acres for every thousand of people employed, against the present average of 70 acres. The outlook for the citizens of another new town, Runcorn, is brighter – there the planners have opted for a high-frequency bus service running on roads freed from other traffic.

Shopping streets and precincts

Most other new towns have been content to establish shopping precincts on the lines of the bold and eminently successful venture in Coventry. Shopkeepers' fears that trade would suffer have everywhere proved unfounded; far from suffering, in fact, trade has generally increased, leading to demands from shopkeepers for pedestrian precincts elsewhere.

This has also happened where important shopping streets have been closed to traffic, like London Street, Norwich. Of 32 shopkeepers who provided figures during the experiment, 28 did more trade, in one case 20 per cent more. Mr Alfred Wood, city planning officer, has described in a report on the scheme (Norwich Corporation £1·05) how he visited successful footstreets in Dusseldorf, Essen, Cologne and Copenhagen before proceeding with the project in his own city. A survey carried out at the completion of the scheme revealed that only 4 per cent were entirely opposed to it.

As there was no legislation permitting streets to be closed to traffic for environmental purposes when this project was prepared, Mr Wood had to invoke a traffic regulation order. The 1968 Town and Country Planning Act now provides the necessary powers. This, coupled with the success of the Norwich venture, has induced a number of other towns to prepare similar plans. Bolton completed a project in 1969 whereby a substantial pedestrian precinct was created out of three existing streets – Oxford and Newport Street, and Victoria Square – in the city centre. York, Leeds and Swindon now have pedestrian streets; Swindon, in fact, proposes to free the whole of its 'new town' central area from traffic within a few years. London has lagged behind. A scheme was drawn up by the GLC for Bond Street, but the council yielded to protests by car owners and modified it considerably. It is now proposed that only one end of the road will be closed, thus limiting the use of the road to local traffic''; and this will only be done when evaluations have been made of experimental one-way traffic flows at present in progress.

Some pioneering projects

One of the most interesting and forward-looking traffic plans was produced by Mr Konrad Smigielski, the city planning officer for Leicester. Mr Smigielski established that full car use in the city centre would necessitate elaborate networks, huge parking areas, much reconstruction and an outlay of over £400 million.

Instead, he proposed that a high-capacity elevated inner motorway be constructed to replace the three ring-roads in the city development plan. Linked to it would be a series of interchange car parks where commuters and other 'non-essential' car users would stop and complete their journeys by public transport, including fast buses and mini-taxis. This project, which, for once in a way, combines the best features of both private and public transport, is now being put into effect. Its estimated cost is far less than the car free-for-all pattern – £135 million.

Liverpool also discovered that full motorisation would be out of the question – it would have entailed roads up to 36 lanes wide! So the city is implementing a combined motorway and new rail system which will considerably reduce the amount of traffic in the city centre – if they can get the money to carry it out.

One of the biggest objections to the use of cars for commuting is that they reduce the efficiency of buses, which carry on average 34 times the number of people who can be accommodated in a car in peak periods. Leeds plans to introduce Britain's first experimental municipal minibus service. It will operate in shopping streets where other traffic will be restricted during the day. Public transport will generally be given priority in the city centre. Express bus services will use the primary road network, taking people to work, shop and home, linked with park-ride services. City centre services will provide easy cross-city connections between bus and rail terminals, and car parks, and there will be the normal stopping service for off-peak travel. The minibuses are intended to be used for the city centre and park-ride services.

By-passes will be built to take out of the business area the 40 per cent of traffic which has no business there, and long-stay parking provided on the fringe of the central area will, it is hoped, encourage commuters to complete their journeys by public transport.

Far too few towns have drawn up comprehensive traffic plans, however. For the most part they are relying on parking restrictions to deter the motorist, which can only be partially effective – they have no influence on through traffic, for instance. The services of a relatively new band of specialists – traffic engineers – have been called upon to speed the flows and the various measures they have devised (one-way schemes, no right turns, etc.) have had the desired effect, though planners have protested that this amounts to pushing still more traffic through existing streets. Certainly they have made life more perilous for pedestrians.

No real policy

The absence of a clearly defined policy is one of the main obstacles to progress on this front. Such a policy should aim at encouraging the wider use of public transport and restricting cars. This could be done by investing in buses and railways rather than roads. The 1968 Transport Act provides 75 per cent Exchequer grants for capital investment in Undergrounds and smaller grants for passenger interchanges and buses. What a boon the Victoria Line in London has been, cutting the travelling time from Euston to Victoria by up to half an hour! Also, there could be more bus-only lanes in city centres and on urban motorways, fares could be reduced (perhaps putting rail and bus travel on the rates), parking restrictions stepped up and possibly some form of road pricing introduced with differential taxes based on horse-power. We should learn a lesson from Stockholm, which is said to have cut congestion and stepped up the use of public transport dramatically by providing a cheap standard ticket entitling the holder to travel where he likes within the city and up to 40 miles outside it.

The most economical schemes will combine the flexibility of the car – its ability to carry you from your very door and back again – with the carrying capacity of buses and trains, by providing interchange stations on the Leicester pattern.

Rigid divisions between investment in public and private transport such as exist at present can only lead to absurdities like rising commuter fares, motorways built without links to an adjoining Tube (like London's Westway) and demands that railways and buses should pay their way – though no such demands are made for cars and lorries.

Surveys have shown that traffic will expand and contract according to the space available for it. The average London car is driven for only about 2 per cent of its life; the rest of the time it is parked, and the extent of this parking is only too apparent. If we build more roads, whether they be motorways or not, and make travel by car easier, we simply encourage motorists to use their cars more widely. This will mean more congestion on approaches to the new roads, with a consequent loss of efficiency for buses and trains, and the new roads themselves could ultimately become clogged. In the United States, and especially in the town of Los Angeles, this self-defeating process can be seen in its most extreme form, with more and more traffic lanes having to be added and with the city being ultimately engulfed in a pall of smog caused by exhaust smoke.

It can be claimed, in any case, that it is the motor car which ought to be re-fashioned to suit the town, and not vice versa. The present vehicle, with its heavy demands on space and its high speeds which cannot be reached in congested conditions, is already an anachronism in city centres. The bicycle can often get there quicker! So why contemplate building new roads and all the upheaval and suffering these can cause to the families displaced, apart from the damage to the environment, when we shall be merely perpetuating an anachronism?

Schemes for wholesale bans on cars, however, would amount to an admission of failure to use a most valuable and widely appreciated technological tool, apart from being socially unacceptable and possibly economically undesirable. But if we are ever going to be able to strike the right balance – to work towards a level of car use at which the car will not interfere unduly with pedestrian or public transport movement, and will not cause too much environmental damage – it might prove essential to limit production in some way. The economic implications will have to be faced. Already there are signs of consumer resistance. Speaking at the 1971 Motor Show in London, Giovanni Agnelli, chairman of Fiat, said that, in general, world market opportunities for the motor industry in the near future would be much more restricted. 'A slow rejection process is under way in highly motorised countries,' he added, 'and the suitability of the car as a means of meeting the need for mobility in large metropolitan areas is under question'.

Clearly, the desirable level can be influenced by the nature of the car itself. If smaller, electrically-powered cars could be developed for use in towns, the level could probably be pitched higher.

We would still be using our cars in a woefully inefficient way, however. Any industrialist who employed expensive machinery for only 20 minutes of the day and then allowed it to become a positive hindrance to his operations would soon be out of business. Any city which permits its public transport services to be impeded by private cars to such an extent that these services have to be curtailed has surely got its priorities wrong.

New forms of transport

Systems are now being tested which would make better use of vehicles and road space. One is a form of taxi service run on guided tracks. You would buy a ticket, insert it into a programmed car and be whisked off to your destination. Unfortunately, it seems to be regarded as a supplement to present facilities rather than a replacement for them, as tracks running over the roads are envisaged.

If road traffic were reduced, why shouldn't the tracks be provided at ground level?

A better idea perhaps, would be to have small runabouts parked at suitable points throughout the city, possibly in parking meter bays. On inserting a coin, you would be able to drive to your destination and leave your vehicle at another meter for the next person to 'activate' it by inserting a coin. This would make the maximum use of the car's flexibility and of the available road space. One condition for its successful operation, of course, would be the widespread provision of off-street parking for private cars.

Nobody expects measures of this kind to meet with rapturous support on all sides. Powerful commercial interests are involved and, let's face it, we do so cherish our very own shiny, sleek automobiles. Nevertheless, we love them less than we did.

Even in the United States, where the car has been worshipped as nowhere else, people are calling for action to reduce the noise, pollution, danger and disruption it causes. The loudest appeals for action come from smog-drenched Los Angeles.

There have been too few soundings of public opinion on this question in Britain, but the results might surprise our leaders. In a poll in the London suburb of Putney, for instance, 81 per cent of those questioned – the majority being car owners – said they would approve restrictions on the use of private cars in peak hours if buses were improved. Governments tend to lag behind public opinion, so it may be some time before they recognise the strength of such feeling; especially with a vociferous motor lobby constantly clamouring for new roads.

We clearly need to see the development, on a national scale, of an equally vociferous lobby to that which emerged in opposition to London's ringway projects, but sufficiently broadly based to present constructive alternatives. It should challenge the degree of priority given to the motorist and the idea that towns be refashioned to suit the car. It should question the massive expenditure on roads and the miserable sums spent on public transport. It should recognise the folly of passively accepting population growth, and should campaign against passive acceptance of more and more cars on our overcrowded roads. It should also ask why manufacturers neglect to build safety factors into cars for the home market while compelled to do so for those meant for export.

It must challenge especially the acceptance of accident rates which, on a European scale, represent as many people being killed on the roads each year as were killed by the atomic bomb on Hiroshima.

Legislation:

Town and Country Planning Act (especially 1968, Closure of Highways)
Transport Act 1968

Mainly responsible:

Planning authorities, county boroughs, county councils (traffic regulation), county boroughs, boroughs, district councils (parking), Department of the Environment.

See also 'Reducing the Racket', 'The Colour of our Lungs' and 'The Mobile Millions'.

5. Homes for the under-privileged

The environment, like charity, begins at home, and if 'home' means a damp rotting basement surrounded by squawling children, the family is unlikely to be very much concerned with the environment outside. And in no other environmental field is the seeker after truth so beguiled by 'lies, damned lies and statistics' as in housing. Figures have been outrageously manipulated to try and suggest that all is going along very nicely thank-you.

Successive governments have engaged in a kind of competition in new construction, raising the target each time and sometimes nearly meeting it, so that the number of houses completed annually has almost doubled since 1945, despite recent setbacks. This enables certain politicians to claim that, with the number of households now exceeding our 17 million houses by half a million, the problem which has defied solution for so long is now virtually solved – apart, they may add casually, from the need for a 'nominal' 200,000 houses a year to provide for replacements, new households and so on.

This blandly ignores the important factor of how far progress made on the housing front measures up to needs. Here we come to another set of figures entirely.

At the end of 1970 it was estimated that over 20,000 people were in hostels for the homeless, about 8,000 more than in 1966 when *Cathy Come Home* was first shown – a trend confirmed by the Greve Report published in May, 1971. More than 190,000 families were on London's waiting lists, compared with 150,000 in 1966. Mr Peter Walker, the Environment Minister, has prophesied that by 1974 inner London could be short of 250,000 satisfactory homes. Glasgow still has 50,000 waiting for homes, Birmingham nearly 30,000 and Liverpool 13,000.

The 1966 sample census indicated that at least 1·6 million people were overcrowded, in what seems a fair definition of the term in relation to modern needs – that is, living at more than 1½ persons to a room, including kitchen – and nearly 400,000 of them were extremely overcrowded.

And while three-quarters of a million slums have been cleared since 1954 – an impressive achievement – there are still 1,800,000 homes officially declared unfit for human habitation and a further 4,700,000 are sub-standard; many require urgent work to save them slipping beyond redemption. Professor Colin Buchanan has estimated that more than 40 per cent of the population live in sub-standard accommodation. In Glasgow, which has one of the worst legacies of bad housing in the country, no fewer than 70,000 homes (one-third of the total) are unfit and there is a similar number of unfit homes in Liverpool. At the highest rate of slum clearance so far achieved – 83,000 a year – it would take over 20 years to clear the 1·8 million alone.

While there may be a crude surplus of homes over households in general terms, this matters little unless the homes are where they are wanted. It is no help at all to the occupant of a Glasgow tenement that homes stand empty in some rural district in the south of England, where jobs cannot be found even if the problems involved in moving house could be faced.

Furthermore, it is clear that our stock of houses includes millions which cannot, by any stretch of the imagination, be termed real homes. The files of 'Shelter', the National Campaign for the Homeless, are full of the most distressing cases. When my small son comes home proudly carrying his clarinet in a case and goes up to his room to practice, I think of those millions of children who haven't got a separate room even to do their homework in, let alone have their minds and senses opened to the satisfying world of music. In one case quoted by 'Shelter', a child had to do her homework in an outside lavatory to get some peace. Seven children lived in this house in Salford, which was damp and rat-infested. There was no bath and all the hot water had to be boiled on the stove. Husband and wife shared a bedroom with the four youngest children, and the three eldest, all girls, took the other bedroom. All the children had suffered from bronchitis and were consistently ill throughout the winter. A 26-year old divorced woman with five children occupied a one-room flat in Liverpool which was 'alive with cockroaches and mice'. The toilet consisted of a bucket in the room. Another family in Peckham, London, had to share a lavatory with 20 others. In yet another London district, Southwark, a woman and three children lived in two rooms which were so damp that the bedding was soaked and the children were ill throughout the winter of 1970.

The social costs

It is difficult to estimate the full social costs of bad housing, but they must be considerable. Newsom and Plowden have both stressed the close links between bad housing and low educational attainment. Plowden specifically referred to the adverse effects of overcrowding, lack of play space, insecure tenancies and the absence or sharing of basic amenities. Bad housing has also been linked with broken homes, juvenile delinquency, adult crime rates and higher health bills.

Mr Gordon Cherry, now deputy head of the Centre for Urban and Regional Studies in Birmingham, carried out a survey in Newcastle upon Tyne, in which he compared the least overcrowded third of the city with the most overcrowded third. He found that in the most overcrowded third t.b. notifications were double, peri-natal deaths 43 per cent higher and venereal disease and offences against the person five times more prevalent. There were seven times as many persons on probation in the overcrowded part, juvenile delinquency was three times as bad, cases of child neglect five to six times greater and of mentally sub-normal persons three times greater.

One social cost can be measured – that of children in care for housing reasons alone. It costs on average £8·9 to keep a child in care for a week, so that if there are 7,000-plus children in care for housing reasons, as there were at the time of writing – the total cost to the country is about £50,000 a week or £2,750,000 a year. For that kind of money you could do a great deal in the twilight areas. In fact, the cost of one child in care is often greater than the total rent the family proved unable to pay – it would be more economical to help them with the rent.

While there are clearly sound social arguments for better housing, it would be wrong to presume that we can solve most of these problems 'at a stroke' by removing people from bad houses and putting them into good ones. For one thing, we would have to be quite clear what we mean by bad and good accommodation. There are slums which provide a more congenial environment for people than many a brand-new council estate, and where you find little evidence of social malaise. Those housing authorities which adopt a 'do-gooding' stance and who feel rejected when the objects of their concern do not respond in the way it is felt they should have only themselves to blame.

Decent housing should not be wielded as a social weapon by those who think they know best, but should be regarded as everyone's birthright.

To attain a reasonable level for everyone, however, we must raise our investment considerably. At present we are bottom of the European 'league' in terms of the proportion of national resources and capital devoted to housing – even Ireland does better than we do, believe it or not.

The most intractable situations occur in the big towns, especially in London. Professor Greve feels that only a regional housing authority (which, he contends, the GLC is not) backed by big government subsidies, could solve the capital's problem, although a proposal by the London boroughs to set up a housing office to match the needs of the overcrowded inner areas with those of the more spacious outer boroughs looks encouraging. There is not only an absolute shortage of houses – in London the deficiency has been estimated at over 300,000 – but a shortage of homes at rents which people can afford to pay.

Those who believed poverty had been reduced to a trifling amount by more than a decade of growth in the economy and social services had a shock when the Ministry of Social Security released figures in 1966 showing that more than one-third of a million adults and a million children were estimated to be in old-standard initial poverty (*Circumstances of Families*, HMSO 1967). And less than one-half of this surprisingly large amount of poverty is being removed by the social security services. With large-scale unemployment, these figures are probably higher today. Such people often cannot afford even a rebated rent, and only one-third of local councils operate a rent rebate scheme.

The Cullingworth Committee on *Council housing purposes, procedures and priorities* (HMSO 75p) concluded that while most local authorities were operating schemes which did not prevent low-income families from becoming and remaining council tenants, there were a number whose rent policies 'might constitute an insurmountable barrier to such families'.

A new approach to rents

In fact, the whole system of housing finance leaves much to be desired. R. A. Parker, in a paper on *The Rents of Council Houses* (Bell, 1968) stated that there seemed a reasonable possibility that local authorities failed to identify their poorest tenants because income was measured in crude terms and little attention paid to income per head. 'The field of council rents is frankly chaotic. They are surrounded by untested assumptions, expediency, convention and lack of basic data.'

However, it seems that this patchwork pattern of subsidies, rebates, supplementary allowances, rent pooling and so on is to be recast. Mr Peter Walker, Secretary for the Environment, outlined the new policies in the Commons towards the end of November, 1970. He said the fair rent principle which was replacing controlled tenancies in the private sector would be extended within that sector and would also form the basis of local authority rents in England and Wales.

He also announced that a comprehensive programme of rent rebates and allowances would be drawn up for both the public and private sectors. This will remove a long-standing anomaly whereby unfurnished tenants of private landlords who are among the poorest and often live in the worst conditions, receive no financial help towards their housing costs. The other important change will be that subsidies will be related to people rather than buildings as at present.

These new measures were not expected to become operative before May, 1972 at the earliest. They certainly represent a bold attempt to deal with the problems. Some effects can be predicted. Rents may be expected to rise generally, as has happened under the 'fair rent' formula in the private sector, but we are told these will be graduated and that the increases will fall on those most able to pay.

The Government's strategy seems to be to 'rob Peter to pay Paul', to see that the better-off pay more, and sometimes considerably more, so that the poorer families can benefit. It may also be in the Government's mind that by exerting financial pressure of this kind it can persuade tenants who can afford to buy houses to do so and thus leave more accommodation for those not so well off. At least one million tenants can buy, according to a report published by the Housing Research Foundation.

It all sounds fine, but one must have doubts about a scheme introduced against a background of cuts in public spending. One of the main aims, it was stated, was to save £300 million a year in subsidies. This will be achieved through higher rents for council tenants. True, many will be entitled to rebates, but previous experience suggests that not all of them by any means will apply. So there is bound to be hardship. Also, will the saving be so great when one has taken into account the cost of the army of bureaucrats needed to work out the rebates? The fact that furnished tenants are not covered is also regrettable, as these are among the most exploited. Another big question mark is whether there will be enough of the more affluent tenants to enable the scheme to work effectively without higher Government subsidies.

Surveys have shown that the stories of council tenants with a boat in the back garden and a Jaguar in the front are grossly exaggerated (only 1 per cent of council tenants have gross incomes of £40·00 a week and over). Most council tenants need a subsidy – and don't forget that owner-occupiers receive a hidden subsidy through tax reliefs. These totalled £222 million in 1968-69.

Government purposes could also be frustrated by rising costs. Construction costs alone more than doubled in the ten years between 1959 and 1968, and land prices have soared astronomically. In Birmingham land costs can account for more than £500 per council house or flat before a brick is laid. In London this figure can be much higher. Land prices in the private sector in London are running at around £31,000 an acre, five times the national average. Mr Ray Thomas, in research for Political and Economic Planning, prophesied that the GLC may be paying £400,000 an acre for residential building land by 1981.

Long before that some Government may have devised an effective formula for tackling the compensation and betterment dilemma (*see chapter on planning*). One proposal is that betterment (that is, the increased value accruing to land as the result of community action) could be collected through capital gains tax and redistributed in the form of special subsidy or housing allowance to poorer families.

There is some hope that in due course industrialised techniques might bring down construction costs; results so far in this respect have proved disappointing. It would be very sad indeed if local authority housing standards had to be reduced, after showing so much improvement in recent years. Council housing in some areas now compares most favourably with the private product, partly because councils have to build to Parker Morris standards, whereas private builders do not.

Better use of existing houses?

With building land in the bigger towns so hard to come by and so costly, it seems evident that the problem will never be solved by relying on new construction alone. Can we not make better use of the houses we have, therefore? Our present stocks are ill-suited to needs. They consist, for the most part, of standard, three-bedroom properties which, with dismal lack of vision, both public and private sectors have continued to build. Now we find ourselves in a situation where nearly half the number of households consist of one and two persons only, which means that many houses are under-occupied and much valuable space unused; at a time when many large families are desperate for decent accommodation. The GLC discovered in a survey of its estates that there would be no fewer than 136,000 rooms for people on the waiting lists if existing over-housed tenants could be persuaded to move. Some 43 per cent, or nearly 100,000 homes, had one or more rooms above the number considered necessary for the size of family. 'Significant' under-occupation was said to have risen from 9·2 per cent to 14·2 per cent in eight years; in 7,000 homes there were three or more rooms going free.

There is evidence of a similar situation elsewhere in the local authority field and, according to Professor David Donnison, under-occupation is three or four times more prevalent in privately rented or owner-occupied accommodation than in council dwellings.

The 1966 sample census gives an estimate of 1,067,150 cases in Britain where single people are occupying five rooms and over. More than 10,000 are thought to have ten rooms and more. And this is in a country where about 2,000 people are made homeless every month and where, at any one time, about 12,000 are living in hostels!

There are also, at any one time, more than 500,000 houses standing empty for one reason or another, and I think it is fair to assume that thousands of these could be put to good use.

What makes the situation even more tragic is that many of the single people occupying these large houses would dearly love to move, if only they could find a smaller house within reasonable distance of where they are now living. The National Old People's Welfare Council is constantly getting inquiries of this kind. Unfortunately, the shortage of smaller houses is so acute that it is difficult to meet such requests. Some local authorities, including the GLC, are well aware of the problem and doing what they can. Most are doing little or nothing, and the private sector, with the exception of housing societies and associations, would appear to be doing even less. If progress could be made towards ensuring a better distribution of housing space, the benefits could clearly be considerable.

However, a good deal is happening in one other respect. Steps are now being taken to arrest the decline of our older houses and prevent them degenerating into slums.

The Government's 1967 survey showed that there were more unfit and sub-standard houses than ever – 3·7 million needed substantial repair and 2·3 million lacked one or more of the basic amenities. Experts have pointed out that improving existing dwellings is much cheaper and quicker than replacing them.

Many of the problems were examined in *The Deeplish Study* (1966) an investi-gation of a run-down area in Rochdale sponsored by the Government. Then the recommendations of a sub-committee of the Central Housing Advisory Com-mittee under Mrs Evelyn Denington were embodied in a White Paper, *Old Houses into New Homes*, and this was followed by the 1969 Housing Act.

The Act created a new structure of improvement grants under which the limits were raised – though the owner still has to find half the money – and local authorities were also given power to declare general improvement areas. This enables them to call for help from Westminster. If it agrees, the Government will find £50 for every house provided the council finds a similar sum. Thus, for 300 houses a total of £30,000 would become available for traffic improvements, landscaping, layout of childrens playgrounds, removal of eyesores and so on.* More important, however, it starts people thinking about the area as a whole and how it might be improved.

It is laid down in the Act that landlords can charge fair rents after the work has been done instead of the old controlled rent, provided the results are satisfactory to the local authority.

Persuasion rather than enforcement is to be the method adopted; compulsory purchase powers are available, but are only to be used as a last resort. This means that close links will have to be established between planners and planned. Local authority officers and members will have to go out into the field to meet people and discuss their housing problems. And they will have to look at *all* housing stocks in the area. This can surely do nothing but good.

Some authorities and housing associations have already carried out improve-ment schemes under previous legislation, one of the most notable being that accomplished by the Urban District Council of Whitworth, Lancashire – known as the Leavengrave Environmental Recovery Project – whereby a derelict district was transformed with technical and financial help from the Ministry of Housing and Local Government. Other projects were carried out by the Civic Trust for the North West at Skelmersdale, by Exeter City Council in its Newtown district, and by the London Borough of Lambeth. The new Act should enable much more to be done on these lines.

'Shelter' neighbourhood project

A most interesting pilot project to see how the Act would work was carried out by 'Shelter' in an unpromising part of Liverpool, which had actually been on the council's list for clearance when they had second thoughts about it.

This Shelter Neighbourhood Action Project might well be taken as a model

* Extra grants for home owners and local authorities in development and 'intermediate' areas were provided for in a Bill introduced by the Government in the summer of 1971.

of how such a campaign should be conducted. The people of the area were encouraged to participate through street groups, democratically elected committees and so on. Studies were made of such questions as vice and vandalism; education and recreation; traffic and landscape; and services. A full-scale survey of the area was carried out.

An advice centre was established where drawings were prepared and grant applications processed.

The results were remarkable. Whereas over the previous 14 years only three grants a year had been paid, nearly 200 applications were submitted in the first nine months. Scores of homes were converted and improved.

The survey revealed that a surprisingly high proportion of residents (65 per cent) liked their houses and 41 per cent also liked the area. An overwhelming majority said they would stay if improvements were carried out.

It made one wonder how many other areas likewise contained within themselves the seeds of regeneration? Do we take sufficiently into account, when considering slum clearance, the value of intricate patterns of human relationships built up over many years? Have we, in other words, placed too much emphasis on buildings and too little on people?

The 1969 Act – surely one of the wisest of all housing measures in recent years – should help to ensure that we get our priorities right. If used in the right way, these powers could aid diversity. Houses not worth keeping can be pulled down and replaced by new dwellings, while others can be improved. How much better the results would be than a one-class council estate!

The success of housing policies in future will turn largely on how far they are directly geared to people's needs. While housing associations may not have made a significant contribution yet in terms of numbers, their efforts have often proved invaluable in being specifically directed towards the elderly, disabled and others who require a special approach. In this respect they have often filled a gap left by the other housing agencies.

To meet people's needs, however, one must first know what those needs are. There is still far too little 'feedback' in housing. Few sustained attempts are made to find out where a scheme has succeeded and failed. More serious still is that real consultations with the users – the potential tenants of an estate, for instance – involving examination of the plans *before* they are implemented, are so rare as to merit headlines in the papers when they occur; this was the treatment given to an experiment conducted by architects and planners of the Department of the Environment who, we learnt, were reported to be shaken by housewives' comments on their ideas. One effective way of bringing the architects and planners down to earth would be to require them to live on their estates for a period as ordinary tenants.

Much unnecessary trouble is caused because people do not know where to go for advice; a point stressed in the Greve Report, which especially recommended examination of the need for community legal advice. Shelter has had an advisory centre going for some years now and the London Borough of Lambeth, which has tackled its manifold problems in a most forthright fashion, set one up in May, 1970, and has been inundated with inquiries ever since. One of the most practical and helpful steps which could be taken in the years to come would be to establish such centres in every town and city.

WHO DOES WHAT?

Because there seems to be much public confusion about the roles of the various agencies in housing, it might be useful to summarise these as follows, bearing in mind that nothing is static . . .

Department of the Environment

Exercises overall control of housing policy, though Lady Evelyn Sharp in her book on *The Ministry of Housing and Local Government* (now part of the new department), feels this is nothing like firm enough. 'What really bedevils housing,' she writes, 'is the lack of any coherent philosophy about its economic basis.'

However, controls are exercised over local authority programmes, chiefly financial ones, based on what the Government feels should be the share of the national 'cake' allocated to housing. The department also pioneers new housing approaches through its research and development group, which publishes somewhat belated accounts of its activities. New building techniques are more directly the concern of the National Building Agency, now almost entirely involved in the housing field.

Local authorities

Their role is generally interpreted as being to meet the needs of the local community in terms of housing irrespective of whether people can afford to pay for the accommodation offered. This involves clearing the slums and rehousing their occupants, providing subsidised housing for the poor, the elderly and the disabled, and meeting the special needs of students and single people. Many councils feel they have a duty to cater for the better off, too – those who can afford to pay economic rents – to provide more balanced communities. They can also stimulate private building and owner-occupation by granting mortgages, and they have an important new role in improving our stocks of older houses. Unlike the private sector, all local authority houses have to be built to Parker Morris standards.

Private builders

They are generally regarded as building for owner-occupation but it may not be appreciated that half of their output consists of houses put up for local authorities. Though not directly controlled by the Government, their operations are influenced by dear money policies, restrictions on land use and other decisions emanating from governments.

Housing associations (not to be confused with housing societies, *see* below)

These voluntary, non-profit-making bodies provide accommodation for those in need, which entitles them to government subsidies and local authority grants. There are around 2,000 associations accounting for about 3 per cent of our housing and co-ordinated by the National Federation of Housing Societies. A notable newcomer to this sector in recent times has been 'Shelter'. Apart from aid through local authorities, societies may also obtain funds from charities and building societies.

Housing societies

Provide cost rent and co-ownership housing for people unable to buy or rent in the usual way, under the aegis of the Housing Corporation set up by the Government in 1964. Up to half the money for approved schemes comes from the corporation as a rule and the other half from building societies. All schemes have to be built to Parker Morris standards.

Legislation:

Housing Acts 1930, 1957 (slum clearance) and 1969. Rent Acts, 1957, 1965. Housing Repairs and Rents Act 1954. Housing Subsidies Act 1967.

Mainly responsible:

Greater London Council, London boroughs, county boroughs, boroughs, district councils, Housing associations and societies, private builders, Department of the Environment.

Historic Buildings

6. Beating the bulldozer

A nation's stock of buildings represents an accumulation of riches beyond price. Each age makes its contribution and whether it be great or small, it will be unique to the period. Later builders may attempt to copy the earlier styles, but in building as elsewhere it is the genuine article which is most valued. The farther back you go in history, the fewer genuine articles you find and thus the greater their value. Other buildings may be unique not because they are old but because they embody the creative genius of great architects.

Britain is a real treasure-house in this respect. We have small churches dating back to Saxon times and our great medieval cathedrals are among the finest in the world. The towns of East Anglia in particular are famous for their timber Tudor dwellings, and people come from all over the world to visit the great houses and estates of the 17th and 18th centuries, to marvel at the baroque splendours of Vanbrugh and Hawksmoor, and at the landscaped gardens of William Kent and 'Capability' Brown.

We shall never see the like again of the work of Inigo Jones, ambassador of the Italian Renaissance, with his masterpieces at Greenwich and in Whitehall, nor that of his disciple, Christopher Wren. And those steel and glass structures of the 19th century – exhibition buildings, railway stations and bridges – are monuments to honest and skilful engineering.

Then there are groups of buildings conceived as architecturally unified schemes, like the squares and terraces of Bloomsbury, Bath, Edinburgh and Newcastle upon Tyne, where the individual buildings are distinctive enough to be singled out for conservation. Secondly, and more commonly in England, are areas which have grown up organically over the centuries and which have considerable group value. Individually the buildings may not be remarkable, but with others they form a unity which brings character and distinction to our towns. Until the Civic Amenities Act was passed in 1967, these areas were not protected.

It is inevitable that over the years this intricate tapestry should undergo changes – some refashioning here, some make-do-and-mend there. Often the changes are more radical, however. Perhaps the town becomes economically run-down – people move out and the buildings fall into decay. Or prosperity may create enormous pressures, making demands for redevelopment almost irresistible.

But every strand of the historic fabric which is permitted to disintegrate represents an irreparable loss. Every weaver's cottage allowed to crumble away means another part of our heritage which can never be replaced.

The 19th and 20th centuries have seen this heritage defiled at a rapidly rising rate. Rows of distinguished buildings have been torn down to make way for factories, roads, supermarkets and tall flats and offices of depressing uniformity. The growth of towns has been marked by a plunge in the quality of their elements. Grace and elegance have given way to brashness and vulgarity. Bloomsbury is fighting a losing battle for survival and Kensington is crumbling.

But this erosion is now being fought. Along with the desire to build a new Britain which marked the post-war period came a resolve to protect and enhance all that was best in the built environment. The 1947 Town and Country Planning Act gave effect to this feeling by requiring the Minister of Housing and Local Government to compile lists of buildings of special architectural or historic interest. Investigators were sent out to make detailed surveys and to recommend structures for listing according to criteria laid down by a standing advisory committee. This was an important first step. Buildings in grades I and II were afforded statutory protection, and a supplementary list – grade III – was drawn up for those not deemed to justify statutory listing but to be worth preserving if possible.

At the end of 1970 there were 120,000 buildings listed, mostly small houses. The first listing took over 20 years to complete, but speedier procedures have now been introduced. The lists are also being revised. Following a recommendation by the 'listing sub-committee' of the Historic Buildings Council, which advises on the criteria to be adopted, the grade III category is being dropped and the more important buildings placed on the statutory list – the remainder are being brought to the attention of local authorities for consideration when exercising their planning powers. You may inspect the lists at The National Monuments Record, Fielden House, Great College Street, London, S.W.1 or The Welsh Office, Summit House, Windsor Place, Cardiff (see also section 24, Directory).

Buildings in grades I and II are now more firmly safeguarded by the provisions of the 1968 Town and Country Planning Act and the Civic Amenities Act, 1967. Owners now have to seek express permission through the local authority to alter or demolish a listed building and must advertise the application. Previously they were only required to notify the authority and could assume it was all right to go ahead if they heard nothing. The penalties for infringement have also been raised to up to one year's imprisonment, with or without a fine related to the profit which could accrue from demolition or had already been obtained. An owner who fails to keep a listed building in good repair risks having it compulsorily purchased by the local authority. Councils also have the power under Section 6 of the Civic Amenities Act to carry out urgent repairs, but as they cannot at present recover the cost from the owner, the teeth are effectively drawn from this provision.

Threats to a notable building which is not listed can be forestalled by the local authority serving an emergency building preservation notice. This gives the building the same protection as if it were listed.

These negative controls are supported by more positive steps. The Department of the Environment spends £800,000 a year to maintain castles, abbeys and other historic structures like Stonehenge, and £200,000 on the Royal Palaces. The Historic Buildings Council for England and Wales has been providing owners with grants totalling around £1 million a year and its Scottish equivalent pays out £75,000 annually.

Grants are given for all kinds of buildings, from windmills to palaces, and although many feel the sums to be totally inadequate, the fact remains that very few major structures have been lost for lack of money in recent times.

Under the 1962 Local Authorities (Historic Buildings) Act, every local council has power to make grants for the upkeep of historic buildings in its area. Very few, in fact, do so. Mr Grenville Powney, a Suffolk business consultant who owns an historic building himself, became so frustrated at trying to interest his local authority that he carried out his own nation-wide survey. He found that grants made by local councils averaged only 84p each during the financial year 1968–69 and that councils in fact spent more on cleaning their offices than on the preservation of such buildings.

In the year ended March 31, 1969, only 148 authorities in England provided any support to owners at all – about 1,090 provided none. Worthy exceptions to this general lack of concern were the GLC and Hampshire, who headed the list with grants totalling £24,000 and £27,000 respectively.

Mr Powney also made the disturbing discovery that three-quarters of listed building owners didn't know their properties were on the list, so weren't aware they had any responsibilities thereto and that they could obtain grants towards their upkeep.

Local authorities have been castigated for their apathy, but until quite recently it might have been contended that public apathy was just as great. There has, however, been a remarkable change in recent times and public interest is growing.

It will surely have been stimulated further by the conservation awards scheme promoted by *The Times* and the Royal Institution of Chartered Surveyors and in which first, second and third prizes in 1971 went to Holywell Urban District Council (for work on some listed cottages), Swindon Borough Council (for rehabilitating its railway village) and the city of Chester for conserving the only remaining row of 17th century terraced cottages aligning the city walls.

Much of the credit for the changed atmosphere must go to the Civic Trust, which has spearheaded the work of some 700 amenity societies and whose president, Mr Duncan Sandys, piloted the Civic Amenities Act through Parliament as a Private Member's Bill.

Nor should the splendid contribution made by the National Trust be overlooked. The trust owns 200 historic buildings and about half a million acres of beautiful countryside and coast. It would also appear that the persistent and determined effort over the years by bodies like the Society for the Protection of Ancient Buildings, the Ancient Monuments Society, the Georgian Group and Victorian Society, the Council for the Protection of Rural England and innumerable local societies is at last bearing fruit.

The number of listed buildings being destroyed annually is falling. In 1970 it was around 200, about half the number four years earlier.

However, it is not sufficient to protect individual buildings. As was pointed out earlier, there are groups of buildings which, though not remarkable in themselves, nevertheless form a collective unity which ought to be preserved, not as some antiquarian exercise, but as part of the normal planning process.

Town schemes

Until the Civic Amenities Act was passed, the only way of ensuring that such groups were properly looked after was through 'town schemes' operated in conjunction with the Historic Buildings Council. Under these schemes grants are made jointly by the Government and local authorities for half the required sum and owners are expected to find the other half. Application for such grants must first be made to the local authority. Many towns are operating such schemes; the biggest so far is at York, where some 400 buildings are involved.

Since the introduction of the Civic Amenities Act, it has been stipulated as a condition of approving such a scheme that it should be within a 'conservation area'. These are areas deemed to be of special architectural and historic value, and whose character should therefore be protected or enhanced. The Act gave planning authorities power to designate such areas and many have lost no time in doing so. By the middle of 1971 there were nearly 1,500 in being and it is expected that some 3,000 will ultimately be established.

Designation by itself is not, of course, enough. It does little more than focus attention on the need for conservation. Indeed, in the early period of the Act it seemed that it could provide no more than paper protection. Great concern was felt about the way buildings in these areas continued to be demolished without any apparent let or hindrance.

However, legislation to see that buildings within conservation areas cannot be demolished without prior planning consent has now been promised. In announcing that this would be done, Mr Peter Walker, Secretary of State for the Environment, described it as 'a long-overdue reform'.

This would greatly strengthen conservation measures, but there are still legislative gaps, as the Preservation Policy Group has pointed out. This group was set up in 1966, under the chairmanship of Lord Kennet, to consider what changes might be desirable in current legal, financial and administrative arrangements for preservation, including the planning and development aspects. In its report – issued in May, 1970 – the group recommended that an Exchequer subsidy be made available to local authorities for the repair of listed buildings and that they should be empowered to charge the owner when they themselves carried out repairs. Also, present legislation should be amended so that' an owner deliberately neglected a listed building to realise its break-up value, the local authority might acquire it at a price which excluded the break-up element.

These two recommendations were accepted in principle by the Government, but a decision on a third – that Whitehall should pay local councils half the annual deficit incurred in new conservation schemes – was postponed until the results were known of pilot projects at Chester, York, Bath and Chichester. These are being carried out following studies of the four cities commissioned in 1966 jointly by the Minister of Housing and Local Government and the city and county councils concerned. The pilot schemes, which will enable conservation theories to be applied, are bound to take years to complete. Thus the Government's decision is most disappointing for all those who had hoped to see money being put into conservation on a truly meaningful scale. The PPG thought a grant of this nature would encourage a comprehensive approach and also felt it anomalous that redevelopment should be encouraged in this way but not conservation.

The group left its financial proposals to the end because 'all else hangs on them'. However, its report also pointed out that, handicapped though they might be by the absence of such general assistance, authorities could still do a great deal of conservation work. For a very small outlay paintwork can be renewed, eyesores removed, rubbish and dereliction cleared up, and perhaps improvement street improvement schemes carried out on the lines so widely demonstrated by the Civic Trust.

Grants are already available for town schemes and for environmental improvements – as well as improvements to individual houses – under the 1969 Housing Act. Some road schemes also rank for grant and so does the provision of public open space.

Whether radical measures like re-siting non-conforming industry and tackling serious economic problems will be feasible, however, remains to be seen, though encouragement may be drawn from the experience, for instance, of Haddington, county town of East Lothian, which has been rescued from stagnation and decay through an overspill agreement with Glasgow.*

The traffic problem

Pilot projects in the historic towns should throw a good deal of light on the practical possibilities. Nobody doubts that the biggest – and most expensive – of all problems to solve will be that of traffic. Heavy lorries thundering through historic streets make a mockery of conservation. Re-creating a peaceful atmosphere in which people can see and enjoy beautiful buildings must be a prior aim. Not only can traffic ruin the visitor's pleasure, but it can result in the area becoming run-down. The effects can most clearly be seen in the shopping areas of some historic cities, and especially in the upper storeys of shops – often aesthetically the most pleasing – which have frequently been deserted and made derelict. One of the main reasons people give for moving out of central areas is the noise of traffic. 'Noise is the curse of York', said Lord Esher in his study of that city. And Professor Buchanan declared, after taking a look at Cirencester: 'It is the traffic problem that dominates all others.'

Among proposals for reducing the traffic load in historic cities is the creation of pedestrian streets on the lines of those at Leeds, Bolton, Leicester and Norwich. These have all been remarkably successful and it looks as if a pilot project in York – where a principal shopping street, Stonegate, has been closed to traffic – will be equally rewarding. In particular, shopkeepers' fears about

---

52   * These and other projects are featured in an excellent film called *A Future for the Past* available from the Civic Trust

possible loss of trade have been proved unfounded. Trade has, in fact, generally increased, with the result that traders elsewhere are now demanding that their streets, too, should be closed to traffic.

Certainly there is no place in any city centre for traffic which merely wishes to get through it to somewhere else. Besides by-passes, ring roads and other measures designed to ensure that only essential traffic is accommodated, we can, it seems, look to the motorways to provide relief. When introducing plans for a thousand miles of new construction by the early 1980s, Mr Peter Walker made a point of declaring that the proposed network would benefit nearly all the historic towns listed by the Council for British Archaeology and which were on trunk roads.

Cost of conservation

Much can be done without costing a penny more. But nothing will be gained by pretending that conservation can be cheaply bought. 'The magic philtre which would enable the streets and closes of this country's oldest towns to keep their charm has one indispensable ingredient – more money,' wrote *The Sunday Times*. This was also the main findings of the Preservation Policy Group. Lord Esher's estimate of the cost of a scheme for York (£2 million) was thought far too low by the city council, who put it at nearly double; a lot of money indeed. The way in which the public rallied to the Esher proposals was encouraging, however, and led to three-quarters of them being adopted.

While preparing to move boldly forward to the next stage of its conservation programme, York City Council has stressed that the financial burden is one which York cannot be asked to bear alone. Other historic centres take the same stand.

The case for a bigger national contribution does not only rest on intangibles. Something like £550 million is being spent annually by about seven million foreign visitors to this country, and our historic towns are among the chief attractions. The total expenditure by all visitors, English and foreign, to Bath is at least £3·56 million a year.

Would that more cities had followed the example of Chester in establishing a special conservation rate! Not all the extra finance needs to come from public sources, however. What happened at York – where £2 million was raised in a relatively short time to save The Minister – and to similar 'self-help' ventures in Lincoln and Shrewsbury shows how much can be achieved when public interest is aroused.

The National Trust for Scotland operates what is known as a 'revolving fund', which was launched in 1961 to encourage the preservation of little houses of architectural merit, individually or in groups. Starting with initial capital of £20,000 – subsequently boosted to £100,000 by grants and interest-free loans – the Trust acquires properties, restores them and seals them under covenant. Proceeds from sales are returned to the fund to finance further work. About 100 properties have been dealt with in this way over nine years.

Some of the 22 historic buildings preservation trusts also use this technique. The Civic Trust has proposed* that the idea could be extended through a national network of preservation agencies having a target of 400 restorations a year. To meet this target, a capital sum of the order of £3 million would be necessary, spread over some 200 local trusts. A National Buildings Conservation Fund could be set up, it is suggested, with a capital float of about £1 million. The

*Report available from Civic Trust (30p, 35p post paid).   53

fund's resources, subscribed by industry and commerce, and guaranteed by Government, would be advanced to the local trusts and repaid on the resale of restored properties. Building societies, local authorities, local appeals and private loans might be expected to provide up to 75 per cent of the capital required for purchase and restoration, with the fund lending the remaining quarter.

One class of building outside the public conservation 'umbrella' at present are the churches, which are subject only to normal planning control, although the State does contribute to the Redundant Churches Fund. Self-help has not proved adequate to keep many incomparable churches and cathedrals in proper repair, and there is much discussion as to possible ways of increasing aid. A private Members' Bill proposes to extend listed building control to all ecclesiastical structures. Finding new uses for redundant churches is often the best way of preserving them. One London church has become a block of flats, another will be a theatre and a third may house a market.

Although State and local authority finance may not be the only source of funds by any means, experience has shown that it is often necessary for such aid to be seen on the ground – perhaps in the form of a new precinct or attractive open space – to spark off a general improvement drive. Public co-operation measures to upgrade run-down districts by means of the increased grants available under the 1969 Housing Act – a valuable new conservation 'tool' – can be most effectively secured by building a couple of show houses in the area.

This is not a job which can be done from above. Everyone must be involved – State undertakings, local authorities, private developers, preservation trusts, amenity societies and the public generally. Only through such a combined assault on erosion and decay can our historic towns and cities continue to delight their inhabitants and attract a steadily rising number of visitors from all parts of the world.

Population growth is threatening standards here as in many other respects. It is a sobering thought that out of 25 English towns, excluding London, which in 1801 had populations of at least 12,000, the only ones to survive to be classified in 1965 by the Council for British Archaeology as having town centres worthy of preservation were mainly those which had grown the least. And historic towns tend to grow the fastest!

But we can take heart from the enthusiasm being displayed by the young to conserve old buildings. Of the scores of people who worked on the York study, all were under 40 and the majority were students.

This has prompted Lord Esher to declare that 'the myth of a golden past, which inspired all the great innovators from Alberti to Pugin – inspired for example, the almost miraculous silhouette of the Houses of Parliament – may yet have some potency in the mind of man.'

Legislation:

Historic Buildings Act 1953
Town and Country Planning Acts 1962, 1968 (part V)
Local Authorities (Historic Buildings) Act 1962
Civic Amenities Act 1967 (part 1)
Housing Act 1969
Redundant Churches Act 1969

Mainly responsible:

Planning authorities, Historic Buildings Council, National Trust, Civic Trust, Historic buildings trusts, Department of the Environment.

Further reading

Cities

Jacobs, Jane, *The Death and Life of Great American Cities*, Pelican, 1964.
Morris, Desmond, *The Human Zoo*, Jonathan Cape, 1969.
Mumford, Lewis, *The Culture of Cities*, Secker and Warburg, 1st edn. (1938)
Osborn and Whittick, *The New Towns: Answer to the Megalopolis*, 2nd edn., Leonard Hill, 1969.
Hillman, Judy (ed.), *Planning for London*, Penguin Special, 1971.
Sharp, Thomas, *English Panorama*, Architectural Press, 1950.

Traffic

Traffic in Towns, Buchanan Report, *HMSO* 1963, Penguin, 1964.
Tetlow and Goss, *Homes, Towns and Traffic*, Faber, 1968.
Wood, A. A., *The Creation of a Foot Street*, Norwich Corporation.
  Foot Streets in Four Cities, Norwich Corporation.
Richards, Brian, *New Movement in Cities*, Studio Vista, 1966.
Ritter, Paul, *Planning for Man and Motor*, Pergamon, 1964
Smigielski, K., *Leicester Traffic Plan*, Leicester Corporation, 1964
Gruen, Victor, *The Heart of Our Cities*, Thames and Hudson, 1965
Road Pricing, The Smeed Report, HMSO 1964.

Housing

Sandford, Jeremy, *Cathy Come Home*, Pan, 1967.
Allaun, Frank, *Heartbreak Housing*, Zenith, Hodder and Stoughton, 1968.
Wilson, Des, *I Know it was the Place's Fault*, Oliphants, 1970.
Cullingworth, J. B., *Housing and Local Government in England and Wales*, Allen and Unwin, 1966.
Face The Facts, Shelter Report, National Campaign for the Homeless.
Donnison, David, *The Government of Housing*, Pelican, 1967.
Burney, Elizabeth, *Housing on Trial*, for Institute of Race Relations by OUP, 1967.
Council Housing: Purposes, Procedures and Priorities, Cullingworth Committee report, HMSO, 1969.
Homes for Today and Tomorrow, Parker Morris report, HMSO, 1961, reprinted 1969.
Our Older Homes, A Call for Action, Denington Report, HMSO, 1966.
The Deeplish Study: improvement in Rochdale, HMSO, 1966.
Old Houses into New Homes, HMSO, Cmnd 3602, 1968, repr. 1969.
Living in a Slum: a study of St. Mary's, Oldham, HMSO, 1970.
Moving out of a Slum: moving from St. Mary's, Oldham, HMSO, 1970.
Housing in Britain, COI reference pamphlet, HMSO, 1970.
Homelessness in London, by John Greve, Dilys Page and Stella Greve, Scottish Academic Press.

Historic Buildings

Preservation Policy Group Report, HMSO, 1971.
Conservation progress reports, *Civic Trust*
Historic Towns: Preservation and Change, HMSO, 1967.
Houses of Historical or Architectural Interest, Gowers Report, HMSO, 1950
Greater London Council booklet on Historic Buildings, GLC, 1970.
Historic Buildings Council annual reports, HMSO
The Continuing Progress: A history of the National Trust, Longman's, 1968.

POLLUTION:

This Septic Isle

By the year 2000 the United Kingdom will simply be a small group of impoverished islands, inhabited by some 70 million hungry people, of little or no concern to the other 5-7 billion people of a sick world. – Paul Ehrlich, Professor Biology, Stanford University, California.

Fred Hoyle, the mathematician and science-fiction writer, calculates that the crash is due in 2250 when, he thinks, world population will have reached 25 billion – but demographers expect this figure to be reached before 2070 at present rates. The population will collapse to a mere 2,000 million and the cycle will repeat itself every 300 years. Personally, I doubt if we shall make it to 2070. – Gordon Rattray Taylor, from his *Doomsday Book*.

These doom-laden prophecies, bursting upon us towards the end of European Conservation Year and the early part of 1971, seemed too contrived and incredible to be valid. Yet we cannot, and dare not, dismiss them.

There is plenty of evidence, in fact, that we could be heading for disaster. The growth of population is proceeding at an alarming rate, threatening world famine. We have poisoned the air we breathe and the water we shall need to drink in the years ahead. We have cast a blight across much of the land with our developments, ripping the earth apart for coal and clay, sand and gravel, and other mineral workings, and often leaving it scarred, pitted and defiled by our activities. We have spread poisons over the land, too, so that mothers in some parts of the world dare not feed their babies because of the amount of DDT in their milk. We have produced deserts by thoughtless farming and the exhausts from our cars blot out the sun and kill vegetation. Our world becomes daily more clogged and clamorous, and life quickens into a furious, frenetic, competitive brawl, catching us up in its currents and whirling us around like scraps of paper in the wind to deposit us where – on civilisation's scrapheap?

That is one side of the picture at any rate and if you project the trends forward a decade, as was done in a recent film, you may have good reason to forecast the end of the ocean late in the summer of 1979, a world agricultural disaster caused by the adoption of a 'miracle' pesticide and consequent mass starvation.

But there is another, more positive, side and I feel this should be emphasized too, because the trouble with prophecies of doom is that, if people believe them, they tend to think the lemming-like rush to destruction cannot be halted and that, therefore, it only remains to enjoy life while they may and let tomorrow go hang; *precisely the attitude which will prove the prophets right!*

57

To my mind we have to latch on to our achievements, take heart from them and strengthen our resolve to carry them forward. And these achievements are considerable. The fact that we have reached the third quarter of the 20th century without destroying the world – though we have for some time possessed the means to do so – may be regarded as an achievement in itself. Furthermore, life in many ways is more agreeable for more people than it has ever been before. I think this is true in the global sense, although the gap between the rich and poor nations is widening in a way which must give rise to the greatest concern.

So far as Britain is concerned, it is true that our cities are more crowded and there is less unspoilt countryside than there used to be, but living conditions within cities have in many ways improved. We are better housed, fed and clothed than we were 50 years ago, and we have more leisure and more opportunities for getting out into the countryside and coast than we used to have.

That we are paying a price for all this, and a heavy one, is now all too apparent, but would we really choose to put the clock back? What must give us sound reason for hope in the present situation is that we now possess the wealth and technological 'know-how' to make a real assault on all these problems.

Indeed, we have been doing so for quite a while, unbeknown to many who have only just woken up to the fact that we have an 'environment' to enhance, protect and conserve. Take the problem of river pollution, for instance. Despite vast population increases giving rise to bigger towns and more development of all kinds and, as a result, greatly increased loads on our sewage works, we have managed to hold our own and even to improve the position considerably in one or two areas. The River Thames, for instance, is now cleaner than it has been for centuries and there are ambitious plans for the Northumberland Tyne which could produce an equally dramatic improvement in the quality of that great river. If we can do it in London, in the heart of the most densely populated part of Britain, surely we can do it anywhere.

The same conclusion follows from the fact that Greater London is now enjoying 50 per cent more winter sunshine and has no had bad fog since 1962. A Londoner can now see three miles farther than he could in 1958. Once it was the North which set the pattern for progress. Now it is the North which has to follow suit. I'm sure it will not be far behind. Sheffield is one city which has shed its grimy mantle and where now housewives can take clean washing off the line.

In Lancashire, the West Riding, Durham and Nottinghamshire they are transforming derelict acres into parkland, recreational areas and farmland, and creating a pleasant landscape instead of eyesores. There are exciting plans for the Lea Valley, The Potteries and South Wales. Worthing, Bolton, Bradford and London are setting the pace in reclaiming waste products. The countryside is protected to a fair degree through national parks, areas of outstanding natural beauty and other planning measures, and wildlife through nature reserves. Most important of all, perhaps, we are at last discussing population control.

Most of this progress has been made at a time when most people were apathetic. Now there has been a great public awakening, reflected in a spate of activity which would have been undreamt of a few years ago. Royal commissions, working parties and study groups covering all the main fields have been set up and we have had a whole string of reports, surveys and recommendations, many of which have been acted upon. We now have, for the first time, a Department of the Environment.

In fact, there has never been a period when development of all kinds has been subjected to such close public scrutiny. Spearheaded by the Civic Trust, hundreds of civic and amenity societies have sprung up. Technological advances which at one time would have been accepted merely because they had been made, are now called into question.

In the last few years at least a dozen measures have been enacted partly or wholly concerned with the control of pollution. They include the Clean Air Act, 1968, the Salmon and Freshwater Fisheries Act, 1965, the Mines and Quarries (Tips) Act, 1969; the Rivers (Prevention of Pollution (Scotland)) Act 1968; the Sewerage (Scotland) Act 1968; the Civic Amenities Act 1967; the Sea Fisheries Regulation Act 1966; the Medicines Act 1968; the Farm and Garden Chemicals Act 1967; the Nuclear Installations Act 1965 and the Public Health (Amendment) Act 1969. We now have a Clean Air Council – set up in 1957 to review progress under the Clean Air Act – a Noise Advisory Council and a Standing Royal Commission on Environmental Pollution.

Government and local government have not been idle by any means. That is not to say that the steps taken have been in any degree adequate. Far from it. We are falling behind in many respects and in the subsequent pages I shall be drawing attention to many of these shortcomings. But there are signs of a new resolve. In May, 1971, Mr Peter Walker, Secretary for the Environment, promised a series of anti-pollution measures – legislation to force firms to pay for damage they did, planning laws to strengthen restrictions on factories polluting air, sea or land, and a nationwide chain of monitoring stations to keep a check on pollution. Promises by politicians who are in office are worth noting.

Without denying that the future of humanity may well be poised on a knife-edge, I hope I have indicated that we have the means to come through. We have at least laid the foundation for a determined assault on these problems and, if only slowly and hesitantly, are beginning to tread the right road.

This movement will grow. I'm sure of that. And human ingenuity, which has triumphed over seemingly impossible odds in the past, will increasingly be brought to bear on these problems.

We need not worry too much about incentives. The greatest incentive of all must surely be the knowledge that, if we fail this time, we are unlikely to get another chance.

Waste Disposal

7. Our prodigal society

The civilisations which create great cities decline as soon as they forget their indebtedness to the soil. – J. C. Wylie, in his book, *The Wastes of Civilisation*

We have come a long way from the situation in the 19th century when the streets swam in sewage and when houses, cellars and yards reeked with such a nauseous stench that it is hard to imagine how people could put up with it. 'Dens of pollution and wretchedness' was how one chronicler described these places.

But we still have a very long way to go. Waste-disposal methods remain far too primitive far too often. We have frequently done little more than shift the refuse a little farther out from our towns, to become 'dumps of pollution and wretchedness'. Most town wastes are still disposed of by tipping, which all too often means disgorging the garbage on the nearest convenient piece of land that doesn't happen to be used for anything else. The resultant repulsive, reeking, rat-infested mounds are a constant affront to local inhabitants and a hazard to streams through seepage and run-off.*

It happens to be the easiest and cheapest way and, like many such solutions, far from the best. Not only can disposal methods be criticised; so can the all-too-common attitude that whatever is in the dustbin is rubbish or garbage to be quickly and conveniently thrown away. The ordinary dustbin may contain much of value to industry – scrap iron, tin cans, rags, bones (which can be processed into animal feeding stuff, manures and glues) and bottles, not to mention waste paper. Cinders may also be useful as a low-grade fuel. As Mr E. W. Ward, chief public health inspector for the county Borough of Warrington, said in a paper to the Association of Public Health Inspectors in January, 1970: 'The logical approach to solid waste disposal is one of conservation, to minimise generation of waste material, to salvage and re-use waste and to dispose of the irreducible amount in a manner which will conserve the disposal site, or if incinerated, produce steam for district heating.'

Yet, as the 1971 report of the Working Party on Refuse Disposal made clear, only a very small amount of waste (not much more than 2 per cent) is reclaimed.

Much of the material thrown away is valuable. It includes enormous amounts of food – one-third of the total prepared for human consumption, according to one estimate. We in Britain are not the only wasters, of course. It has been said that the Americans, for example, throw away enough food to feed the people of Britain – quite a thought when you bear in mind all the hungry people in the world.

Furthermore, at a time when the steel industry is avid for scrap, tons of it are wasted. Only one-third of local councils recover scrap in an organised way. A great deal has to be imported – in 1969, for instance, 290,000 tons of ferrous scrap at a cost of £5,672,000.

Lord Delacourt-Smith, Minister of State for Technology, said in the Commons in March, 1970, that the recovery of scrap could make a valuable contribution to the balance of payments. The total value of scrap and waste used annually in industrial processes had been estimated at £1,000 million.

It's much the same story with waste paper. Despite an enormous demand – waste paper accounts for more than 40 per cent of the consumption of the paper board industry – yearly collections have fallen to about half of the 400,000 tons gathered during the war. It is shameful that we are also having to import paper at the rate of about 50,000 tons a year at a cost of £880,000.†

Mr Frank Flintoff, an associate in a firm of engineering consultants, has pointed out that as paper accounts for 65 per cent by volume of all domestic

---

* Perhaps the situation will improve following the issue of a circular from the Department of the Environment (DOE 26/71, HMSO) giving a code of practice for waste tipping.

† One body which will collect your waste paper and use it for a good 'amenity' purpose is the Inland Waterways Association, defender of the canals, whose address can be found at the end of the book.

refuse, and this is expected to grow, the best hope for substantially reducing the amount to be disposed of lies in the separate collection and return to the board and paper mills of as much as possible.

He concedes that collecting waste paper has proved unprofitable at times 'through poor organisation and lack of incentives to manual workers'. But more often the alleged unprofitability has been due, he asserts, to 'departmental' accounting which takes no note of the interaction between services. The authority which sells separately collected waste paper avoids entirely the refuse-disposal cost of that weight of paper. This is a real saving, says Mr Flintoff, which can vary from a few shillings to £3 a ton.

Mr Flintoff hits the nail squarely on the head. And so does the technical committee on the disposal of solid toxic wastes when it gives the economist's definition of waste as 'that which is cheaper to throw away than to make further use of', and goes on to declare that this definition is inadequate because it concerns one user only. It might be economic for him to throw something away but uneconomic for mankind. This is surely where society has to take a hand and persuade, cajole and induce (perhaps through subsidies) local authorities and manufacturers to go in for reclamation on a bigger scale.

Certainly there are many private specialist reclaimers who do very good business indeed in both the scrap metal and waste-paper fields. But it is reported that the waste-paper dealers are now working to capacity, and that any major rise in the amount salvaged must come from domestic sources.

World supplies of raw materials are not unlimited – in fact, a universal shortage of timber, ores and oil has been predicted by the end of the century. Copper could be the first to run out, followed by lead, tin and zinc. Not only are the affluent nations consuming vaster and vaster quantities, but the under-developed countries will be making increasing calls on these supplies. Britain, which depends so much on imports, is especially vulnerable in this respect.

Waste and pollution

Yet we still talk about refuse *disposal* rather than *reclamation*. We are still a long way from regarding waste as part of a cycle which can benefit our economy and improve the quality of life. The extent of pollution in all its forms is a measure of our failure to deal properly with waste products.

Not only domestic waste, either. A technical committee on 'The Disposal of Solid Toxic Wastes' has pointed out that – although little evidence has been found at the moment – there could be a major pollution hazard to our rivers and underground supplies, and hence to our drinking water, through existing disposal methods.

Nobody should under-rate the size of the problem. The 30-40 million tons of domestic, trade and commercial and industrial waste handled in England and Wales in 1971 has doubled in 20 years and could double again in volume within a decade, largely through the rise in packaging materials and 'planned obsolescence'. The cost of collecting and disposing of it has been estimated as £250-£400 million annually. This does, however, underline the importance of salvaging as much of value as possible.

Still, attitudes are changing and several councils at least try to put their wastes to good use by compacting them into landfill for levelling derelict sites and land-scaping them, and returning the land to agriculture. Much of London's wastes, for instance, are absorbed in reclaiming the river marshes. Details of the work of other authorities will be found in my review of derelict land.

Some authorities sort their waste by hand before tipping or extract scrap metal by magnetic means. Still others burn or pulverise it, and some councils go in for composting, selling the product to farmers and gardeners. There are various permutations of these processes.

Among authorities showing the way are Worthing, in Sussex, where Mr V. Gosling, cleansing and salvage superintendent, has drawn up a truly integrated waste-management programme. According to the March, 1970, issue of the journal, *Public Cleansing*, the following materials had been salvaged since 1955 – 3,650 tons of paper, which realised £38,150; 680 tons of tins (£3,850), 426 tons of ferrous and non-ferrous metals (£4,595), 240 tons of rags (£3,900) and 3,800 tons of fine dust (£400). All this represented a total income of £51,170 – not an inconsiderable 'windfall' for the ratepayers.

Most of the remaining refuse goes to a composting plant, where it is combined with sludge from the nearby sewage works to produce 35 tons of compost a day. Some of this is used on council landscaping schemes and some is sold.

The city of Bradford provides an interesting example both of the potential in this field and of what local authorities can do when they have to. Bradford has a unique sewage purification problem arising from its position as a centre of the wool industry. About three-quarters of all the wool, both 'home grown' and im-ported, is taken to the city for scouring. The city's sewage is thus excessively loaded with emulsified wool grease and industrial detergents. It is therefore necessary, before carrying out any normal purification process, to treat the sewage with sulphuric acid to remove excessive quantities of grease.

This means that the treatment costs are much higher than usual. However, the council has found it possible to produce by-products which find a market cur-rently running at the rate of some £250,000 a year. The department's engineer and manager, Mr R. E. F. Gardner, is careful to point out that although this does not represent a profit, it does make a very considerable contribution to the reduction of exceptionally high treatment costs. It certainly represents a most commendable initiative on the authority's part.

Bradford, incidentally, has also gained a notable reclamation success by con-structing a first-class sports stadium on a foundation of city refuse.

Cars into scrap metal

One of the most important potential sources of scrap metal are the half a mil-lion or so motor cars abandoned each year, but until recently this scrap could not be relaimed because the presence of 'contaminants' like upholstery, leather, glass, wood and so on made it almost useless for the steel industry – balers could not separate the metal.

Technology has come up with one answer in the form of the Proler Cohen plant, now in operation for the GLC at Willesden. This has had quite a dramatic effect, transforming a curse into what might almost be called a blessing virtually overnight. The plant produces clean, easy-to-handle pieces of steel which are nearly as pure as the original and therefore command a high price. It can deal with four-fifths of the total number of cars scrapped each year and can produce about 5,000 tons of scrap metal a week. Other large items, like washing machines, refrigerators, cooking stoves and water heaters can also be effectively dealt with.

A Japanese firm, the Tezuka Kosan Co., has developed a method of reclaiming industrial and household refuse which seems worth examining for possible use in this country. Giant presses take scrap metal, timber, paper and assorted garbage, and produce five-ton square blocks as hard as concrete. These are used to build dams, dykes and to reclaim land.

On the compost front not so much is being done as one would like to see. With farming becoming more and more intensive, the need to return nutrients to the soil is doubly important. And there are experts who will argue strongly that the best and safest way of doing this is through organic manures. Although we have a tradition of good husbandry in this country and have managed to avoid creating 'dust bowls' like those in the United States and elsewhere, some disturbing evidence has been produced recently of the impoverishment of certain soils in the Home Counties. Nor are we free from soil erosion through winds and floods, especially in the Fens.

Nature requires three hundred to a thousand years to build up one inch of topsoil and this can be swept away by wind or rain overnight if the land is worked thoughtlessly.

Only a small fraction of sewage sludge is composted. 'The rest', says Mr J. C. Wylie, 'is allowed to spread over meadows to form lakes of putrefaction alongside our towns or is dumped in rivers or the sea. We spend thousands, perhaps millions, of pounds a year in advertising our seaside resorts and in making them attractive, and then allow the tides to wash back on our beaches a mess of accumulating and dangerous filth that has been discharged into the sea through sewers or from sludge boats. We rob our soils and pollute the waters around us because we have not the will to add the offending wastes of sewage to the dry organic wastes of refuse by methods which have been proved in practice to be reliable, to make organic manures, which every farmer, smallholder and gardener throughout the country wants.'

Municipal compost is richer than farmyard manure and some products, like 'Tottenham Pudding' – produced from kitchen wastes only, supplied to the then metropolitan borough of Tottenham by 14 adjoining authorities – became quite famous. Thirty-three thousand tons were distributed to farmers in 15 countries at one time.

Artificial fertilisers and pig foods produced by industry now compete strongly with such products, but there is still a big demand in certain areas, as can be seen from booklets produced by Lawrence D. Hills, director-secretary of the Henry Doubleday Research Association. These have been called ' "Which" guides to the best buys at the sewage shops' and include information on the councils marketing compost, how it can be bought, how much it will cost and how good it is. His first *Sludge Guide*, produced in 1961, sold nearly 10,000 copies, went to a second edition as *Fertility Finder* and was later issued as *Fertility Finder Number Two* (17½p from the association).

Among the fascinating titbits of information given by Mr Hills is that Toronto is the only city in the Commonwealth to sell leaf-mould made from dead leaves, and that Manchester and Cardiff are the only corporations which will deliver

63

loads of leaves to ratepayers. The author feels that not only is burning dead leaves a deplorable waste of humus but also creates an obnoxious form of pollution.

The price of packaging

While local authorities could certainly do more on the reclamation front, the behaviour of manufacturers is often far from helpful; in one or two cases it is downright irresponsible.

If society is to be called upon to accept a mountain of packaging – much of it of doubtful utility – then society should demand that it be in a form which can be dealt with. To unload on the community millions of plastic cups and containers which, because they are virtually indestructible by natural processes, are left to litter fields, hedgerows and beaches for an indefinite period, and even turn up in the bellies of codfish, is quite indefensible.

If we must have these disposable articles, surely paper would do just as well and would not be open to this objection. Manufacturers should either be required to produce a biodegradable plastic – one that can be broken down by bacteria and other natural elements – or to change over to some less objectionable material. They should certainly not be permitted to put products of this kind on the market with a deplorable lack of concern as to how they can be reclaimed.

Perhaps we need a national reclamation agency to 'vet' new packaging materials in much the same way as pesticides and drugs are vetted?

There is an urgent need for action on this issue. An avalanche of these disposables will be decending upon us in the next few years. The number of non-returnable plastic milk bottles could reach 32 million a day, and the number of disposable cans for soft drinks could strike the 700 million mark.

The situation wouldn't be so disturbing, of course, if we had a truly litter-conscious community, but in fact we throw rubbish about to the extent of 250 lb per head per year. Shall we make much progress in this direction without stricter penalties? It might be noted – as the CPRE points out – that substantial fines levied on the spot by the police in Canada make it difficult to find a single toffee paper in the 70 miles between Toronto and Niagara.

Every advance on one front seems to be accompanied by a retreat elsewhere. For instance, the 1967 Civic Amenities Act could help reduce the number of old bedsteads, mattresses and cookers deposited in laybys and hedgerows, and on farmland, and the number of old 'bangers' dumped by the roadside, because it gives local authorities powers to remove abandoned vehicles and to provide dumps where bulky items may be taken free of charge, and to impose penalties on anyone dumping such refuse. This is not by any means an ideal arrangement – one would like to see a clear statutory duty on councils to collect such items – but it does represent a big step forward. On the other hand, this explosion of disposable items could increase the amount of long-term litter enormously.

The situation will not be improved by piecemeal measures. We need a thoroughly comprehensive approach, looking at production and reclamation as a complete cycle and thinking the whole process through to make the maximum use of the materials at our command. The status of reclamation must be lifted well above the 'Steptoe and Son' level.

This involves a critical and questioning attitude to technological innovation. We can no longer afford to act first and ask questions afterwards. We must be prepared to assess the *overall costs* as far as possible, not only in terms of development but in terms of the impact on amenity. To what extent can we afford to reclaim what we cannot use and how much pollution is likely to result?

Local authorities say that by and large reclamation doesn't pay. In other words, it doesn't pay them to transport waste, say, 20–30 miles to fill in a gravel pit or quarry, or to turn it into compost and try and sell it to farmers in a highly competitive market, or again to install expensive reclamation plant. But I hope I have shown that there are gains for the community which ought to be taken into account. The answer would again seem to lie in the establishment of a reclamation agency able to pay grants for approved schemes.

Decisions will never be easy. A certain amount of risk must always be allowed for, or we would never do anything. But if we'd had comprehensive cost-benefit studies would be have gone ahead with the Concorde? (latest estimate of cost, £885 million), or with nuclear power?

Nuclear power produces a waste which is odourless, tasteless and dangerous, as Walter C. Patterson, M.Sc. points out in that excellent magazine, *Your Environment.* He declares – and it seems a good note to end on:

'If we want the undoubted benefits of nuclear power, radiotherapy and the many other applications of man-made radioactivity that are becoming part of everyday life, we must recognise what we are buying, and what we are paying for it. Unfortunately, some of the bills may not arrive until it's no longer possible to return undesired goods.'

Legislation:

Public Health Act 1936
Civic Amenities Act 1967
Litter Act 1958

Mainly responsible:

All local authorities, private reclamation firms, Department of the Environment.

8. The colour of our lungs

People can find as many excuses for failing to tackle the public scourge of air pollution as for not giving up their own more private form of pollution – smoking. There is an equally overwhelming case against both, but in general I find the excuses for smoking more acceptable. At least this is a pleasurable activity, whereas nobody can pretend to enjoy breathing poisoned air. And you give up breathing at your peril.

Some of the excuses for inaction on the clear air front are quite ludicrous. Local authorities in mining areas, for instance, say they are reluctant to deprive ratepayers of concessionary coal – nearly 300,000 miners are accorded this privilege. These 'perks' are traditional and doubtless there would be an outcry if

65

they were withdrawn. But surely the concession could be given in some other form – perhaps some monetary consideration or, when supplies become more abundant, in smokeless fuel? It is nonsense that people have to be encouraged to pollute the air because we are afraid to break with established practice.

Depriving miners of free or cheap coal might cause some hardship, but they wouldn't die as a result, whereas many do die from air pollution. Chronic bronchitis kills 30,000 Britons a year, incapacitates many more and is responsible for some 35 million lost working days. If you look at a map showing where most bronchitis sufferers live, you will discover a remarkable 'coincidence' of the disease and smoke-polluted areas. In fact, the so-called 'English disease' is far more likely to strike an inhabitant of Middlesbrough than someone living in Worthing. To claim that there is something peculiarly English about it is to ignore the evidence gathered throughout the western world, showing that 'where there's muck there's bronchitis'. In 1968 England and Wales had 57·5 deaths per 100,000 from the disease, compared with 4·7 (France), 4·5 (Norway), 6·3 (Sweden), 7·6 (Denmark), 12·3 (Holland) and 17·3 (West Germany). If we could reduce our level of air pollution to the level of West Germany, for instance, it is estimated that we could save 20,000 lives a year.

Any remaining doubts about the link between air pollution and bronchitis should be dispelled by the falling death-rate figures in this country as we make progress towards clean air. In 1958, there were nearly 14 more deaths per 100,000 than there were ten years later.

Air pollution not only aggravates bronchitis but reduces the life span. Professor P. J. Lawther, director of the Air Pollution Unit, Medical Research Council, has stated that smoke *in any concentration* is undesirable and could well constitute a hazard to health. Clothes, buildings, crops, plants and wildlife can also be affected. Damage to Britain's agriculture alone has been estimated at about £10 million a year. Smoke sends laundry and painting bills soaring, pollutes rivers and streams, and leaves deposits of grease and grime on everything with which it comes into contact. If you can visualise a ton of polluting matter, multiply that 125 times and you will have an idea of the amount of filth deposited in some parts of Britain per square mile.

All these effects have been known and recognised for a long time, but it was not until the 'smog' disaster of December 1952, when more than 4,000 people died, that any real action was taken. Four years later the Clean Air Act was passed. This placed restrictions on the emission of dark smoke from factory chimneys and gave local authorities power to establish smoke control areas in which only smokeless fuel could be burned and certain types of stoves and boilers installed.

But local authorities are not the only enforcement agencies in this field. Many industrial processes come within the purview of the DoE's Alkali Inspectorate, a government-appointed agency for industrial clean air. The Inspectorate has the task of ensuring that any new plant is fitted with adequate dust-arresting apparatus and that the specified chimney heights for dispersing gases are adhered to. Unfortunately, the Inspectorate's ability to prosecute firms which are poisoning the air by emitting, not only smoke, but dust, grit and fumes has been frustrated to a great extent by a legal ruling that only what is economically feasible can be insisted upon.

Tall chimneys are often erected as a compromise, but they merely spread the pollution more widely. Gases may also accumulate in the atmosphere and reactions dangerous to health may occur in certain climatic conditions.

Progress at first was slow – only about $2\frac{1}{4}$ million premises were covered by smoke-control orders by the end of 1964 – and although this rate later increased, the situation was felt to be so unsatisfactory that in 1968 another Clean Air Act was passed giving the Secretary for the Environment power to require local authorities to draw up smoke-control programmes and, if necessary, to make orders himself. It also restricted the sale and delivery of smoky fuels in smoke-control areas. The shortage of smokeless fuel has prevented these powers being exercised, however. On the contrary, smoke-control orders have had to be suspended and the clean air campaign has suffered a setback. It was ironical that this should have happened in European Conservation Year.

The present situation is that, although much progress towards clean air has been made in Greater London, with more than 72 per cent of the polluted districts cleaned up, nearly half the premises in the black areas of England are still not covered – more than a score of authorities have no smoke-control programme at all. Whereas one-quarter of industrial premises in London are covered. more than three-quarters in the north of England remain uncontrolled. Little or nothing has been done in Wales.

So far as industrial pollution is concerned, the situation is regarded as far less satisfactory than it should be by the Association of Public Health Inspectors. It will not be altered, they say, until local authorities carry out regular inspections of industrial premises, not only to ensure that proper equipment has been installed but that it is being properly maintained.

Clean air benefits

When one looks at some of the benefits already realised in some areas, one finds it all the more inexplicable that so little has been done elsewhere. The inhabitants of Greater London, for instance, are now enjoying 50 per cent more winter sunshine and there has been no bad fog since 1962. Visibility has also improved dramatically – a Londoner can now see nearly three miles farther than he could in 1958. London suburbs like Woolwich are reported to have lower smoke concentrations than parts of seaside resorts like Brighton and Eastbourne. Hundreds of varieties of plants now flourish where previously only privet, laurel and plane tree would grow, and well over 100 species of birds now visit the capital – twice as many as a decade ago. Seven London boroughs have completed their smoke-control programmes and the remaining 26 are scheduled to complete theirs by 1978.

Sheffield is shaming its northern neighbours who have done little or nothing. So vigorously has the authority set about its task that already the city has lost its grimy image of terraced housing seen against a background of chimneys belching smoke. It has become a place where housewives can take clean washing off the line and where buildings are no longer black with soot. The amount of smoke is estimated to have dropped by 80 per cent in 11 years. The number of foggy days has been more than halved. By 1972, when the last smoke-control order is due to be made, the city air will be as clean as that of Eastbourne, it is claimed.

Anti-pollution measures have to be paid for, and nobody pretends that clean air can be got on the cheap. The cost is divided among householders, who normally have to pay 30 per cent of the sum spent on conversion to smokeless fuels, and local authorities and the Government, who find a further 30 and 40 per cent respectively. In 1968–69 alone, the Government paid out more than £3 million, at a time of financial restrictions.

Nevertheless, measured against the cost of doing nothing, this expenditure is piddling. According to a report prepared by the GLC Research and Intelligence Unit for the London Boroughs Association, Londoners have paid no more than 15p each per year for their brighter, healthier and warmer capital.

Now, even if one takes the Beaver Committee estimate of £250 million a year as the direct cost of air pollution to the nation – which Sir Hugh later admitted to be a serious under-estimate – this would give a cost to London of around £50 million a year or £5 per head. Should the expense of remedial measures have to be doubled or trebled to clean the air entirely, it would still be a gilt-edged investment, even more so if one were to accept later estimates of the cost of air pollution – around £10 per head per year.

That some authorities should need prodding to get on with cleaning the air takes some understanding in face of these figures. With the shortage of smokeless fuel reported to be over, there is no valid technical or economic reason for failing to act; it is often nothing more than prejudice and inertia which holds them back. I have in front of me an article from *The Times* of March 25, 1970, headed 'Clean air? We don't believe in it' and quoting such comments as these . . .

'I just don't believe in smokeless zones. . . . There is nothing like a good coal fire. I just do not believe that domestic coal causes damage to health.' – from the civic head of a town often described as 'the muckiest place in the north'.

'I am sure that the Minister will come down on us soon and make us do something. But I told my public health inspector to write and tell them we were giving the matter urgent consideration. That is one way of putting them off.' – council chairman in a northern town, which seems to be relying on fresh breezes from Southport to blow its smoke into someone else's territory.

This example shows how impossible it is to confine the problem – it cannot be tackled on anything less than a regional scale. Perhaps the reform of local government will help to eliminate sectarian attitudes of the kind illustrated above.

International co-operation will also be required, as the fall-out from nuclear explosions has revealed – air pollution knows no frontiers. Sweden's rain has become more acid recently and foreign sources are blamed, including British ones. We might learn something, too, from the Danes, who have been greatly aided in their fight against air pollution by the widespread adoption of district heating. Some 400 Danish towns with a population totalling two million take their heat from a central source. This has cut the pollution by half – although it was admitted at a clean air congress in London that the original aim was pure and simple economy. The efficiency of an average district heating plant burning heavy fuel oil can be as high as 90 per cent. The advantages of having one central, closely-controlled unit instead of thousands of separate domestic fires seem obvious, but we in Britain have been slow to appreciate them.

Car exhaust fumes

Much attention has been focused in recent times on the growing pollution by car exhaust fumes. In California regulations have been passed cutting down the amount of carbon monoxide permitted to be poured out of new cars and a similar ruling will come into force nationally by 1980. According to the annual report for 1970 of the Atomic Energy Authority, Los Angeles type 'smog' – caused by the action of sunlight on petrol fumes – is possible in Britain.

Vehicles exported from the UK will have to conform, but unless we take similar action, new cars on our roads will still be able to poison the air to the same extent as now and, of course, there will be many more of them. Even today concentrations of carbon monoxide approach and sometimes exceed the danger level for periods in busy streets. Lead from exhaust fumes can be inhaled by humans and large amounts are being absorbed into the soil and vegetation. Recent Swedish studies suggest that the safety margin between present levels of lead absorption for city dwellers and that which gives rise to chronic damage in man is very small. Clearly we, too, should be considering action on American lines as a matter of the utmost urgency. The oil firm, B.P., has announced that it is ready to provide lead-free petrol as and when required.

If lead-free petrol were banned and cars fitted with what one knows as 'catalytic converters', noxious emissions could be cut by 90 per cent, it is claimed (see the journal, *Engineering*, March, 1971).

Mr Peter Walker, Secretary for the Environment, said in May, 1971, that tests were being made to see if traffic fumes could harm children playing in the streets. This followed a study in traffic-congested parts of Germany showing that dustmen were suffering more harmful effects from the dirt they handled than from the air they breathed.

Perhaps the real answer, however, lies in some form of electric transport in towns. Recent developments have shown that a battery car could be built for about £450, with a running cost of 0·4p per mile; future advances are sure to give it greater range.

Action by Governments and local authorities can be powerfully reinforced by the ordinary householder. While black smoke pouring from factory chimneys is more obvious, the ordinary domestic coal fire does more damage, and householders who change over to other forms of heating are contributing to the clean-air campaign. But not entirely, it seems. Whether coal, coke or oil is burnt, sulphur dioxide is produced in huge quantities (about six million tons of it are pumped into the air each year), though the biggest offenders in this respect are power stations, oil refineries and chemical concerns. Sulphur dioxide combined with water vapour forms dilute sulphuric acid which corrodes buildings and harms plant life. There is no reason to believe that it affects humans, but the possibility cannot be ruled out. Dr Frank Taylor, former president of the Institution of Heating and Ventilating Engineers, has described the emission of sulphur dioxide as 'the biggest single air pollution problem' – and he fears it might be getting worse.

Here, too, however, we could be within sight of a breakthrough. Gulf, one of the world's leading oil companies, has announced the development of a new refining process which can cut the emission of sulphur oxides dramatically. There are also systems for extracting sulphur dioxide at source which could help to recover millions of tons of sulphuric acid each year. Most of them are only in the experimental stage but they are charting the way forward.

In fact, the frequency with which technology comes up with an answer as soon as the community demands that one be found, makes the case for prior examination of all new industrial processes that much stronger. Either the technology exists for minimising pollution or it can be developed. Failure to consider both possibilities before going ahead with new processes may mean enormous social and economic costs to the community.

Providing a legislative framework is usually the most effective way of ensuring that such considerations are borne in mind. At the time of writing, for instance, the City of London has a Bill before Parliament which would restrict the use of oil fuels in the City to those with a low sulphur content.

Even so, there are signs that industrialists are becoming more alive to their responsibilities. One hears more news now of voluntary action to stop pollution. A recent example is that of the Goodyear Tyre firm, which plans to spend £300,000 at its Wolverhampton factory to convert coal-fired boilers to ones using North Sea gas. Mr Kenneth Bull, the engineering division manager, is reported to have said: 'We shall have very clean exhausts from our chimneys, absolutely free from grit. We have a very vigorous responsibility for the environment and are fully prepared to accept our share.'

Town planners, too, have an important role in reducing the effects of air pollution. By seeing that noxious industries are kept away from people's homes, by creating traffic-free town centres and by consulting those best equipped to advise on these matters before going ahead with developments, they can ensure that while troubles are being eliminated at source, the nuisance and health risks to those living in the vicinity are reduced. They can also insist on proper landscaping of new developments, including the planting of trees, which themselves help to cut air pollution.

The prospects generally are not unpromising, therefore. But the pall of smoke which hangs over the Swansea Valley and the industrial districts of the north is a constant reminder that still far too many of those areas' inhabitants who have created, and continue to create, so much of the wealth of this country, are taking air into their lungs which is not fit to breathe and which may lead to their premature deaths.

Legislation:

Public Health Act 1936
Clean Air Acts, 1956, 1968
Alkali Works Regulations Act 1966

Mainly responsible:

All local authorities except county councils, Alkali Inspectorate, Clean Air Council (advisory), Department of the Environment.

9. Conveyor belts for poison

Scientists of the Water Pollution Research laboratory at Stevenage took a rainbow trout and placed it in the Billingham Beck, a tributary of the River Tees. It died instantly. Supposing a child fell into the stream and swallowed some of this highly toxic liquid? And supposing any cow or dog or horse drank it?

Some streams are full of phosphoric acid – an official taking a sample burnt his hand – and others contain deadly poisons like cyanide. While we take the utmost care to label any poisons used in the home as clearly as possible and do our best to keep them away from children and animals, we accept, as a matter of course, the existence of toxic effluent flowing through our cities and industrial areas. Sometimes there are warnings against bathing in such streams; more often there is no obvious sign that the water is dangerous. And animals can't read anyway.

Polluted streams are a public menace and not only for the reasons given. Many rivers are important sources of drinking water – two-thirds of London's supply comes from the Thames system, for instance – and with the continual growth in the demand for water, more and more abstraction is taking place from the polluted lower reaches. There must be risks involved, as the Institution of Water Engineers confirmed in its evidence to the Central Advisory Water Committee. The Institution pointed out that modern technology is advancing so fast that the chemicals used by industry were often not known and conventional techniques frequently failed to detect them. Detergents are an obvious example, because they cause frothing on rivers, but they also increase the phosphate content of waters, which can have more serious results. (Actually a Government ban on the foaming agent would remove one problem at a stroke; the foam plays no useful role anyway.) Recently detergents have been developed which are 'biodegradable' – that is, can be broken down by natural processes.

Apart from the risks involved from poisoned effluents, there are many other reasons why clean rivers and lakes are desirable. The farmer's need to water his cattle has already been touched on, but he also requires clean water for irrigation. Commercial salmon fishermen want rivers clean enough for fish to run up them to spawn, and trout farmers, too, need clean water. Other commercial fishery and boating interests are involved. Under common law all riparian (that is, river bank) owners are entitled to have water flowing past their land in its natural state of purity and they can take civil proceedings if they don't get it.

Rivers and lakes are more valued than ever as sources of recreation. There are reckoned to be close on three million anglers in this country and they, more than any other section of the community perhaps, are aware of what pollution can do to their sport. But boating and sailing enthusiasts are an ever-growing army, too, and they shun filthy, evil-smelling waters. Then there are the indefinable numbers of people who are fascinated by water and who derive great joy from just sitting and looking at lakes or streams, walking along their banks or having a picnic with the family, followed, perhaps ,by a swim or paddle on a hot day. Obviously they, too, will want their water clean.

How often will they and the other interests referred to be satisfied and how often will they be repelled by the state of our waterways? Up-to-date figures of the extent of river pollution were not available at the time of writing, although they were expected shortly. However, it seemed unlikely that they would point to any overall marked improvement in water quality since the informal survey covering some 20,000 miles of non-tidal rivers in England and Wales was carried out in 1958. This showed that about 73 per cent of river miles were unpolluted or recovering from pollution, 15 per cent were of doubtful quality and needing improvement, 6 per cent were of poor quality and 6 per cent were grossly polluted and incapable of supporting fish life. For canals the figures were 58 per cent (clean), 25 per cent (doubtful), 9 per cent (poor) and 8 per cent (grossly polluted).

In other words, some 2,500 miles of river and 250 miles of canal were in a poor or grossly polluted state, with the situation in the industrial areas of the North-West and the Midlands being far worse than the national average.

Towards the end of 1970, Mr Eldon Griffiths, the then Minister for Sport, said he didn't agree that rivers were dying – on the contrary, there had been 'a remarkable improvement'. Nevertheless, the figures he gave were little different from those quoted.

Whether a river or lake holds fish is a fair measure of its cleanliness. No fish can live in water containing less than 3·3 parts of oxygen to a million parts of water. A really clean river has ten parts of oxygen per million. Heating the water reduces the oxygen supply, which explains why fish die in warm weather. Anglers, therefore are fair judges of the state of our rivers.

Mr Richard Walker, who is probably the best-known angler in the country, disagreed sharply with Mr Griffiths: 'Every river that I have known and fished for the last 20 years has deteriorated to a greater or lesser degree. Every experienced angler with whom I have discussed this tells me that his experience is the same.'

It may be contended that this is an unscientific view – though Mr Walker is certainly not unscientific in his angling – and that the figures we have do show that the situation is at least not getting worse. However, I wonder whether these broad categories (unpolluted or recovering from pollution, etc.) can reveal the true situation. Rivers may still hold fish, but do they grow as big and as fat as they used to? In most cases the answer is no.

The upper Thames is a case in point (I shall refer to the situation on the lower river shortly). Above Teddington there are plenty of fish, but evidence collected from anglers by the River Thames Society suggests that their size has gone down. One fisherman wrote: 'We, the anglers, have noticed the decline in the fine-leafed water plants such as water buttercup, mirofoil, starwort and elodea. Their place has been taken by cabbage lily, the thistle of the underwater world. The insects and crustaceans are fast vanishing. How many stretches of the river now yield crayfish for bait? Can you pull out a bunch of water plants and find them teeming with shrimp and caddis? These fine-leafed plants were the nurseries and the larders for the fish population.'

Even if we accept official assurances that the position is being maintained, there is still much cause for concern. Some of our major waterways – Tyne, Trent and Tees, Irwell, Mersey and Ribble – are grossly polluted for much of their course, and the fact that this pollution occurs near large towns means the consequences are especially serious. Millions of city dwellers have to put up with the odious appearance and nauseating stench of what are often little more than open sewers. Not only that, but if they want to fish, take out a boat and have a picnic they must travel long distances to do so.

Pollution has also deprived us of food in the form of salmon and trout. Salmon was once relatively cheap; now it is a luxury. The Trent and Thames were both fine salmon rivers, but none could hold a candle to the Northumberland Tyne, which in the 1870s produced more than 130,000 salmon in one year! Today the Trent and Thames are devoid of salmon; the Tyne has a few which manage in times of flood to penetrate the barrage of estuarial filth – truly a tribute to the determination of the fish. Polluted estuaries also prevent the passage of the sea-trout, or salmon-trout as it is sometimes known, and whose flavour is incomparable. Scores of brown trout streams have been destroyed.

The Yorkshire Don, the Mersey and Birmingham Tame are among the foulest. The Tame has been aptly called 'the waste pipe of the West Midlands'. Not even the lowest forms of river creature – the loglouse and bloodworm – can exist in its murky waters. The Warwickshire Avon and Stour are not much better and there are countless smaller streams which are simply used to carry away the poisonous wastes of tanneries, dye-works, chemical concerns and so on. Often they flow into more important rivers and pollute them as well. The Churnet dares to assault the delectable Dove, where Izaak Walton fished for trout with his friend Charles Cotton – though I understand that, due largely to the campaigning by the Anglers' Co-operative Association, the Churnet is improving.

How it happens

Pollution can arise in many different and, regrettably, more varied ways. It most commonly occurs through the discharge of effluents from sewage works and industrial concerns. Some of these industrial wastes are relatively harmless, some extremely dangerous. Many are discharged into the public sewers for a fee, a practice which is encouraged because in this way they can be more easily controlled than if industrialists carry out their own treatment before releasing effluent directly into the rivers.

Farm wastes – and, with intensive cultivation these are growing – provide special difficulties, because sewage authorities are loath to accept the foul slurries produced and farmers claim they cannot afford to treat them to the standards required.

Under the 1951 and 1961 Rivers (Prevention of Pollution) Acts, the 29 river authorities in England and Wales who are responsible for pollution control have powers to prohibit any discharges into rivers which do not conform to a required standard. The standard usually demanded is one recommended by a Royal Commission way back in 1912 and is generally regarded as too low, especially with the volume of effluent constantly increasing. Some rivers consist almost entirely of sewage effluent – and their numbers are growing. Furthermore, the Royal Commission standard envisaged a dilution factor of eight times for sewage effluents and this is frequently not possible under today's conditions.

Despite the inadequacy of the standard, however, it has been estimated that more than half the discharges do not even conform to it. Various explanations for this have been put forward. It is suggested that because most river authority members are also members of local authorities, they are reluctant to take enforcement proceedings against their own kind. This has been hotly denied, but the fact remains that prosecutions are rare. However, even where prosecutions are brought, the penalties are derisory. For instance, when cyanide killed 63,000 fish in the Essex River Chelmer, from which public water supplies had to be suddenly stopped, the firm responsible had to pay a fine of only £25! It cost Birmingham corporation £1,000 and three months' effort to trace a firm which had caused pollution by pouring acid down a drain. The firm was fined £60, plus an analyst's fee of £20! A sewage authority can always appeal to the Minister on the grounds that the proposed standard is unreasonable and governments have been inclined to look favourably on such appeals because of the costs involved in meeting it*.

If the controls for non-tidal waters are inadequate, then those applying to estuaries are still more so. The 1960 Clean Rivers (Estuaries and Tidal Waters) Act only covers new (i.e. post-1951) discharges, and most of the pipes now pouring torrents of filth into tidal waters were installed well before then. Forty million gallons of untreated sewage is allowed to be poured into the Tyne every day. The Jeger Committee on Sewage Disposal, which reported in July, 1970, urged that tidal waters and estuaries be brought under similar controls as non-tidal rivers. This is an area where there is the greatest scope for improvement. There is hardly an estuary of any size which isn't polluted to some extent. Most of them are in a disgusting state, with the filth perennially flowing backwards and forwards on the tide.

The same committee referred to another cause of pollution which has become common on the Norfolk Broads, for instance, in recent times – the discharge of sewage from boats – and recommended that this practice be prohibited in waters used as sources of public supplies or recreation.

Of more general concern, however, is the relatively recent form of pollution caused by the run-off of rain-water into the rivers. At one time rain could be seen as a blessing, as it brought health and life to streams and lakes. Even floods could have their positive side in giving rivers a good scour. Now the rain washes fertilisers and pesticides off the land. These chemicals can either poison lakes and streams or produce what is known as 'eutrophication' or enrichment, the effect of which is to cause algae and other plant life to thrive to such an extent that they take up too much oxygen and cause the death of insect life and fish.

According to the Soil Association, Thames Valley reservoirs are producing patches of algae for the first time and the phosphate level of the Thames itself has increased a hundredfold. Lake Erie in America is the oft-quoted example of eutrophication in its most extreme form. Formerly crystalline and rich in fish, this lake now supports nothing but vast quantities of weeds, and the US Government will have to spend enormous sums to rehabilitate it.

This kind of pollution is most difficult to control. Indeed, the only satisfactory way of controlling it is at source, through fewer and less toxic pesticides, and fertilisers which don't wash out of the soil in heavy rain; better for the farmer, too. Research into these matters is continuing.

The discharge of hot water from power stations is another possible source of trouble, as the amount of oxygen water can hold decreases as its temperature rises. Then there are mechanical effects, like the release of china clay which has ruined Cornish trout streams by making the water cloudy and preventing life-giving sunshine from getting through.

74   * Mr Peter Walker said in a Commons reply in November, 1971, that unlimited fines or imprisonment would become available for the worst pollution offences.

It is clear from glancing through river authority reports, however, that much pollution arises from what are termed 'accidental' causes, although how far they are accidents and how far sheer carelessness is a matter for speculation. Could release of the chemical which decimated the Rhine have been prevented? Would tighter controls and higher penalties produce fewer accidents? Anyway, the consequences can clearly be disastrous. It is a sobering thought that a trace of the chemical which did the damage to the Rhine, endosulphan, was reported to have been found in Walton's Lea. And in the same river there were 69 oil spills in one year recently against only two or three a decade ago.

Lower flows mean more pollution

The degree of dilution is a vital factor in determining the quality of river water. Every scheme to abstract water, therefore, increases the pollution risk. Many lovely waterways have already been sucked dry. Even more splendid ones are threatened – the chalk streams of Hampshire, Wiltshire and Dorset, for instance – as Mr D. S. Martin made plain in an article in *The Ecologist* (April 1971).

There are alternatives to raiding the sensitive and sparkling upper reaches. Abstraction could take place lower down where water volumes are big enough to bear it; there could be much greater re-use of water, or water might be obtained from the sea by desalination. Usually such alternatives are more costly, so again there is a price to pay.

One might well conclude from this survey of what can happen that it is a marvel our rivers survive at all. On the other hand, let us not overlook the more positive aspects. Technical advance may have brought more pollution, but it has also made it possible for us to deal with it. As Lord Molson said in the House of Lords, 'It is technologically possible to treat any waste water to a condition where it is restored to virtually the same state of purity as natural clean water'.

This is largely a matter of cost. For two or three times the £100 million a year now being spent we could clean up our rivers. We can only speculate on whether people would be prepared to pay this price. The fact is that they have never been asked – just as they were never asked whether they wished to afford the Concorde. Perhaps the question in future will be: Can we afford not to find the money, in view of the cost of purification to meet public water demands?

The 'miracle' of the Thames

The GLC – and its predecessor, the LCC – is one authority which *has* found the money, and the results have been dramatic. A century ago Members of Parliament became aware that they had a problem right under their noses, so to speak – both Houses had to adjourn because of the smell from the river. Despite a hundredfold increase in population and industry since then, the water quality has improved to the extent that fish are returning in good numbers to the lower reaches and no stretch of river is totally devoid of oxygen.

When you think that the GLC provides main drainage for about seven million people over 500 square miles and deals with around 500 million gallons of sewage a day, this is a remarkable achievement by any standards. Indeed, if anyone is thinking of handing out an environmental award, the GLC – and the Port of London Authority, which is responsible for pollution in the tidal river – would assuredly qualify for it.

Mr Alwyne Wheeler, of the Department of Zoology, British Museum (Natural History) has established that fish are present in the river in considerable numbers from Fulham to the estuary, a stretch probably devoid of all fish life, apart from eels, from about 1920–60. No fewer than 31 separate marine species have been identified in the brackish water of the estuary and the usual freshwater species higher up. The presence of lamprey, smelt and shad has been clearly established, and a run of haddock up the estuary sent anglers scurrying for their rods.

The money to bring this about – nearly £20 million by the GLC and its predecessor since 1949 – has been spent largely on the rationalisation of sewage works, involving the closure of small plants and the modernisation of others. When major extensions at Beckton are finished in 1973, a further rise in river quality may be expected.

If the Thames, why not any other major river system? Why not indeed? It is generally agreed that the path to progress lies along the lines of GLC operations. There are no fewer than 5,000 separate sewage plants in the country and many of them are too small to do the job properly. A reduction in the number of sewage authorities from the present 1,300 would also help, but perhaps this will have to await the reform of local government.

Meanwhile other moves are afoot. Up on Tyneside a score of local authorities have got together to produce a £30 million scheme which could achieve equally dramatic results in the condition of the river by the year 1977. A clean Tyne within a decade is the objective, and who can say it isn't realisable given the success down south?

Planning and research

Highly sophisticated equipment is being used to monitor and analyse water quality in the Trent Valley as part of a £½ million research study aimed at reducing pollution on that river system, too. Those rivers of the north-east, the Aln and Wear, are reported to be much improved following better sewage treatment. There is also a £2 million scheme to clean up the poisoned River Ebbw, a tributary of the glorious Usk in Wales.

Establishment of the Water Resources Board, under the Act of 1963, has opened the door to better national planning of water resources. One outcome has been some interesting projects for improving water quality by increasing flows in dry weather, rather than improving effluents. This can be done either by transferring water from areas where it is abundant to those where it is short (the Ely Ouse scheme is one) or by pumping clean water from underground sources into rivers to augment their flow. Self-purification in storage lakes is another possible method – experiments are taking place with this in the Trent Valley.

A key role in the clean rivers campaign is being played by a dedicated team at the Water Pollution Research Laboratory at Stevenage, and anyone interested would find a visit to the laboratory most rewarding. The laboratory's scientists monitor new developments throughout the world. One of them which has aroused much interest is a new disposal system being used in Dieppe involving the joint incineration of sewage sludge and garbage. It is said to be practicable for cities the size of London.

But there will be no 'miracle cure'. If we are to do more in future than keep abreast of the situation, more money must be made available, along with wider enforcement powers for river authorities, and a rationalisation of sewage works. Industry, too, must make a bigger contribution. In the heavily industrialised Ruhr Valley of Germany a method of taxing industries according to the level of pollution they create has led to a much cleaner Ruhr. This could be worth looking at.

The divided responsibilities entailed by the present system of separate sewage authorities, water undertakings and river authorities has been criticised, but the Central Advisory Water Committee, which looked into this, was not prepared to make a firm recommendation. One of the main arguments put forward by the committee for continuing the present arrangements is that it is valuable to have a separate 'watchdog' for river pollution rather than one body concerned both with sewage disposal and pollution control. One would only comment that this is all very well, but the dog must be able to bite.*

Given much-needed reforms, however, there seems no reason to be despondent about the future. Mr Hugh Fish, the respected chief purification officer of the Thames Conservancy, predicted at a congress of river authorities that 'a very considerable advance overall in the quality of waters in rivers generally will be made in England and Wales over the next 30 years or so'.

Let us see to it that he is right.

Legislation:

Rivers (Prevention of Pollution) Acts 1951, 1961
Clean Rivers (Estuaries and Tidal Waters) Act 1960
Water Resources Act 1963

Mainly responsible:

River authorities, Port of London Authority (lower Thames), Water Resources Board.
Sewage disposal authorities – GLC, London boroughs, county boroughs, boroughs, district councils.

The Seas

10. Fouling our lifeline

A Norwegian ocean research vessel, operating in the North Sea, took ten hours to steam through a mass of dead fish, covering 70 miles in all. An analysis showed that the fish had been killed by a chemical thought to have come from a viny-chloride factory in Britain or on the Continent.

This mass fish kill is but one of many signs that nations cannot continue with impunity to tip, heave, pour or propel into the oceans whatever they find difficult or inconvenient to dispose of by other means. The seas are not only expected to accommodate all the rubbish and poisons we pour or tip directly into it, but millions of gallons of effluent, much of it highly toxic, which end up in the ocean from those 'conveyor belts for waste-disposal' – the rivers.

The death of 10,000 birds in the Irish Sea is another warning sign – again

* Government proposals for all-purpose regional water authorities, to be responsible for both pollution control and sewage disposal, were announced as this book went to press.

chemical residues from plastics manufacture were found – and one may also cite the heavy fish kills by cyanide off South Wales in the summer of 1969 and the landing of pollack and cod along the south coast which were reported to be 'riddled with ulcers and horrible scars'. More recently came news of the discovery by a Bristol University survey team of limpets containing 550 parts per million of cadmium in the Severn Estuary off Portishead. To eat even a handful of these would have been fatal, it was stated. The cadmium, which is many times more poisonous than arsenic, was thought to have come from a big zinc smelter at Avonmouth; there is always some of the metal in zinc ores. Although limpets are rarely eaten by humans, they are eaten by fish, which could find their way on to our plates. The limpets were analysed by Dr Graham Nickless, of the university's chemistry department, who also found high cadmium concentrations in crabs; other shellfish might be affected, it was stated. In November 1971 it was reported that thousands of flatfish had been contaminated by drums of a chemical dumped in the Channel. At least a score of the drums were trawled up. They contained cyanuric chloride which produced blisters on the hands of fishermen and coastguards who dealt with the containers.

These are all examples close to our own shores. Many more, and often worse ones, could be drawn from other parts of the world. The pollution of the ocean is, in fact, global. It arises from the unprecedented scale of the disposal of all kinds of junk and waste material into the sea from populations which have grown so rapidly since 1900 that two-thirds of all those who have ever lived have been born since then.

Speaking on behalf of the secretariat of the United Nations conference on the human environment, to be held in Stockholm in 1972, Professor Jacques Piccard, the Swiss oceanographer, said many experts believed life in the seas would be extinguished within the next 25 to 30 years if man were not prepared to pay the price of stopping pollution. He said that five to ten million tons of petroleum products were getting into the oceans each year. About 1,800,000 tons of this, including 200,000 tons of lead, came from vehicle exhaust emissions and a further million tons from oil tankers. Mercury from paper mills – about 5,000 tons of it a year – and pesticides from the land were other major hazards identified by the professor.

Not only are increasing amounts of waste of higher toxicity than ever before being disposed of into the sea; but some which were sealed in containers and deposited on the sea bed a few decades ago are threatening to burst and release their contents. The Swedish nation was informed in June, 1969, that concrete containers with 7,000 tons of arsenic were crumbling away on the bottom of the Baltic. The arsenic had been dumped in the 1930s by a metal company. A Stockholm newspaper said there was enough of it to kill all the people in the world three times over.

The Baltic was one of the seas referred to in the cautiously worded report of our Royal Commission on Environmental Pollution as having shown major changes due to pollution, including a decline in oxygen. It is reported that the Danish Food Institute is to check whether Baltic fish are still fit to eat, following a Swedish ban on the sale of Baltic cod liver because of its high DDT content. The Baltic and Black Seas are already commercially fished out and the countries around them are frequently caught pirating fish from the territorial waters of other lands. Jacques Cousteau, French oceanographer, diver and marine biologist, has warned that at the present rate of exploitation and pollution, all the oceans could be fished out within a decade. Lobsters, crabs and shrimps are especially vulnerable to insecticides washing off the land. Many of them were developed specifically for use against land creatures like themselves.

Something like 175,000 tons of phosgene and mustard gas are known to have been dumped in containers by the British Navy in the North Sea and Atlantic. Are these crumbling away, too, and what would the likely consequences be if their contents were released? The ferric chloride canisters washed up on the Isle of Wight make one wonder about the scale of such military dumpings.

The Mercury Menace

Professor Piccard referred to mercury from paper mills, but some also probably enters from streams and run-off from the land, as mercury is also used in seed dressings. Mercury has contaminated tuna fish and frozen swordfish in America to such an extent that the American Government felt it necessary to take large stocks off the market.

The most infamous case of mercury poisoning was the Minamata affair in Japan in 1953, when 46 people died and around 100 suffered brain damage, progressive blindness, deafness and loss of co-ordination by eating shellfish from a bay in which a plastics company (yet again) had dumped its wastes.

You can die merely by inhaling mercury compounds, and Professor Barry Commoner, of Washington University, has described methyl mercury as a bigger threat to human life than radiation fall-out from nuclear tests in the atmosphere.

Baby seals which died off Cornwall in January, 1970, were found by the Natural Environment Research Council to have no less than 8·3 p.p.m. of mercury in their livers, 80 times the poison content of the tuna fish recalled. The research council's conclusion that the seals had died from natural causes did not allay concern. Levels of 6 to 10 p.p.m. will kill adults, and mercury also tends to concentrate in unborn children, causing nervous disorders and physical deformity.

The seal's diet consists largely of shrimp and small fish, foods which also sustain many large fish, including cod, whiting, bass, mullet, salmon and sea-trout – as John Piper pointed out in *Anglers' Mail* (Jan. 16, 1971). 'Are we to accept that seals absorb these massive doses, but that fish in the sea around them show no trace of the poison?' he asked.

Later it was announced by Mrs Thatcher, Secretary of State for Education and Science, that tests had been carried out by scientists of the Natural Environment Research Council in the six months following the discovery and that nothing had been found to cause concern. The Ministry of Agriculture also carries out regular sampling of fish. Even so, the question remains as to how the food of these seals came to be contaminated. The fact that the mercury level had built up to such an extent from what must have been very small amounts in shrimps and the like shows the degree to which poisons can become concentrated the higher you go up the food chain, and is a further reason for a cautious approach to 'permissible levels' of toxic wastes.*

---

* When fish caught off the Northumberland coast were sampled by public health officers, every one was found to contain traces of methyl mercury — report to Northumberland County Council in December, 1971.

The Royal Commission on Environmental Pollution estimated the extent of the dumping of industrial waste around Britain's shores at three million cubic metres a day. And the signs are that it is growing. One British company was reported by *The Observer* (April 18, 1971) to be planning to start a massive European business, using a newly commissioned £500,000 custom-built waste ship. It was proposed to dump some material in the outer Thames Estuary and also to use dumping grounds off the Continent. A spokesman for the firm, John Hudson Ltd, was reported to have stated: 'We are confident we are on to something big here.' It seemed the company was hoping to pick up some lucrative business when a ban on all dumping on the Rhine came into effect in the following May – one source of additional ocean waste.

Nevertheless, the firm was planning its operations with the approval of the Ministry of Agriculture, and it was stated that Ministry scientists at the Fisheries Laboratory, Burnham on Crouch, would 'police' the dumping. It occurs to me to wonder in all this who will police the policemen, since Governments are themselves – through various agencies and their dedication to the armaments race – among the worst dumpers.

In this particular case much will depend on the degree of independent testing carried out and on the monitoring of sea water in the dumping area.

This company's operations could, in fact, be more strictly supervised than many other activities of this kind. Controls of dumping can only be enforced within the three-mile limit through the bye-laws drawn up by the Sea Fisheries Committees. Because enforcement is so difficult, it must be presumed that illicit dumping takes place within territorial waters. Beyond them there are no statutory powers of control, although a voluntary consent system operates through the Ministry of Agriculture, Fisheries and Food, and is believed to be working well – though this again must be largely conjecture in view of the difficulty of policing the seas.

The Technical Committee on the Disposal of Toxic Solid Wastes, reporting in mid-1970, did not think there was a case for changing the present arrangements. 'If a method of doing something fails now and again,' they stated, 'the correct thing to do is not to abandon the method but to find out why it fails and what makes it succeed, and then to develop techniques of operations, or adopt the necessary precautions, so that it will not fail.' The committee also declared:

'We believe that there is a good case for expanding the practice of sea disposal (as distinct from ocean disposal but in many cases well beyond the three-mile limit) particularly for semi-solid and for certain liquid toxic wastes. But we do not think it should ever be adopted without careful selection of disposal sites in relation to the nature and quantity of the waste, and evidence sufficient to meet the circumstances of the case that it would be safe and satisfactory.'

The committee's attitude seems much too complacent. If it were merely a case of one or two small, isolated incidents of sea pollution by such dumping, there would be something to be said for their reaction, but 70 miles of dead fish can hardly be termed small or isolated. Nor can we shrug aside the deaths of thousands of sea-birds, the strange happenings to cod and pollack off the South Coast, the fish kills by cyanide off Wales or mercury in the seals off Cornwall.

Clearly the present system is not adequate to prevent such occurrences or to track down and punish offenders. It will not be adequate until we can put hand on heart and say we know precisely what and who is dumping where, at least within our own territorial waters.

Every ship leaving a British port with the intention of dumping toxic material in the ocean, wherever it may be, should at least be required by law to notify his intention to the Ministry of Agriculture, so that the information can be recorded.

The Scandinavian countries would like to go much further. Towards the end of 1971 they were planning to introduce legislation prohibiting the dumping of certain poisonous materials in international waters altogether, and they expected that all those who had signed the North-East Atlantic Fisheries Convention – Britain is among them – would follow suit. Mr Peter Walker, Secretary for the Environment, said there was great urgency for Britain to find solutions because 'the North Sea and Channel were at great risk'.

Not only more toxic wastes, but more radioactive wastes, are going to be disposed of in the sea in future. Wesley Marx, in his book, *The Frail Ocean* (Ballantine Books Inc.) states that within a few decades the world will be faced with the disposal of one thousand tons of high-level waste fission products annually. The West Pacific Ocean is vast, deep and sparsely populated by man and affords, he feels, a good test of the ultimate limit to the ocean's ability to handle such waste products. In the US atom bomb tests in 1954, mixed fission products of the order of half a ton were introduced into the upper layer over a short period. Within no fewer than a million square miles, tuna and other fish were found with sufficient radioactivity to render them unsafe to eat.

Stricter control over sea dumping would enable us to use it in a more positive way. Many fishermen's marks are in the vicinity of wrecks, which afford shelter for fish and salvation from predators. Dumped junk could offer a similar refuge. Some wastes, especially sewage sludge, can be beneficial to fish populations by introducing phosphates into the water and we might direct these to certain areas.

Oil and water don't mix

That this commentary has had an international flavour is inevitable – pollution of the seas is truly an international problem and can only be tackled at that level. Nowhere can this be more obvious than in regard to oil discharges.

With around 260 million tons of oil being carried by some 800 ships a day through the English Channel, the busiest sea route in the world, the risks are great. If fuel oil used for dry cargo vessels is taken into account, the total amount of oil moving around the British Isles exceeds 350 million tons per annum and is increasing by roughly 10 per cent a year.

The problem was, of course, highlighted by the *Torrey Canyon* disaster, when 100,000 tons of crude oil poured into the sea off the Isles of Scilly, and there have been many accidents of a less serious nature since. Indeed, hardly a week goes by without some collision in our congested shipping lanes, a new slick being sighted and beach authorities being alerted along some part of the south or east coasts.

At an international conference in June, 1970, it was stated that although catastrophic spills aroused public alarm, the real danger to the ecological balance of the oceans were smaller, continuing pollutions. Nature could restore the balance after one or two spills, but continual small discharges could change the whole situation.

We know that oil kills and incapacitates thousands of sea birds and fouls beaches, but little is known about its effects on marine life generally. Some scientists believe it has little effect on fish, for instance, as they are able to go deeper or to swim away from it. But Dr C. M. Tarzwell, director of the National Water Quality Laboratory in America, called for a more cautious attitude at the conference referred to. He gave an interim report on work showing that cancer growths had been found on the lips of croakers, a bottom-feeding fish caught in the Pacific Ocean in an area polluted with carcinogenically potent wastes from a nearby refinery.

He also quoted the results of studies with 29 oil dispersants, showing that they generally made oil more toxic. This has been backed up by tests made by our own Field Studies Council, stating that beach cleaning with emulsifiers must be regarded as the deliberate tipping of poisons into the sea.

However, it seems clear that some belated research by industry will produce results in the shape of harmless disposal agents in time – although coastal authorities still hold large stocks of the toxic BP 1002, sprayed on the *Torrey Canyon* site.

The chief hope for improvement lies in the strengthening of the 1954 International Convention for the Prevention of Pollution of the Sea by Oil. Enforcement is one problem, the imposition of proper penalties another. In 1968 there were 62 convictions under British Acts embodying the convention and they yielded only £9,000 in fines. Amendments to the convention extend the controls on discharges to all sea areas and in effect make the 'load-on-top' system mandatory. Under this system ships keep most oily residues on board. There are also provisions making tanker owners liable to pay compensation for damage of up to £6 million a time.

Even so, enforcement is bound to remain a problem. Unless a ship goes aground and leaks oil, like the *Torrey Canyon*, how can you tell who is responsible for a particular slick?

Well, it seems that the Swedes have an answer to this one, too. Their coastguard service was expected by the end of 1971 to have 15 oil-fighting vessels, equipped with jets to shoot out dispersants and various types of boom to round up the oil. Nor is that all. The coastguards can call up other ships, helicopters and private companies with specialist knowledge should an oil slick be sighted. The Swedish Atomic Energy Company has also found that radioactive iodine can be used to trace where the oil came from – a spot dropped into a ship's tank is enough.

Here, surely, is the answer for us. Such a fleet could not only be used to fight oil slicks and track down offenders, but to keep an eye on illicit dumping of toxic wastes. Helicopters could be used as spotter planes, too.

Sewage in the sea

But ships do not have to put to sea to enable illicit dumping to take place. Manufacturers may be able to persuade coastal authorities to accept toxic waste into their sewers and, as there is no control whatever over the discharge of sewage into the sea, they may be able to sidestep the rules which would apply if they tried to dump the waste separately.

Again this is an area where stricter supervision is required. Most of the sewage poured into the sea by some 220 coastal councils is untreated and although the tendency in recent years has been to insist on the use of long outfall pipes, many councils still use pipes extending only a short way below low water; beach contamination inevitably results and leads to complaints from the public. One Member of Parliament convulsed the House with his suggestion that swimming in such conditions merely amounted to 'going through the motions'.

Those who will avidly seize upon any excuse for doing nothing have laid great store by the four-year investigation by the Medical Research Council which, reporting in 1959, stated that the problem was largely an aesthetic one and that health risks could be largely ignored. Even if this were accepted – and many doctors disagree – the aesthetic objections are still powerful ones and should weigh heavily with authorities dependent on the tourist trade. Evidence has also been produced of damage to marine life, especially by detergents.

The Royal Commission on Environmental Pollution said it would be 'comparatively simple' to extend the powers of river authorities to include the control of sea discharges, and there are sound reasons for taking such a step.

In the long run, however, a better answer may lie in reclamation. Wesley Marx stated that the extension of sewage outfalls farther and farther out to sea was becoming an increasingly expensive way of deterring inshore pollution, especially when the specific catalysts of this pollution were poorly understood. Some districts were learning to re-use effluent rather than dump it into the ocean; treated effluent was a cheaper source of water than desalination.

This is the kind of approach we shall have to adopt more extensively in future. If we want to go on enjoying the fruits of the ocean in the widest sense of the term, we must see to it that those fruits are not destroyed by thoughtless actions. What has happened to Lake Erie and the Great Lakes shows that sheer size will not by itself provide protection. The seas, too, can be killed – the process just takes a little longer. In fact, we are informed that if an accident had occurred over or on the sea while defoliants were being transported to Vietnam, the results could have been catastrophic.

This island race of ours is sustained by the sea. We owe our lives to it in more ways than one. In the years to come we shall look to it increasingly to feed us and to meet our needs for recreation and enjoyment. But we shall also be calling on the sea to bolster our water supplies.

Keeping all these options open must have prior claim on our energies and resources.

Legislation:

Oil in Navigable Waters Acts 1955, 1963
Sea Fisheries Regulation Act 1966

Mainly responsible:

Coastal authorities (sewage disposal), Sea Fisheries Committees, Department of the Environment, Ministry of Agriculture, Fisheries and Food.

11. Reducing the racket

Many people's notion of hell would be some kind of bedlam. Few, I suspect, would see it as absolute quiet. Yet man has become conditioned to accept a certain level of noise and would probably be driven just as crazy by complete silence as by a devilish din.

Noise has been defined, in fact, as any *unwanted* sound, and it is clear that in this respect attitudes can change with time. For instance, trains make quite a lot of noise, but recent research has shown that people have come to accept the conventional sounds, though not those made by the new diesels. On the other hand, soft sounds, like the scampering of mice, can be most disturbing to some.

City dwellers become used to higher sound levels than their rural counterparts. The sounds themselves are also of a different nature. Townsfolk are thus frequently disturbed by the comparative peace of the countryside. Some cannot bear it. With noise levels rising sharply in the towns and not-so-sharply in the countryside in recent years, the differences have become more acute, so that one finds even short-term visitors to rural retreats taking their noise with them in the form of transistor radios and seeking out noisy spots for picnics, like the verges or traffic islands on busy main roads. Some people have to keep their radios on all the time while they are at home. It seems a kind of neurosis.

Advances in sound-deadening techniques have made it possible to reduce noise in offices to almost nothing, but firms which have created such conditions for their executives have received no thanks. On the contrary, there have been so many protests that they have either had to reduce the insulation or to introduce noise through tape recorders or electronic sound generators.

Certain kinds of noise are beneficial. Music, for instance, not only soothes the savage breast but also increases productivity. The sounds of nature are generally soothing. Recordings of surf on the seashore, the rustle of trees or corn and the song of the birds are played in sanatoria and mental homes. The lullaby is as old as time.

American research has suggested that music may even produce bigger crop yields. Maize grown in a hothouse in which music was played around the clock was found to grow faster and to have 20 per cent heavier stalks than maize grown in an identical hothouse without the music. It has been suggested that sound energy may increase the molecular activity of the soil, raising its temperature and influencing micro-organisms. Sounds have also been used to control pests.

On the other hand, much noise can be regarded as a form of pollution. It can cause mental and physical disturbance. Cotton workers, riveters, building workers, pneumatic drill operators and anyone subjected to noisy machinery over long periods is liable to sustain hearing loss. Research at Southampton University has suggested that no fewer than 100,000 workers might be entitled to compensation for hearing damage if it were included under industrial injury benefits. Young 'pop' fans have been found to have the hearing of the middle-aged. Traffic and aircraft noise can also hamper work in hospitals and schools.

The Russians have found that the noise produced by a jet plane can kill bee larvae and has a depressant effect on adult bees. It is said that if you place a carnation near a radio set and turn the set on at full volume it will wither. (I haven't tried this myself.) Noisy milking machines and even noisy milkmaids are stated to have caused lower milk yields and to reduce weight gain in pigs.

Investigations in Russia and elsewhere have revealed that noise can not only affect the human ear but can also cause many diseases, including cardiovascular afflictions. Its psychological effects – irritation, loss of sleep and so on – are well known. Cases have been recorded where abrupt noise has caused blindness, stammering and even epileptic fits. Where the background level is too high, warning noises cannot be heard and this may lead to accidents, breakdown of machinery and so on.

Town and countryside are becoming ever noisier. Traffic roars along motorways and through city streets; bigger and bigger jets thunder and whine overhead, and soon the sonic boom may reverberate; noisier machinery invades factory and farm; and diesel trains trumpet like herds of charging elephants. Life whirls along faster and faster, and the noise grows louder and louder.

It is disturbing more and more people. The Wilson Committee, which reported on the noise problem in 1963, referred to a survey showing that more than twice as many people were disturbed by noise in 1961 as in 1948, and who can doubt that the trend has continued to rise? In fact a survey by *The Observer* in 1971 found that city noise had grown 50 per cent louder in nine years.

Traffic most disturbing

Research has shown that traffic noise disturbs most people. 'Nothing would make a greater contribution to improving the quality of life in our cities than the development of a noiseless, fumeless motor car engine', says Mr Walter Bor, past-president of the Town Planning Institute. When the Westway motorway in London was opened in 1970, complaints about the noise from those living nearby were so great that the complainants were very quickly rehoused.

No action on traffic noise was taken, however, until July, 1968, when the Ministry of Transport introduced the Motor Vehicles Construction and Use (amendment) Regulations which were published as consolidated regulations in 1969. These made it an offence for any vehicle to generate a noise greater than 92 decibels at a distance of 25 feet. A year later this limit was cut to 89. It is now proposed to reduce it for goods vehicles and motor tractors of less than 200 horse-power to 86 decibels after 1973. On the other hand, the limit is being raised to 92 for vehicles of more than 200 horse-power until 1973, after which it is proposed to reduce it to 89. The limit for cars from 1973 onwards will be 80 dBA and for light goods vehicles up to 3½ tons gross weight 82 dBA. These revised rules will apply to vehicles manufactured after April 1, 1973.

The number of lorries of the heaviest class (over eight tons unladen weight) increased six times – from 6,000 to 40,000 – from 1956 to 1968 and at that rate there will be 14 times as many heavy lorries on the roads in 1980 than 1956. So it will be apparent that the total noise they make will probably be at least as great despite the reduced individual levels.

The existing limits – although better than any so far produced on the Continent – are still way above what the Wilson Committee regarded as acceptable, which was within half a decibel on either side of 80, and although the committee felt this level might be impracticable at the moment, it recommended an interim ceiling for all new vehicles, except motor cycles, of 85 decibels.

The decibel, it should be explained, is not a unit in the sense that volts, metres or grammes are units. It is merely a convenient form of measurement where the range of values is too great to be measured otherwise. It is essentially relative and works on a logarithmic scale. A doubling of sound intensity gives an increase of three decibels. A normal conversation is rated at 60 decibels and the scream of a jet taking off at 120. The Wilson Committee measurements included an 'A' weighting which makes them more closely attuned to the behaviour of the human ear. On this scale, an increase of 10 dBA corresponds roughly to a doubling of loudness.

The Noise Abatement Society, which was founded in 1959 and has been a pioneer for peace and quiet, has called for a maximum permitted noise level of 80 dBA at 12 feet – 'the farthest distance to which a pedestrian can normally retreat'. Its chairman, Mr John Connell, has rightly stated that present testing procedures are so complex that it's no wonder the regulations are not being enforced – the only real action being taken by the police is over defective silencers which is the subject of thousands of prosecutions a year. Mr Connell has suggested that a more practical method of enforcement would be for police officers and traffic wardens to carry a small 'noise torch' which would show when a prescribed level was exceeded. The registration number of the offending vehicle could be taken and the owner required to produce a certificate from a garage testing station proving that his vehicle complied with the regulations. In an address to the Royal Society of Arts, however, Dr E. J. Richards, Vice-Chancellor of Loughborough Institute of Technology, advocated tighter limits on vehicles at source, plus an annual check on silencers.

There is more than a crumb of comfort in the Government's decision – announced in December, 1970 – not to allow an increase in the 32-ton maximum weight of lorries (44-tonners had been asked for). Mr John Peyton, the Transport Minister, said he shared the concern about the effects of heavy lorries on the environment made to him from many quarters, including local authorities and amenity societies.

In a later speech, however, he hinted that this restriction might be relaxed when road improvements made this possible. There is also the possibility of Britain having to conform with the higher Continental tonnages if we enter the Common Market. At the time of writing concern is already being expressed that Continental 'juggernauts' are not having to meet British weight standards. There is a widespread feeling that the only way to deal with this problem is to confine lorries to specific routes – and to set aside special parking areas so that they do not have to park in residential streets.

But much tougher enforcement measures are called for, especially when unnecessary noise is being created, as with the removal of silencers on motor cycles. Both the French and Swiss impose lower noise limits and see that they are adhered to. The French will even confiscate the cars of persistent offenders and in Switzerland it is an offence to slam a car door loudly.

The building of more motorways raises special problems in relation to noise. Not only are levels on these roads very high, but there is a growing tendency for more night travel. This has meant that noise levels on some motorways between midnight and 6 a.m. are only about five decibels below the average daytime level, and it is predicted that there will eventually be very little difference.

Unless special steps are taken to insulate motorways – by the provision of acoustic barriers, for instance – people living nearby could be plagued by the noise, day and night. Much has already been made of this, and rightly so, by opponents of London's proposed ringway system.

Anguish near airports

While traffic noise is more general, aircraft noise can be more intolerable for those living near airports or under the flight paths. It disturbs people's sleep, making them nervous and irritable, and ill-prepared for the day's work, cuts down the pleasure of relaxing in the garden and interferes drastically with education and conversation generally. Though a step forward, the banning of night take-offs during the summer at Heathrow will have only a marginal effect on the noise nuisance. For one thing, landings are not banned; for another, the ban will increase the build-up in the early morning, which is already tremendous. From about 6 a.m. onwards in the summer months thousands of people are assaulted by the roar and whine of powerful jets. No sooner has the sound of one flying monster died away than another is heard in the distance, coming closer every second. Hundreds are jerked from their beds, finding sleep impossible. The Sunday morning lie-in is a thing of the past.

And it doesn't make the sufferers feel any better to discover that some of the planes shattering the peace are empty – Pan American operates a score of empty flights a day between the United States and Europe, TWA 22 and BOAC six.

Thousands of complaints pour into Heathrow every year – even pilots living at Windsor are said to have grumbled that aircraft noise stops them sleeping! In 1956, when planes had propellers, there were only 87 grumbles. Millions of householders and their families are being driven frantic because of the inept planning which put Heathrow where it is. And those living around Gatwick are in some ways worse off, because they have to take the night jets which are refused permission to land at Heathrow.

Noise take-off limits are supposed to be restricted to 110 decibels by day and 102 by night,* but there is evidence that they are often violated. Mr Geoffrey Holmes, chief public health inspector for Windsor and technical adviser to the Noise Abatement Society, claims that in two years recently there were more than 2,000 violations of these rules, but that in only one case was action taken against the pilot. The Department of Trade and Industry, which is responsible for the control of aircraft noise and which monitors take-offs, admits infringements of around 0·5 per cent.

Grants for sound-proofing their houses are available to Heathrow residents but not, at the time of writing, to people living near Gatwick. Applications can be made to the local authority, but the grant is paid by the British Airports Authority. The scheme has been a failure, with only about 4 per cent of those entitled to grants applying for them, chiefly it is thought because people object to paying £150 or so to abate a nuisance caused by air travellers and which they should be paying for.

One of the big snags, of course, is that the windows have to be kept closed. It

* Measured in perceived noise levels (PNdB) which give special weight to the higher frequencies, e.g. the scream of a jet.

was reported to a British Acoustical Society conference that the owners of a London office block forgot this when deciding to install double glazing at a cost of £28,000 – in this case to reduce traffic noise. On realising that the windows would have to be kept shut, they were forced to install air conditioning at an extra cost of £212,000.

A new housing estate built by the GLC for £3·4 million at Beaver Farm, Hounslow, and consisting of 631 dwellings, overcomes the problem of having to keep the windows closed in summer by providing a mechanical heating and ventilating system which is claimed to provide satisfactory internal conditions with the windows shut. The site lies directly in the eastern approach flight path to Heathrow, but heavily insulated panels and double glazing are said to give lower noise levels than in conventional houses several miles away.

It is all right, of course, if you don't want to go outside in summer and if you don't care about hearing the benevolent sounds of nature.

But this is no real way of tackling the problem – far better to reduce noise at source. What hope is there of this? An agreement reached by the International Civil Aviation Organisation means that the new generation of jet airliners coming into service in the 1970s will be a few decibels quieter. This is welcome, but may do no more than hold the balance, in view of the increased amount of traffic predicted. In 1963 there were 60,000 jet movements. Today there are more than 200,000 and the forecast for 1978 is 350,000. By 1980, for instance, it is prophesied that 300 jumbo jets a day will be landing at Heathrow. And they alone will disgorge 12,000 travellers, most of whom will want to travel into the centre of London somehow.

Engine manufacturers are under continual pressure from governments and public throughout the world to build in noise-reduction factors, and this will undoubtedly lead to much quieter aircraft in due course. It is hoped that even the Concorde will be no noisier than existing jets. Vertical take-off and landing aircraft may come in sooner than we think. They would probably increase the noise for people in the immediate vicinity, but would reduce it considerably for others.

What one might call 'traffic management' schemes – changing routes, switching runways and so on – have already brought relief to people living under the Heathrow flight paths, and more may be possible along these lines. It seems elementary justice, too, that people should be able to submit claims against airline operators for damage arising from their activities, as they can in America. We might also follow Tokyo's example in banning night flights entirely. Laws against sonic booms have been passed in some countries, and might be extended.

But perhaps the biggest hope of relief lies in siting future airports along the coast, so that they can take off and land over the sea. The decision to build a third London Airport at Foulness makes it possible in time to phase out Heathrow, despite the huge sums invested there and the opposition of Mr Peter Masefield, chairman of the British Airports Authority, who thinks that people who hope for such relief are living in 'cloud cuckoo-land'. Mr Masefield has been proved wrong more than once in recent years. Mr Peter Walker did say, in fact, that 'one of the main objects of a third London airport is to reduce the nuisance at existing airports'.

The law on noise nuisance

Finally, a word about the law relating to noise nuisance from factories and offices, radios, lawn mowers and so on. This type of nuisance falls into three categories – public, statutory and private. The first two are crimes and the last one is a civil offence. Public nuisance is deemed to affect people in general and private nuisance only individuals or a group. Statutory nuisance is defined by the Noise Abatement Act 1960, which brought noise within the scope of the 1936 Public Health Act. It gives local authorities (i.e. public health inspectors) the right to serve an abatement notice where they are satisfied that a noise nuisance exists, and to take action in a magistrates' court if the nuisance is not stopped. Statutory undertakings like British Rail and the National Coal Board, and aircraft noise are excluded. If three separate occupiers of land or premises are disturbed they may also complain to the magistrate. A working group of the Noise Advisory Council – set up by Mr Anthony Crosland, when Secretary of State for Local Government and Planning – has declared that the legislation is inadequate for modern conditions and needs strengthening.

The most common remedy is to seek an injunction, but the disturbance complained of must be substantial to have any hope of success. But public health officers and factory inspectors achieve a great deal 'behind the scenes' through negotiations with noise-making concerns.

Again sound planning, which keeps noisy operations away from residential areas or ensures that the noise is reduced at source, can prevent much trouble arising. And spare a thought for the poor factory worker, who may have to stand a deplorable din every minute of his working day. According to Mr F. Reynolds, chief air pollution and noise abatement inspector, Birmingham, the loss due to inefficiency and lack of concentration caused by noise in the working environment has been put at £1,000 million. There could be some comfort for factory workers in the news that a £1,500 grant for research into reducing noise in factories has been awarded to the University of Birmingham by the Science Research Council. It is thought likely, too, that Britain will follow America's lead in limiting the maximum steady noise to 90 dBA for people working an eight-hour day. This is still pretty loud – equivalent to the kerbside noise of a diesel at full throttle – but would represent an advance on the conditions often applying at present.

Tougher action to reduce noise has been promised by the Government at the time of writing. One measure worth carefully considering is the establishment of noise control zones, on the lines of smoke control zones, as suggested by the Association of Public Health Inspectors. This would help to meet the difficulty posed by higher traffic levels producing more noise than at present, even though individual levels are not exceeded.

Robert Koch, German bacteriologist and Nobel Prize winner, said at the turn of the century that some day mankind would be forced to combat noise as resolutely as it combats cholera and plague. While noise has since grown to almost plague proportions, the resolute action to combat it has yet to be implemented.

Legislation:
Public Health Act 1936 (part III)
Noise Abatement Act 1960

Motor Vehicles (Construction and Use) Regulations 1969
Heavy Lorries Regulation 1970
Civil Aviation Acts 1949, 1968
Town and Country Planning Act 1962

Mainly responsible:
Local authority public health departments, police, Noise Advisory Council, Department of the Environment.

Pesticides

12. The sprays of death

'We are losing half the subject matter of English poetry,' Aldous Huxley is reported to have remarked after reading Rachel Carson's *Silent Spring*, a book which more than any other has aroused public alarm about the indiscriminate use of pesticides.

Strange, is it not, that time and time again it is the immeasurable values which are lost? Half the subject matter of English poetry – how do you assess the song of the birds, the hum of insects in midsummer or the wayward flight of the butterfly? We know they give us enormous pleasure. We cannot envisage a world without them. Yet we are unable to put a price on their heads, whereas yields per acre can be weighed and costed, and neatly slotted into accountant minds.

Well, what's a few birds or insects or poetry, after all? We wouldn't die without them, whereas we couldn't survive without food. If we don't do it our competitors will, so you see, we have no choice. Anyway, if we make enough at it we'll be able, if we wish, to spend our holidays in some under-developed country and have our fill of bird-song. It will give us something special to look forward to.

There are people who think like this – who see the issue before us as a straight choice between economic survival and the retention of what they regard as dispensable luxuries. 'On the farmlands of these crowded islands,' wrote Sir William Slater, FRS, former secretary of the Agricultural Research Council, in the *New Scientist*, 'food production must come first. We cannot sacrifice the efficiency of our food production in order to avoid the loss of a few birds and mammals killed by chemicals, which is only a minute fraction of those due to natural causes or the guns of sportsmen.'

This was written in 1961, soon after the deaths of thousands of birds had been reported – pheasants, partridges and finches, kestrels, sparrow hawks, buzzards and owls – and when it looked as though some species, like the peregrine falcon, would be entirely liquidated.

In the winter of 1960, a strange epidemic swept through fox populations, causing convulsions, coma and apparent blindness. They lost their fear of man and one is even said to have strayed into the yard of the Master of a Hunt!

It was some time before Authority accepted that insecticides were to blame. When the evidence could no longer be disputed, a voluntary ban on the use of spring-sown seed dressings containing aldrin and dieldrin was imposed. This seems to have been generally observed and the mass deaths ceased. Nor did our agricultural economy suffer unduly, be it noted.

However, it emerged that the matter was much more serious than had at first been imagined. Pesticide residues turned up in so many widely varying situations that it soon became apparent that the whole environment was contaminated. These substances are extremely persistent. They can stay around for years in the soil and can be passed along the food chain in ever more concentrated form until predators, for instance, may receive lethal doses. Kenneth Mellanby, director of the Monks Wood Experimental Station (Nature Conservancy), says it is difficult, if not impossible, to find a field in England which does not contain a detectable amount of pesticide or a bird or mammal without residues in its tissues. All of us have pesticide residues in our body fat. Americans are said to have more DDT in their blood than is permitted in meat and such high concentrations have been found in breast milk in some parts of the USA that women have been advised to bottle-feed their babies. Spot checks of restaurant meals have shown that all contained DDT. A study made in 1966 for the Ministry of Agriculture, Fisheries and Food found that lard, apples and potatoes all held residues above the recommended levels. DDT even turned up in the flesh of Antarctic penguins.

An article in the *British Medical Journal* dealing with cases of impotence among farm workers stated that doctors found that in one year on the farm where the affected men worked, no fewer than 17 different chemicals had been applied to the land, of which four were deadly poisons.

'Along with the possibility of the extinction of mankind by nuclear war,' wrote Rachel Carson, 'the central problem of our age has therefore become the contamination of man's total environment with such substances of incredible potential for harm – substances that accumulate in the tissues of plants and animals, and even penetrate the germ cells to shatter or alter the very material of heredity upon which the shape of the future depends.'

Some experts think this is going too far. Dr Mellanby points out that even ingesting relatively large amounts of DDT has not caused any noticeable harm to humans – though all agree that we just do not know how things will work out in the long-term.

Already, chemicals previously thought to be relatively harmless, like the fungicides used for spraying fruit and potatoes, have produced some disturbing side-effects. The earth beneath trees sprayed over a long period has been found to be devoid of worms, for instance, and it is acknowledged that fish can be killed should the substance get into streams in any quantity.

Nor can we any longer be sure that these substances, too, do not build up in food chains. It is thought that widespread mercury poisoning among wildlife in Sweden might be due to fungicides used in seed dressings. American research has indicated that forage crops can and do take up insecticides from the soil and pass them into grazing cattle and thence into man.

When it became clear that the persistent organo-chlorines, as they are called, were getting into foodstuffs and reducing the number of predators, the Advisory Committee on Pesticides urged in 1964 that further restrictions be placed on their use. Again this was done on a voluntary basis – the use of aldrin and dieldrin in garden chemicals and sheep dips was phased out. Five years later manufacturers and users undertook to co-operate in withdrawing persistent pesticides from a large number of farm and home uses. Several products containing

DDT are no longer being supplied to distributors, and farmers and growers have been strongly recommended to use alternatives.

In addition, the manufacturers of pesticides have joined a voluntary Pesticides Safety Precaution Scheme whereby they undertake, before placing a new chemical on the market, to supply details of its properties, including toxicity, to the Ministry of Agriculture, so that the data may be studied by the Advisory Committee on Pesticides.

The Ministers concerned also have powers, under the 1967 Farm and Garden Chemicals Act, to make regulations to ensure that the active ingredients in all chemicals are named on the container, and that the label bears a distinguishing mark to indicate the extent of any hazard to human or wildlife. Recently there has been talk in Parliament about permission from the Department of Industry and Trade being required before crops are sprayed from the air.

Can a voluntary system really work?

This is all to the good, but it will be seen that the system throughout is almost entirely voluntary. Dr Mellanby agrees it is not perfect, but says it does seem to work. Nevertheless, there are clearly several flaws. For instance, should a manufacturer market his product as an industrial chemical, he is not obliged to submit it for approval under the Ministry scheme. There was a case not so very long ago where inadequate labelling led to a chemical getting into a stream and killing hundreds of fish. Many other chemicals are known to be marketed in this way.

The Advisory Committee itself pointed out in 1967 that the voluntary system although working 'remarkably well' could not be comprehensive, covering all distributors, and did not take account of ingredients which had been on the market for some time and might slip through the net. The committee thus concluded that the Government should have full power of decision and should not have to rely on the voluntary co-operation of commercial organisations, however responsible they might be.

With this view the Royal Commission on Environmental Pollution, which reported in February 1971, concurred, stating that 'reports already published convince us that mandatory control is desirable and will in the end be inevitable.'

The Council for the Protection of Rural England has declared that the situation would be more reassuring if our public analysts at local level regularly tested foods for poisonous residues and published the results where we could all read them. It might be cheaper to pay analysts today than doctors and hospitals tomorrow.

Most people seemed to think dieldrin, aldrin and even DDT were nearly finished, added the Council, but aldrin could be applied to strawberries with seed beetle, dieldrin to potatoes with wireworm and DDT in many circumstances with Ministry blessing, such as with BHC in smoke only two days before harvesting food crops. 'It may be easier to grow food with the help of these poisons, but is it ethical in the absence of more precise knowledge of the consequences?

Some countries – including the whole of Scandinavia – have already banned pesticides like aldrin and DDT, and many think Britain should follow suit. Others point out that bans would grievously harm agriculture, that some chemicals have brought great benefits to mankind, and that it is really a matter of finding the right balance. The people of each nation will have to decide for themselves whether they feel such pesticides are so valuable to them that they are prepared to risk any long-term harm.

What may weigh more heavily against chemical applications in future is that their use is often self-defeating, in the way that building more roads to cope with ever-increasing traffic often is. Case after case has been recorded of pests which were thought to have been wiped out re-emerging in greater numbers than before. Pesticides not only kill pests but the insects which feed on them. Pests can also build up a resistance, so that stronger and stronger doses are required, involving bigger and bigger threats to wildlife and, possibly, humans as well.

There are all kinds of alternatives which would be more satisfactory and probably in the long run more effective. Frequently less toxic sprays are available which are just as effective and no more expensive to employ. Plants resistant to pest attack can be developed, or planting can take place at a time when the pests will not be about. More selective pesticides might be produced and although they would probably be less economic the Government could provide financial incentives to their use.

Benefits of biological control

Then there is biological control, either through the release of vast numbers of sterile males, or through the introduction of some species which feeds on the pest. An Australian ladybird beetle introduced to California gave complete control over a citrus scale insect – until insecticide sprays killed off the ladybirds.

Garth Christian, in his book *Tomorrow's Countryside*, pointed out that American scientists examining the benefits of strip farming found that the population of aphid-eating spiders increased by almost one million to the acre; parasites preying on wasps multiplied to 217,000 per acre and the number of ladybirds rose by 380,000 in the same area.

Not only farmers use these chemicals, of course. The gardening store is full of them, and gardeners are buffeted on all sides by inducements to use them. Even the Ministry of Agriculture is a party to this. It issues a booklet called *Chemicals for the Gardener*, in which the reader is advised to buy a wide range of substances. Dr Mellanby calls the book 'a rather frightening compilation'. An unsprayed garden usually gives reasonable crops, he points out; biological control goes on all the time. If you start upsetting the balance, you could well do more harm than good.

In other words, are all these chemicals really essential in our gardens? Would our produce suffer to any great extent if we didn't use them or kept their use to a minimum?

What cannot be doubted, as Dr Mellanby says, is that if our gardens were kept free from at least the more dangerous pesticides, the effect on wildlife might be enormous.

Rachel Carson said that the 'control of nature' was a phrase "conceived in arrogance, born of the Neanderthal age of biology and philosophy, when it was supposed that nature exists for the benefit of man."

If we assault nature we assault ourselves. This we are learning slowly from bitter experience.

Legislation:

Agriculture (Poisonous Substances) Act 1952

Farm and Garden Chemicals Act 1967

Mainly responsible:

Local authority public health departments

Ministry of Agriculture, Fisheries and Food

Advisory Committee on Pesticides

Derelict Land

13. New uses for old workings

While we may console ourselves with the thought that if existing supplies of raw materials ran out, alternatives could be found, no such consolation is possible with regard to land. Once it is used for one purpose or another, it is no longer available. Unless we can reverse present trends and reclaim land from the sea or devise economic techniques for large-scale building over the ocean – not very likely – we must regard the supply of land as strictly limited.

It might be presumed, therefore, that any country with such a limited land supply as our own would cherish every acre and see that it was put to the best possible use. We are constantly being reminded about the pressures – 50,000 acres of farmland and open space taken every year for building of some kind or other, for instance, when England's half an acre per person represents all that is available for food production, compared with three acres in France and 12 in America. Then there is the rise in population at the rate of a thousand a day which, coupled with greater expectations in terms of living standards, means still more pressure on land – new houses, shops and schools, more motor vehicles and so on.

Yet, according to Government estimates, which are demonstrably under-estimates, some 95,000 British acres have been scarred, pitted, gashed and generally rent asunder for the extraction of minerals, and left in that condition to demean the landscape, depress the inhabitants and make the land unusable for other purposes without treatment.

The industrial revolution left its trail of havoc in the mining areas of Lancashire and Yorkshire, the Midlands and the North-East, in South Wales and in the Scottish counties of Lanark and Fife, and, to a lesser degree, in Cornwall, where tin was once much sought-after, and may be again. In the county of Northumberland alone the tips cover 1,437 acres and contain 63 million cubic yards of material. More recently the desecration has been added to, by brick-making in Bedfordshire, sand and gravel workings in the Thames Valley, the fantastic 'moonscape' created by china clay operations in Cornwall, the scarring of much beautiful countryside in the Peak District of Derbyshire by limestone extraction, slate-quarrying in Wales, and so on.

It is not denied that these operations are economically essential and that our prosperity has been built on them. But we are paying a high price for their activities and one which could and should be reduced. That the extent of the spoliation is greater than the Government says can hardly be denied. For one thing, the definition on which such figures are based is a narrow one – 'land which is so damaged by industrial or other development that it is incapable of beneficial use without treatment.' In April 1970, Mr Duncan Sandys, president of the Civic Trust, told a conference at Stoke-on-Trent – which has quite a dereliction problem itself* – that the definition didn't include land on which excavation or tipping was taking place with planning approval, nor extensive areas which were degraded and unusable, and offensive to the eye.

It fails to embrace the mess caused by the National Coal Board dumping of four million tons a year of pit refuse on Durham beaches, the large-scale sand and gravel workings, urban squalor or wirescape, spoil heaps on which tipping is still taking place and land scheduled for further development in the foreseeable future.

And the Government apparently assumes that planning conditions regarding restoration will, in fact, be enforced, although this doesn't by any means follow.

If everything of this nature were taken into account, an even more alarming picture would emerge – dereliction could amount to as much as 250,000 acres. How many houses might be built on such land, how many crops might we grow on it, how much might be set aside for playing fields?

Not only are we failing to deal with the backlog effectively, but we are falling well behind in our efforts to keep pace with the blight. According to Civic Trust estimates, this is increasing by about 3,500 acres a year, which means that by the end of the century there could be a further 100,000 acres to add to the total of a quarter of a million.

Modern reclamation techniques

This is all the more unforgivable now that we have new techniques for transplanting mature trees and for growing vegetation on inhospitable shale, and when modern earth-moving machinery can achieve dramatic transformations almost overnight.

There is no technical reason, and no insuperable economic one, why the brooding barriers of spoil and slag which have enshrouded the mining areas for generations should continue to confine and depress the spirit and, as the Aberfan avalanche so tragically demonstrated, threaten the very lives of those beneath. The mountains can be moved or their contours so shaped that, with the aid of grass and birch, pine and sycamore, they may become man-made hills safe for climbing and walking, and a joy to gaze upon.

Alternatively, they can be levelled and returned to farmland or used for recreation; when near towns they might become small country parks of the kind envisaged by the Countryside Act. Wet pits can, with a little preliminary planning and suitable landscaping afterwards, become venues for some of the three million anglers and for the rapidly rising number of boating enthusiasts. Or they may, at very little cost, be set aside as nature reserves. As John Barr suggested, worked-out quarries might be used for industrial developments which would otherwise spoil attractive stretches of countryside – gasholders, transformers,

---

* Stoke in fact has more dereliction within its boundaries than any other county borough in England—over 1,700 acres or nearly one-twelfth of the city area. But it is energetically tackling this problem and won a 1971 conservation award for its Central Forest Park Reclamation project. The award was presented under a joint scheme sponsored by *The Times* and the Royal Institute of Chartered Surveyors.

even small factories, adapted as adventure playgrounds or used to conceal a sprawl of caravans.

Whatever the form of reclamation decided upon, the cost would not be stupendous. Indeed, it has been estimated that the 'hard-core' dereliction could be dealt with for no more than £50 million spread over ten years, or about 10p per head of population per year, far far less than we spend on cigarettes to poison ourselves and pollute our surroundings.

Not only that, but the hard economic returns could be considerable. 'Beauty has an economic value, ugliness an economic cost', as the Civic Trust has pointed out. Yet because they are difficult to measure, these costs are often ignored when departments do their accounting. If the rise in property values when landscape is rejuvenated, the increase in recreational revenues from angling, boating and so on which could result, and the less tangible but nonetheless real benefits in terms of recreational and aesthetic pleasure were taken into account, the balance sheets would have a very different look. The kind of question we might ask ourselves is how many industrialists have been deterred from investing in the development areas by the sombre scene of dereliction which too often greets them? – and throw that sort of item into the reckoning.

If we, as a nation, could clearly afford these costs, it is a pity that all of us are not called upon to pay an equal share. Under the present system, Exchequer grants of 85 per cent of the cost of reclamation are available to local authorities in the development areas and 75 per cent in a national parks or area of outstanding natural beauty. Elsewhere, 50 per cent grants are available, except for the intermediate or 'grey areas', where 75 per cent payment may be made under the 1970 Local Employment Act.

What this means is that, although the whole nation has benefited from mining and quarrying, the areas which have suffered most are being asked to pay much of the cost of clearing it up.* This is not only unjust but unworkable, because by and large these poorer areas, with many other problems of this kind to solve, simply cannot afford to find the sums involved. All local authorities have, in any case, been subjected to a severe economic squeeze in recent years.

Leading the way

Nevertheless, there have been some striking achievements in such counties as Lancashire, Durham, West Riding and Nottinghamshire, in which not only the local authorities but the National Coal Board (especially the Opencast Executive), the Central Electricity Generating Authority and other industrial concerns have taken part.

Lancashire County Council has won a well-deserved reputation as a go-ahead authority in this respect. Boys are playing football on what were once colliery shale tips. Council houses stand where pit heaps stood before. Much 'lost' territory has been restored to agriculture. More than a million trees have been planted on derelict sites.

But this county, at any rate, does not pretend to have acted entirely of its own volition. Mr U. Aylmer Coates, who, as Lancashire planning officer, won a well-deserved reputation for his work in this field, has stated that reclamation had to be undertaken as there was just no other land available – no less than 40

---

* This remains true, despite slightly bigger grants (more than 90 per cent in development areas) announced by Mr Peter Walker, Secretary for the Environment, in May, 1971.

per cent of the urban district of Ince-in-Makerfield, for example, was officially classified as derelict.

The Opencast Executive of the NCB has been no less active. It claims to have spent about £1 million a year on reclamation projects covering close on 100,000 acres. One of the most impressive is at Polesworth, Warwickshire, where a large recreational area is planned, including parkland, sports fields, boating lakes and other facilities. The project is the outcome of negotiations between the Executive, the local water board (which wanted a reservoir and has been sold a relatively inexpensive 'hole' by the NCB) and the West Midlands Sports Council, which is pleased to see a regional sports centre included. It also shows what a splendid opportunity there can be for creative land use in the derelict areas.

If other mining agencies had done as much to reclaim land as the Opencast Executive, the problem would be much nearer solution. Nevertheless, coalmining has a very big community bill to meet, as one other local authority has good reason to know. For many years now Fife County Council has been labouring with commendable energy to raze its 'dark satanic hills' of coal and industrial waste. And with a good deal of success. Another authority with the right ideas is Bolton, which plans to reclaim the degraded landscape of the Croal and Irwell valleys, turning them into linear parks stretching from Bolton to Manchester with the aid of cash from an incinerator plant.

Among the prizewinners for 1971 in the conservation award scheme sponsored jointly by *The Times* and the Royal Institution of Chartered Surveyors was the borough of Workington for its St. Helens reclamation scheme. On a 20-acre site, long derelict, consisting of pit-head areas, small tips, railway sidings and the relics of an old ironworks, the borough has created a pleasant area of grass and trees, with a series of small hills to the north, within which there is a site for a factory and two small, well-concealed car parks. Total expenditure was £25,729, for which an 85 per cent grant was obtained from the Ministry and a 15 per cent grant from the county council. 'We applaud the monumental efforts of such a small local authority,' said the judges in their report. By its initiative, they added, Workington had shown that industrial blight could be tackled and this 'pathfinding project' should encourage others to take action.

Among the projects commended by the judges was an interesting plan by Lanarkshire County Council to convert a disused railway line and spoil heap into school playing fields and a site for light industry. The scale of dereliction involved by the closure of railway lines is not widely appreciated. Every year an area sufficient to build a new town for 80,000 people falls into disuse and much of it can remain derelict for years.*

One general but important point made by the panel was that where districts have been disfigured by mining operations and where someone other than the operators are to carry out the reclamation work, the land should be made available to the reclaiming authority on favourable terms. This seems elementary justice.

Lea Valley and Lower Swansea projects

But the schemes which have really captured public imagination in recent times have been those for the Lea Valley and Lower Swansea Valley. The

---

* See report for Countryside Commission on Disused Railways in the Countryside of England & Wales (HMSO £1.00).

Civic Trust graphically labelled the Lea as 'London's kitchen garden, its well, its privy and its workshop'. After surveying the area, the Trust drew up a plan for a 10,000-acre linear park, and local authorities joined together to promote a parliamentary Bill setting up a regional park authority to make the scheme a reality. The Bill became an Act in December 1966 and the first steps to implement it have been taken.

Would that similar energy had been shown regarding Swansea University's land reclamation project which would transform a wilderness of slag and spoil into parks and recreation grounds. Although this highly imaginative plan was well received in South Wales, there has been no great rush to put it into effect. Why this should be one can only surmise, but as John Barr stated 'The Lower Swansea Valley today is a stark monument to thoughtless and ruthless exploitation, and while it remains in its present state it is a standing reproach to each generation which shrugs its shoulders and looks the other way.'

One of the most economical approaches to dereliction is to link heaps and holes, so that at one stroke, as it were, two problems can be solved – the disposal of unwanted waste and the removal of dereliction. Town refuse, power station ash or builders' rubble can be tipped into gravel, clay or chalk pits, covered with topsoil and returned to agriculture, made into recreation grounds or whatever is deemed appropriate.

Something on these lines is being done through an arrangement between the CEGB and the Midlands brickmakers whereby the Board is tipping ash (at a price) from its Trent Valley power stations into brick pits so that, with suitable treatment of these and the wet pits, whole areas can become recreational parks. The possibilities in this respect may be appreciated by taking a walk through the Fletton 'knotholes' and seeing how attractive some of these lakes can be once trees and grass have grown and the wildlife has become established. Yet the only members of the public who have been able to enjoy such surroundings for years have been a restricted number of anglers. Thousands of acres have been dug up and the air is polluted by smoke and fumes, but until recently little has been done to restore worked-out land to the public in general.

There are many similar examples of this 'heaps and holes' collaboration, mostly of a less ambitious nature, like Liverpool's controlled tipping of house refuse to reclaim hundreds of acres of playing fields and farmland. Domestic refuse tipped on the Mersey foreshore in compacted layers actually laid the foundation for a promenade.

Halted by transport costs

In too many other cases, however, fine chances have been lost because of a few shillings on transport costs. A hundred million tons of sharp sand are available from china clay workings in Devon and Cornwall. These could augment supplies of building aggregate and in particular ease the pressure on sand and gravel, which is rapidly running out in the south-east of England. (Furthermore, it has been estimated that some 47,000 acres will have to be set aside for gravel workings by 1977.)

But the problem is to transport the sand from Cornwall to London and other areas where it is required, and this works out at more than those concerned can afford to pay. Thus a useful product goes to waste, which raises the question of whether everything should be subordinated to the need for British Rail to balance its books? Cannot we devise a system for ensuring that the overall national interests can be weighed in the balance on questions of this kind – surely some kind of subsidy to make the scheme feasible would be a good investment?

If there were an agency able to allocate funds for such purposes and to oversee the problem generally, this would be an enormous help. As the Hunt report (Cmnd 3998, April 1969) pointed out, the present organisation is fragmented, slow and cumbersome, and there is no proper way of establishing priorities. Whether the proposed body should be a Derelict Land Reclamation Agency, as the committee suggested, or whether it should be broadened to take in reclamation generally – in view of the close links between waste disposal and land use – is a matter for discussion, but the case for something along these lines seems irrefutable. And it would be sensible, in view of the doubtful future of the Opencast Executive with the rationalisation of the coal industry, to use their expertise in the new agency.

The Labour Government opted for something more modest – the setting up of a central group like the derelict land unit in Wales which has done some very fine work since the tragedy of Aberfan focused attention on the problem.

To operate effectively, however, any agency would need to overcome certain anomalies or have them cleared away by further legislation. The Council for the Protection of Rural England has pointed to several, including the lack of power to vary planning conditions – which means that authorities cannot take into account the changes which may take place during lengthy mineral operations – the difficulty of obtaining filling materials and the practice of requiring payment for the right to tip (the holes and gashes produced can actually be regarded as 'assets'). The CPRE has also underlined the need for more research into the use of industrial waste as aggregate, to ease the pressure on sand and gravel.

The operators, it seems, can have their cake and eat it, with one notable exception. Ironstone extractors are required by law to restore the lands they tear up. Where reclamation costs exceed a certain figure, they can draw on the Ironstone Restoration Fund, established in 1951, to which they pay a levy and to which the Exchequer contributes a smaller sum.

This arrangement has worked very well. It enables the mining wounds to be progressively healed and this is surely what we want to see done generally. There seems a good case for extending the principle to all mining operators – for putting the burden of restoration largely on the shoulders of those who do the damage and ensuring that they conform with the tenets of good husbandry and that, after they have got what they want out of the land they leave it in a decent condition for those who come after.

Measures of this kind become much more urgent as one looks ahead. Mineral operations are unlikely to diminish. Estimates suggest that by the end of the century the world will need 13 times as much aluminium, 11 times as much lead, nine times as much copper and seven times as much iron.

Legislation:

Industrial Development Act 1966 (grants for development areas)

Local Authorities (Land) Act 1963 (authorised councils to do reclamation work on private land, provided consent obtained).

Local Employment Act 1970 (grants for intermediate or 'grey' areas)
Local Government Act 1966 (50 per cent grants for all areas)
National Parks and Access to the Countryside Act 1949 (75 per cent grants for national parks, etc.)

Mainly responsible:
County and county borough councils
Department of the Environment

Further reading

Pollution – General
Royal Commission on Environmental Pollution, first report, HMSO, 1971.
Lord Kennet, *Controlling Our Environment*, Fabian Society, 1970.
Pollution and our Environment, Labour Party report, 1970.
Protection of the Environment: The fight against pollution, HMSO, Cmnd 4373, 1970.
Urban Pollution: special issue of Municipal Review, April 1970.
Disposal of Solid Toxic Wastes, Report of Technical Committee, HMSO, 1970.
Refuse Storage and Collection, Working Party report, HMSO, 1967.
Refuse Disposal, Working Party report, HMSO, 1971.

The Air
Craxford, Weatherley, Gooriah, *Air Pollution in Urban Areas in the United Kingdom*. (Available to members of Standing Conference of Co-operating Bodies Investigating Air Pollution from Warren Springs Laboratory of the Department of Trade and Industry at Stevenage).
Weatherley and Gooriah, *National Survey of Smoke and Sulphur Dioxide – The Greater London Area.* (available as above).
An Examination of Sulphur Dioxide as an Air Pollutant, National Society for Clean Air, 1964.
Lawther and Commins, *Pollution from Road Vehicles and Health*, NSCA, 1970.
Air Pollution, Departmental Committee on, Beaver Report, HMSO, Cmnd 9322, 1954, repr., 1966.
Annual Report of Alkali Inspectors, HMSO.

Rivers
Prevention of River Pollution, Report of Rivers Pollution Prevention Sub-Committee, HMSO. 1949,
Taken for Granted, Report of Jeger Committee, HMSO, 1970.
Anglers' Co-operative Association Handbook.
A. L. Downing, *Pollution Control and Related Research in the U.K.*, Work of Water Pollution Research Laboratory, HMSO.
B. A. Southgate, *Water: Pollution and Conservation*, Thunderbird, 1969.
River Authorities' annual reports, from authorities concerned.

The Seas

Marx, Wesley, *The Frail Ocean*, Ballantine, USA, third printing March, 1970.
Control of Radioactive Wastes, HMSO, Cmnd 884, April, 1968.
Sibthorp, M. M., *Oceanic Pollution:* A survey and some suggestions for control. David Davies Memorial Institute of International Studies, London 1969.

Noise

Final report of the Wilson Committee, HMSO, Cmnd 2056, 1963.
Taylor, Rupert, *Noise*, Penguin, 1970.
Stephenson, R. J., *The Noise Problem*. Paper to Association of Public Health Inspectors, June 1971. (APHI)
Action Against Aircraft Noise, Board of Trade, HMSO, 1969.
London Noise Survey, HMSO, 1968.
Review of Road Traffic Noise, Road Research Laboratory LR 357, Department of the Environment, 1970.
Law on Noise, Noise Abatement Society.

Pesticides

Carson, Rachel, *Silent Spring*, Penguin, 1965.
Graham, Frank, *Since Silent Spring*, Hamish Hamilton, 1971.
Mellanby, Kenneth, *Pesticides and Pollution*, Fontana, 1969.
Coleman Cooke, J., *The Harvest That Kills*, Odhams, 1965.
Review of Persistent Organochlorine Pesticides, Ministry of Agriculture Advisory Committee report, 1964, HMSO. Supplementary report, HMSO.
Toxic Chemicals: Report of Research Committee, Agricultural Research Council, HMSO, 1964.
  Supplementary Report, 1965.
Moore, N. W. (Ed), *Pesticides in the Environment and their Effects on Wild Life*, (supp. to *Journal of Applied Ecology*, 1966).

Derelict Land

Barr, John, *Derelict Britain*, Penguin, 1970.
Derelict Land, Civic Trust, 1964
The Rhondda Valley – Proposals for Transformation, Civic Trust, 1965.
Opencast Coal – A Tool for Landscape Renewal, National Coal Board, 1967.
Hunt Report on Development Areas, HMSO, Cmnd 3998, 1969.

Note: *Many of the books listed here and elsewhere in this volume are obtainable from The Ecology Bookshop, 45 Lower Belgrave Street, London, SWIW OLS (Tel: 01-730 8603).*

THE OPEN LANDSCAPE

Swan-song for Old England

*If the Government and the people really want the big increase in agricultural pro-
duction aimed at, then they must at the same time face the fact that the old England
we have known, with its little homesteads and its miniature countryside – a great
tourist attraction – will totally disappear.* – Colonel G. R. Judd, chairman of the
Royal Institution of Chartered Surveyors agriculture and forestry committee, at
a conference in London

The passing years have lent credence to Cowper's dictum that 'God made the
country and man made the town'. With the towns becoming uglier, noisier and
more congested, the countryside and coast have acquired an increasingly seduc-
tive quality. Townsfolk are apt to view it much as ageing males view a decorative
addition to the typing pool – any blemishes pass quite unnoticed.

While God may well have made the lady in question, however, He did not
formulate the pattern of the countryside as we know it. This is largely man-made,
and it takes but a moment's thought to realise that this must be so. Nature could
never have created so trim and ordered a landscape. Just as one's own garden
soon becomes rampant with weeds if left to Nature, so the countryside would
have assumed an altogether wilder air.

The mosaic of field and hedgerow, copse and woodland to which thousands
from all over the world pay homage was fashioned by farmers and landowners.
The great estates of the 17th and 18th centuries were purposefully planted and
laid out by landscape gardeners like William Kent and 'Capability' Brown. Even
those stretches of moorland and heathland resulted from the medieval destruction of forests and woods, so could hardly be described as natural.

It is interesting to speculate on the reasons why man, who with rare exceptions
has behaved so clumsily and tastelessly in the towns, should have created so
beautiful a rural landscape, and that when he built in the countryside he built
well. Perhaps it has something to do with the fact that he was using natural
materials, like timber and stone, which help to make his buildings look as if they
belong, whereas in the towns he turned as a rule to synthetic and manufactured
components such as steel and concrete.

But there must be more to it than that, because when he used brick – which,
after all, is only baked clay, a natural material – he used it to much better effect
in the villages and country towns. Of course, adding one or two houses to a
village is a vastly different proposition from putting up a large housing estate in
a town with all the facilities needed to service it. In the former case, there is time

to think very carefully of what you are doing; in the latter, you are working under considerable pressure.

One suspects, however – though it would be hard to prove it – that the real reason is that the Englishman especially has always felt that his home is in the country to which he will return when his temporary sojourn in the town is over.

Be that as it may, man's role in the countryside is not a static one – he is constantly changing, adapting and renewing the rural fabric. Until recent times these changes have been slow and gradual, so that the countryside has seemed to wear the same familiar raiment, changing it only with the seasons, which is right and proper.

Now its very structure is being radically transformed. We are in the throes of an agricultural revolution which will alter the appearance of the country scene to a degree not matched since the enclosures of the 18th and early 19th centuries. Farm mechanisation has not only forced workers to abandon their cottages and seek employment elsewhere, but has led to bigger and bigger holdings on which machinery can be used to the best advantage.

14. What's in a tree ?

Encouraged by Ministry of Agriculture 'improvement grants', farmers are ripping out the hedgerows at an ever-increasing rate. Some estimates suggest we are losing 10,000 miles a year, mostly in East Anglia and the Midlands. The habitat of many species of birds, animals, insects, wild flowers and plants is rapidly being destroyed. According to estimates in a Government report issued in 1955, we could eventually lose some 21 per cent of our standing timber.

While Governor Ronald Reagan, of California, may believe that 'A tree's a tree; what do you want to look at more than one for?' most people will regard these changes with the utmost dismay. There seems to have grown up in most British breasts a reverence for trees as deep-rooted as the oldest oak. The axe which brings a stately elm crashing to the ground, or which chips and chops in the crudest way at the branches of suburban plane trees, so that they look like a procession of hat stands, also strikes deeply into our hearts, for reasons which are as old as time.

Nevertheless, those who wield the axe in such a way with no apparent pain or anguish cannot be few in number. They have done so to such effect over the years that whereas in neolithic times woodland occupied some 40 million of the 57 million acres of England, Wales and Scotland, by the middle of the 18th century this had sunk to an all-time low of around two million acres. Since then it has risen somewhat to reach about three million acres, but we could do with much more. In fact, Britain has fewer trees than any other Western European country, which seems astonishing for such a reputedly tree-loving nation. Woodlands account for only 7·6 per cent, less than a quarter of the European average of 29 per cent.

Trees are a superb investment. They cost so little, yet contribute so much. As well as nourishing the spirit, they have immense practical value. They act as windbreaks, conserve moisture and help to purify the air by taking in carbon dioxide and discharging oxygen.

Apart from the agricultural assault on them, our traditional hardwoods are threatened as never before by pollution, road-widening schemes and other development, and by land drainage. Many are, of course, dying from disease – Dutch elm disease is causing havoc in Kent and East Anglia, for instance – and from plain old age.

The biggest sufferer is undoubtedly the oak. This symbol of British trust and reliability is fast vanishing from the scene. In 20 years it could be a rare sight. Oaks take so long to grow that they are not an economic proposition, especially as metals, concrete, plastics and chemically treated softwoods have largely replaced oak as a structural material.

A new, treeless prairie landscape is emerging, fashioned for the machine and undeniably more productive and profitable in the short-term. So far as the long-term prospects are concerned, however, there are some big question marks.

For one thing, hedges act as windbreaks. If they are torn down, the wind can play havoc with the soil. Nature requires 300 to a thousand years to produce one inch of topsoil, yet thoughtless farming could result in it being swept away overnight. What this might mean in future, in a world of possibly unprecedented food shortages, hardly bears thinking about.

We don't in this country suffer from 'dust bowls' as they do in the North American prairies, for instance, but we could be creating 'dust-bowl' conditions. History has some painful lessons for those who have abused nature. The Sahara, for instance, was once a fertile plain and the ruins of great cities lie beneath the Libyan Desert.

The very areas now being denuded of hedgerows are precisely those which have been prone to soil erosion in the past. In March, 1968, the east of England had its worst dust storms in living memory. Their effects were felt far beyond their usual Fenland boundaries, in areas which had never experienced them before. These were the regions where hedges which could have broken the wind were no longer there. Rolling clouds of dust filled the sky and one expert was reported as saying that 'a minor dust-bowl situation exists on the prairie farms of this country'.

Slowly the rich black soil of the peat fens of Cambridgeshire and the Isle of Ely is being blown or drained away. Mr A. K. Astbury, in *The Black Fens* (1958) forecast that most of the peat fibre would have vanished within a century.

While we remove our hedges, others are protecting theirs. Holland, Germany and Denmark have all passed laws to stop trees being felled and hedges being pulled up, and grants are given for new planting. It is claimed that the returns have been considerable, as crop yields have increased by up to 24 per cent. When new farms are reclaimed from the sea, the first action taken by the Netherlands State Landscape Service is to plant hedges and shelter belts.

Garth Christian, in *Tomorrow's Countryside*, pointed to the value of hedge-rows in reducing evaporation of moisture from the soil. 'Is it purely coincidence', he asked, 'that in areas of East Anglia, the removal of hedgerows has been followed by an urgent call for more costly irrigation schemes?' He added that hedgerows also harbour insect predators, parasites and pollinators.

Whether these arguments will weigh very heavily with farmers remains to be seen. Some success is reported with attempts to persuade them to leave untouched those corners of fields here and there which cannot in any case be reached by the tractor. Twelve-foot willow hedges are being introduced into some parts of the Fen Country and Dr Max Hooper, of the Nature Conservancy, has suggested that this practice might be extended.

So far as tree preservation is concerned, local authorities may make preservation orders, not only for individual trees but groups of trees, including woodlands. If a tree, subject to an order, is destroyed or dies, the owner must plant another of the same species in the same place. Amenity societies can help here by organising tree surveys. This not only draws attention to the trees, but provides valuable data for action by the local authority.

Grants for planting are available to farmers and local authorities but they aren't being taken up on anything like the scale required. However, all planning authorities now have a duty, under the Civic Amenities Act, to see that proper provision is made for the preservation or planting of trees in new developments. In this connection the technique of transplanting semi-mature trees promoted by the Civic Trust is invaluable.

It would certainly help to increase tree stocks if the Forestry Commission had an 'amenity' section devoted to the planting of hardwoods, as has been suggested in some quarters. And the Automobile Association, by calling upon its members to 'drive to plant a tree' is on the right road.

But the real answer lies in more positive tree-planting policies by landowners generally; a need made more urgent by the decimation of our glorious elms. Where is the modern John Evelyn who will fire the nation with the kind of planting fervour which followed the publication of *Sylva?*

The ailing soil

High-pressure farming is also threatening the very structure of the soil. The Soil Association had been warning of the dangers for many years to little effect; then, in the summer of 1970, an official inquiry into the health of farmland soils revealed that in some parts of England and Wales their fertility and structure had been reduced to 'dangerous 'levels.

It was stated that their organic content was often as low as 3 per cent, against the Ministry of Agriculture's recommended minimum of 8 per cent. Cereal crops would not grow and the soil was easily compacted in wet weather by heavy farm machinery, making it virtually unworkable. As a result, something like half a million acres, mostly in the Midlands, were virtually out of production in 1968–69.

Will those farmers who have blithely flogged their soils to the point of complete exhaustion, now be ready to heed the warnings? Will the Soil Association and biologists who have expressed concern about the excessive reliance on pesticides and fertilisers now be listened to?

What is perhaps even more to the point, will the Government take some of the pressure off the farming community and make it easier to resist the lure of short-term gain in favour of genuine, long-term prosperity?

Without such assistance, voices like those of Mr Emrys Jones, chief scientific adviser to the Ministry, could be crying in the wilderness. Mr Jones has said the only cure for the ailing soils is a return to traditional systems of mixed farming and rotation cropping, with much more land turned over the grass and livestock.

How far is this possible in the present economic climate and what is the Government prepared to do to facilitate such a changeover?

With the Common Market in the offing at the time of writing, the situation becomes even more urgent. The coming decade could well see an intensification of the pressures which have led to the removal of hedgerows and the impoverishment of the soil, as more and more farmers face the alternatives of either increasing their exploitation of the land or facing economic ruin.

We saw in the 18th and early 19th centuries how unbridled economic forces ravaged our towns and cities. Even though we now have more power to control these forces, we cannot against such a background view the future with equanimity. Having the power is one thing, being prepared to use it to the required extent is another.

There will be a price to pay and it could be a heavy one. What is the preservation of the countryside worth to us? How many of those who are always declaring their love for it prepared to give concrete expression to that love?

We shall find out in the decade ahead. Let us hope those ardent suitors do not turn out to be feckless and irresponsible when the banns are called.

What price beauty?

To say that we must pay a price to safeguard our countryside is not enough, however; the real question is, how much? How can we measure its value in terms which will impress an inspector at a public inquiry who has to assess it against the measurable claims of housing or industry? Sacrilegious though it may seem to try and translate spiritual feelings about the countryside into material terms – like quantifying a Renoir painting in relation to what it will fetch at Christie's or Sotheby's – the job has to be done in this hard-headed situation. Many a campaign has foundered on this particular rock.

Fortunately, the rock does not now appear so immovable as it once did. Dr E. J. Mishan showed in an article in *Encounter* (December, 1969) how these intangibles could be measured, and the department of town and country planning at Manchester University will doubtless be looking into his suggestions during their three-year study of landscape evaluation techniques for the Countryside Commission.

The Roskill Commission, which inquired into the third London airport, attempted to put a price on amenity factors in its 'cost-benefit analysis', but many will quarrel with its assessments. For instance, Stewkley's 800-year-old church, described by Nikolaus Pevsner as 'the most splendid piece of Norman parochial architecture in Buckinghamshire, was entered as worth £51,000, its fire insurance value!

A break-through here would, of course, apply more widely than to farming economics, but it would be an enormous help in finding the right balance in agriculture between food production and amenity. At present, food production always takes priority, Many people feel that the price we have paid in environmental terms has been higher, in some cases, than the gains in food production and could be higher still in future. The problem is to prove it.

If only we could assess the value, for instance, of well over a million acres of grassland ploughed up in the last decade, involving the loss of beautiful downland scenery. Among the casualties in the county of Dorset have been Eggardon

Hill, Hambledon Hill and downland tracts bordering the lovely Purbeck coast. The turf is being stripped off, destroying plants and insect life which nourish communities of animals and birds. Earthworks are being razed out of existence. Of 871 recorded round barrows in South Dorset, it is estimated that less than 5 per cent remain unaffected.

And the Ministry of Agriculture is encouraging these operations by giving special ploughing grants. The Ministry is supposed to weigh the merits of amenity and natural beauty against those of agriculture in making these grants, but in Dorset at any rate no grant has ever been withheld for amenity reasons.

I am with Brian Jackman when he wrote in *The Observer* (May 16, 1971): 'Farmers have always claimed they are the rightful custodians of the land, whose prime purpose is the production of food. But there are other factors to be considered. Nowadays those who work the land represent less than 3 per cent of the national labour force.

'Surely then it is not unreasonable that the other 97 per cent of us, who pay the farmers' subsidies, have a right to expect a pleasant countryside in which to relax and enjoy ourselves?'

Recreation

15. The mobile millions

Although 80 per cent of British people live in towns of 10,000 population and over, the countryside occupies a very high place in their thoughts.

This is shown by the massive week-end exodus from cities throughout the warmer months. It was estimated that no fewer than 29 million people were on the move during one recent Whitsun holiday. What proportion of those who leave the towns have any purpose apart from a vague desire to get away we don't know, except that outdoor recreations of all kinds claim many more supporters. Angling, for instance, is said to have about three million disciples and to be our largest participant sport. Organised walking and rambling claims 960,000, golf 750,000 and boating 700,000. There has been an astonishing growth in the numbers taking camping and caravan holidays – caravanners have grown from a mere handful in 1951 to around the four million mark today, which poses some obvious problems of providing sites. Millions more visit beauty spots and stately homes.

And although there has been a tendency for more people to go abroad for their holidays, some 30 million still take them at home and there has been a threefold increase in the number of overseas visitors to this country – from two million in the early 1960s to around the seven million mark today.

What this can mean for popular centres may be gleaned from the fact that Loch Lomond is visited by $1\frac{1}{2}$ million people each year; that the Norfolk Broads, which had 80,000 visitors before the war, now attract 300,000, and that the New Forest has to cope with 86,000 sightseers – 30,000 more than six years ago.

These figures are constantly rising as more people have more leisure, more money and more motor cars. New motorways are making parts of Britain more accessible. When the present network is completed, there will be five million people within an hour's travelling time of the Yorkshire Dales and 16 million within two hours. No fewer than 21 million will be able to get to the Lake District and back in a day – nearly half the population! Construction of the Severn Bridge has brought the Brecon Beacons National Park within an hour's run of Bristol. The Beacons Mountain Centre, which was planned for about 8,000 visitors a year, will now have to cater for around 80,000. It has been estimated that within 10 years the number of people living within a 3½-hour journey of Exmoor will leap from nearly five million to nearly 19 million.

The planners say the predicted traffic levels would be unacceptable, but what can be done? Doubtless there will be demands for new and better roads, but experience has shown this to be a self-defeating process. It simply means more cars and fewer opportunities for people to enjoy what they go there to find.

Various traffic management proposals have been put forward – one-way schemes, the creation of scenic drives on the American pattern to channel traffic along certain routes, strict limits on parking and the diversion of through traffic from areas of high landscape value. Some form of road pricing may become necessary or tolls may have to be charged for entering national parks.

Already such a proposal has been made for the use of public rights of way in Snowdonia National Park. The Ramblers' Association has called it 'outrageous'. But if this suggestion is defeated, others are sure to be made unless some better way can be found of handling the huge influx of visitors expected. There are ominous signs from America, where a fee of seven dollars a year per family for admission to all national forests, parks and monuments has been instituted and the proceeds put towards the purchase of more parks and recreation areas. Hefty admission prices are forecast for the years to come. 'Soon getting into a national park will be considerably more difficult than obtaining tickets for the biggest Broadway hit', write the authors of *Moment in the Sun*.* 'It will be a case of waiting until your number comes up on a list – perhaps years from when you want your vacation.'

None of these measures would stop cars penetrating the most remote regions and interfering with the pleasure of those seeking solitude. It is astonishing how even the most inhospitable-looking byway will carry its quota of wheeled traffic. Some motorists will drive wherever their cars will take them – on verges, beaches and village greens; nowhere is sacred, it seems.

Perhaps the best solution would be to classify landscape on the basis of its existing character and possible future use. This classification could broadly follow the lines proposed by the Countryside Commission, ranging from high-density areas near towns, which could be used for recreation, to unique natural areas, wild regions and historic sites. Management policies could be formulated accordingly.

The high-density districts near towns could become country parks as proposed in the Countryside Act of 1968. These, it was stated, would serve three purposes. They would make it easier for town dwellers to enjoy their leisure in the open, without travelling too far and adding to the congestion on the roads; they would ease the pressure on the more remote and solitary places; and they would reduce the risk of damage to the countryside, aesthetic as well as physical. At the time of writing about a score of country parks have been approved.

There is also plenty of scope for more recreational facilities within the green

108   * Robert and Leona Rienow, Ballantine.

belts. Side by side with developing opportunities of this kind, however, should go policies for restricting access to places which are either especially vulnerable to damage from greater use or which it is desired should be kept aside as peaceful havens for those who like to get away from it all. Motor traffic within these regions would be severely curtailed or banned altogether. Powers to take such steps have been strengthened by the Road Traffic Regulation Act of 1967 and by the Countryside and Transport Acts 1968.

There are already one or two interesting precedents. A motorless zone has been operating for more than a decade in the Cannock Chase (Staffordshire) area of outstanding natural beauty, and with considerable success. When tourists – most of them motorists – were asked in 1964 what they thought about it, 87 per cent supported the idea and only 6 per cent opposed it.*

There has been almost unanimous approval for a scheme operating in the Goyt Valley (Peak District National Park), under which four miles of road have been closed to traffic on summer weekends. Car parks have been provided on the edge of the motorless zone and mini-buses operate between them. Picnic sites, footpaths and a nature trail have been laid out. The scheme is run by a project supervisor, working from the national park planning office, and is supported by a grant from the Countryside Commission.

Only through positive planning of this kind, involving encouragement in one direction and discouragement in another, will it be possible to cope with the numbers who will be invading the countryside in the years to come; to see that they can really enjoy what they are seeking and can return to work refreshed by the experience and not frustrated and bitter through having to battle with thousands of others for limited facilities.

Conflicts on water

Water as well as land will have to be subject to careful management. Some uses are clearly incompatible – motor boating or water-skiing with angling, for example – and steps must be taken to keep them apart. Separation can be achieved by place or time. Certain stretches of a river or parts of a lake may be reserved for fishing only, or fishing allowed to take place when motor boating is barred and vice versa.

The aim should be to provide the maximum possible use of a river or lake without the users getting in each other's way. Grafham Water, near St. Ives, is a good example of multiple use – part of it is set aside for sailing, part for a nature reserve and the rest is available to trout fishermen.

This is one way of increasing the amount of water available for recreation. Another is to make wider use of the innumerable wet pits being created by gravel digging. It is sad to see many of them being filled in when recreational demands are so great. With proper landscaping they can become an asset to the landscape instead of an eyesore.

Many more reservoirs could be made available, too. Fishing is permitted in only half the 400 in existence, sailing on a mere 43 and canoeing on six. Only half a dozen out of 60 in the Peak District National Park are so used. The Government has urged water undertakings to extend these facilities. Main objection to doing so is that public water supplies might be contaminated, but experience has shown this to be a groundless fear. All reservoir water is subsequently filtered in any case.

* See *Public recreation in national forests* (HMSO 1968) by W. E. S. Mutch.   109

Canals in future

There is also great recreation potential in the 2,500 miles of canals mostly administered by the British Waterways Board, with a few in the hands of local authorities. They pass through some of our loveliest countryside. Canals are popular with anglers and boating enthusiasts, and towpath hikers – even though there is no public right to use towpaths.

Many have become disused and neglected, however, with broken lock-gates, weeded waterways and damaged banks. It is fortunate that it costs so much to fill them in, because this, coupled with their usefulness as sources of water supply for industry, agriculture and fire-fighting, and the energetic championing of them for both navigation and recreation by the Inland Waterways Association, has led to many being reprieved which would almost certainly have been lost.

The 1968 Transport Act broadly divided canals into three groups – *Commercial*, *Amenity* (to be developed mainly for recreation) and *Remainder* (waterways whose future had yet to be decided). Provisions were included for grants to be paid to restore canals for recreation. And there are, it seems, any number of voluntary helpers ready and willing to take part in this work.

It is they who have largely been responsible for restoring the Stratford-on-Avon and Pocklington Canals, and who are expected to play an increasingly important part in future, not only in practical work but in providing local information for the Inland Waterways Amenity Advisory Council, which advises the Waterways Board and the Department of the Environment on the use and development of non-commercial waterways.

The full potential of our canal system has yet to be realised. We are certain to see the establishment soon of more picnic sites, fishing lodges, fish farms and caravan and car parks, all of which will, of course, have to be carefully integrated with the rural scene.

A three-year respite for the *Remainder* canals expired at the end of 1971. There was certainly no lack of support for their retention, but it was clear that a lot would depend upon how much anglers, boating people and others who use the canals would be prepared to pay for their recreation.

Forest parks

The experience of other countries suggests that the Forestry Commission could do much more than it does to open its doors to the public. At the time of writing it had provided seven forest parks, about 50 nature trails and many picnic places; not a very impressive contribution.

But the situation is changing here, too, and plans drawn up by the commission would mean opening more than a million acres of forest land and streams to the public. Among the choice offerings being made, we are informed, is a proposal to hire log cabins to holidaymakers in forest beauty spots.

As several local authorities and the Opencast Division of the National Coal Board have shown, many of the 150,000 acres of derelict land could be restored and used for recreation. There must also, surely, be some recreational use to which our disused railways can be put?*

Legislation (Recreation):
National Parks and Access to the Countryside Act 1949
Countryside Act 1968

* See *Disused Railways in the Countryside of England & Wales* (HMSO).

Town and Country Planning Acts 1962 (parts III and IV), 1968 (sections 89-97)
Road Traffic Regulation Act 1967
Transport Act 1968
Caravan Sites and Control of Development Act 1960
Caravan Sites Act (1968)

Mainly responsible:

Countryside Commission, National Park authorities, local planning authorities, local authority public health departments (caravan sites inspection etc.), National Trust.

Legislation (Canals):

Transport Act 1968

Mainly responsible:

British Waterways Board, few local authorities, Department of the Environment.

Legislation (Forestry):

Forestry Act 1967
New Forest Act 1949, 1964
Trees Act 1970

Mainly responsible:

Forestry Commission, private owners, local planning authorities.

Services use of land

16. Barbed-wire Britain

Among our biggest and most tenacious landowners – they erect barbed wire to keep out visitors – are the Services. The Army alone has 'captured' some 609,000 acres of country, 146 miles of coastline and 42 miles of creeks and estuaries. With the 50,000 acres held by the Navy and Air Force, an area the size of Cheshire is blocked off.

It includes miles of glorious coastline in Dorset and Pembrokeshire, 30,000 acres in Dartmoor National Park and 56,000 acres in Northumberland National Park. There are fewer soldiers now than there were in 1938, but because they have greater mobility and longer-range weapons, they take up two-and-a-half times as much land as they did.

This land is churned up by tanks and littered with 'temporary' huts, shacks and miscellaneous debris which the Services, as a rule, make no attempt to demolish or clear up when their period of occupation does come to an end – although the troops would probably welcome a constructive 'clean-up' operation of this kind. It should, in any case, be made obligatory.

The question is often asked as to why the Army has to take over so much of crowded southern England instead of wilder Scottish parts, for example, where their presence could give a valuable boost to the economy. The answer, it seems, is that it would be too expensive to build new barracks.

The value of the land they sterilise at present could be far greater than the cost of building elsewhere. And it is a value which is appreciating all the time as the pressures become more and more intense. In July, 1968, the Government issued a blue paper which envisaged a substantial reduction in service establishments and training areas in the United Kingdom, and a committee headed by Lord Nugent is looking into the whole question.

Let us hope we shall see the Forces surrendering much of this occupied territory to the public in the near future.

Common Land

17. Saving 'our last reserve'

Hardly anywhere in Britain is far from a green, common or heath. The Royal Commission on Common Land estimated that there are well over $1\frac{1}{2}$ million acres of commons in England and Wales. Some of them are household names like Hampstead Heath, Epping Forest and Wimbledon Common in London, Town Moor in Newcastle or The Strays in Harrogate. Others are familiar village greens.

But what does the term really mean? What are we talking about when we speak of a village green, common, heath or moor? We probably all think we know and the chances are that we are wrong.

A common – and this is pretty well synonymous with a heath or moor – is widely thought of as a parcel of land which is publicly owned and which anyone can use as he pleases. This is not so. Most are privately owned, even though who has the title to what is often lost in antiquity. Indeed, it has been estimated that only about 20 per cent of commons are legally accessible to the public and that most of these are in urban districts. Many commons are vested in, or are under the control or management of, local authorities and the National Trust. The Trust has acquired large tracts in the Lake District, for instance.

A common is simply a piece of land on which people other than the owner have certain rights. It derives from the village 'wastes' where local people, or commoners, could graze cattle, dig turf or peat for fuel, take reeds, heather, bracken and other materials for various purposes and, more rarely, fish in ponds or streams.

Often these rights have become so little valued that they have ceased to be recorded and attempts have been made to replace them with others more suited to modern needs. The 1925 Law of Property Act provided that commons in built-up areas should be open to the public for air and exercise. The Act also made it possible for rural districts to be included in these provisions through the execution of a deed by the owner or lord of the manor.

However, such measures have only succeeded in checking a general decline, and this has understandably aroused concern. Commons have been described as 'our last reserve of uncommitted land'. They have formed a barrier against development and have effectively prevented areas from becoming completely built-up. With the growth of towns and traffic, and the noise, smoke and fumes that go with them, the value of having a 'citizen's lung' of this kind can hardly be over-estimated.

But commons provide much more than opportunities for fresh air and exercise. Their economic value is considerable. What would the hill farmers of Wales, the Pennines and Lake District do without them? Could the ponies, sheep and cattle which now graze contentedly on Dartmoor and Bodmin Moor easily be found pasture elsewhere? Should we lightly disregard the timber which commons produce through widespread afforestation?

There is also the fact that wildlife forced to retreat before the tide of building and traffic have found homes in the chalk downs and woodlands, heaths and commons. If we permitted these sanctuaries to be swamped, too, we would not only lose the animals, birds and insects they harbour, but one of the essential elements in our incomparably varied landscape.

To save the commons, however, a proper policy of management and conservation is required. The failure of commoners to exercise their rights has meant that in many cases nobody is bothering to look after these open spaces. Many commons have become deplorably run down; rank with weeds, disfigured with litter, sometimes a veritable eyesore and sometimes so overgrown with thorn and bramble that they are quite inaccessible. Cattle straying on the roads present a traffic hazard, too.

The village green all too often falls far short of the ideal picture of a rich sward on which white-flannelled cricketers entertain the locals on a hot summer's day. Its grass may have grown long and coarse, traffic may have mutilated the edges and part of the green may be used as a rubbish dump. In the absence of proper management, motorists who want a path across it or cricketers who would like a new pavilion can find no-one to negotiate with. Parish councils may be reluctant to do anything in case they interfere with some long-forgotten private interest.

Land which is neglected is also more likely to fall into the hands of developers who present a continuing threat, and indeed this form of encorachment is by far the most serious. It is symptomatic of the concern for commons, however, that there are provisions for giving exchange land for any part appropriated. Such exchanges can mitigate, if not completely off-set the harm done. There have also been applications to fence in commons. A number of these are clearly reasonable and arouse little opposition. Others provoke demonstrations, as when 50 men, women and children sat down on a golf course to protest against the fencing-off of the course, which they claimed was on common land.

Sometimes heavy recreational pressure can itself cause serious damage. Frensham Common in Surrey has taken such a hammering from the public over the years that the heather on the fringes of the Great and Little Ponds has been obliterated. This common was declared a Site of Special Scientific Interest by the Nature Conservancy, but it cannot be so interesting to the botanist and ornithologist today.

A Royal Commission set up under Sir Ivor Jennings, Q.C. in December, 1955, found that the commons were indeed 'a wasting asset'. In its report, issued in 1958, it recommended that the existing ones should remain common land, even where rights had lapsed, and that local planning authorities should register all claims and see that the valid ones were preserved as far as possible. This would help to unravel the legal tangle, it was pointed out.

One of the Commission's most important proposals was that all common land, including village greens, should be open to the public as of right, on condition that they didn't leave litter, light fires or drive cars across the land.

The Commons Registration Act of 1965 gave effect to that part of the Commission's proposals concerning registration. County council registers were opened on January 2, 1967, and for three years claims were submitted and registrations made if the authorities were satisfied after hearing any objections. Ultimately over a million acres of commons and greens were registered.

Having placed the facts on record, it now becomes necessary to consider the second part of the operation – proper management. Whatever pattern finally emerges, this will be no easy task. Those responsible could find themselves balanced more and more precariously on a tightrope of competing interests as the years go by.

Legislation:

Metropolitan Commons Act 1866
Commons Acts 1876, 1899
Law of Property Act 1925
Commons Registration Act 1965
Commons Registration (New Land) Regulations 1969
Countryside Act 1968

Mainly responsible:

County councils, County boroughs, Greater London Council, Department of the Environment.

Footpaths

18. On the beaten track

The same pressures which have led to the registration of common land have influenced the mapping of footpaths and bridleways in England and Wales by county councils. The maps provide conclusive legal evidence that the rights of way shown were in existence at the date of the survey. They will have to be revised every five years.

Pressures of this kind were, of course, unknown to our ancestors, who simply took the most convenient route to a local meeting place or the next hamlet, skirting a swamp here, a wood there and crossing a stream at a suitable place. This is how our footpaths system began. Some of these early tracks – probably dating from pre-Roman times – can still be followed. They include the Icknield Way, The Ridgeway in Berkshire and the Pilgrims Way from Hampshire to Canterbury.

Custom and usage is one method of establishing a right of way. Section 34 of the 1959 Highways Act defined a period of 20 years' undisputed use of a path over freehold land as sufficient proof that it had been 'dedicated' to the public, unless there was evidence to the contrary.

Other paths have been established by statute. It might have been a condition of an enclosure award that a right of way be granted, or paths can be established by agreement between local authority and the landowner. Local authorities also have powers to create footpaths compulsorily.

As with common land, it has become apparent in recent years that all is far from well with our footpaths system. Some paths appear to have outlived their purpose and haven't been used for a long time. Many have become overgrown and obstructed, often deliberately. There have been frequent complaints about inadequate signposting and publicity.

Ploughing-up has especially caused concern. A farmer who wishes to plough the whole of a field across which a footpath runs is required to give notice of his intention to do so to the highway authority not less than seven days before the operations are due to begin. Then, within six weeks after ploughing has been completed, he is required to restore the path.

Not only have these provisions often been ignored, but farmers have frequently sought to deter people from using footpaths by 'Trespassers will be prosecuted' and 'Beware of the bull' notices. The former has no legal validity and pasturing a bull over 12 months old in a field where a footpath runs is illegal in most areas.

A much more serious form of encroachment, however, has taken place with the increased scale of building. Rights of way have been built over and sometimes lost for ever. Developers are required to apply for an order from a magistrates' court to divert or stop up a highway, including a footpath, but there have been cases where building has taken place regardless of the existence of a right of way.

All these discontents signify a growing interest in footpaths. This has been brought about partly by a general desire to get away from it all and partly by the weight of traffic forcing walkers off the roads. Along country lanes a few years ago a hiker would have been more likely to meet a cow than a car. Now many of these lanes have become major thoroughfares. There is little pleasure in walking when you have to scramble on to the verges every few minutes, when every bend becomes a real hazard and when the air is polluted by petrol fumes.

Footpaths provide an escape from all this; no cars to pester you, no noise or fumes and only the good old country smells – with, it must be confessed, some not-so-good new ones – to assail the nostrils. It is hardly surprising that many motorists are parking their cars somewhere and striding out across country. So that when a path is found to have been ploughed up or otherwise obstructed, or when it is not properly signposted, more people than ever are likely to be affected.

Mapping is one way of seeing that footpaths are used and are not interfered with. But mapping leaves unresolved many other important matters, such as whether certain paths are really suited to modern conditions, whether new ones are needed or not, what sort of signposting is required and who should be responsible, and so on.

It was to consider questions of this kind that the Government set up a committee under the chairmanship of Sir Arthur Gosling, KBE, CB, in April, 1967. The committee's report, issued a year later, was widely welcomed as meeting many of the complaints. One of its most important recommendations was that footpaths and bridleways be regarded as aspects of land use and placed within the orbit of the planning rather than the highway authority. The committee felt this would be a useful step towards making footpaths less of a Cinderella among local authority cares and would encourage forward planning as an integral part of the wider and more responsible use of the countryside by the public. Publication of the plans, carrying rights of objection, would permit footpath proposals to be properly debated.

The popularity of horse riding and the difficulties met by cyclists on today's crowded roads were brought to the committee's attention. It was stated that a census taken in the Greater London area during 1966 had produced the surprisingly large estimate of some 25,000 people a week who went riding.

While opposed to horses being allowed on public footpaths because they would tend to churn up the paths and create a hazard to walkers, the committee strongly urged that more bridleways be provided. It was also recommended that cyclists be allowed to use footpaths and bridleways.

Stronger measures for restoring paths after temporary ploughing were advocated and the committee proposed that all rights of way should be marked by signposts or waymarks where they left the road, with a hint that such signs be decently designed. The responsibility for maintaining stiles and gates should rest with landowners and occupiers, it was stated, but they should receive a reasonable contribution to the cost from public funds.

Some of these recommendations have been incorporated in the 1968 Countryside Act and others have been accepted by the Government in principle.

With footpaths becoming more important for their recreational value than as a means of getting from one place to another, attention has been focused in recent years on the creation of long-distance routes through scenically attractive areas.

Routes covering 1,414 miles have been approved by the Government at the time of writing, following proposals drawn up by the Countryside Commission. The longest is the Pennine Way, which runs for 250 miles from Derbyshire to Scotland. Then there is the 168-mile long Offa's Dyke Path, the Pembrokeshire Coast Path (167m) and the North Downs Way (141m). Five sections of the southwest peninsula coast path through Dorset, Devon, Cornwall and Somerset, and totalling 515 miles have also been approved, along with others for the South Downs (80m) and the Cleveland Way in Yorkshire (93m).

These examples reveal the scale of current thinking on footpaths. They show that more and more people are realising that pounding the beaten tracks can bring delights of a kind which travelling by car or train can never hope to match.

Legislation:
National Parks and Access to the Countryside Act 1949 (parts IV and V)
Countryside Act 1968
Town and Country Planning Act 1968 (s. 89)
Town and Country Planning (Public Path Orders) Regulations 1969

Mainly responsible:
All local authorities, Countryside Commission, Department of the Environment.

19. Less fun beside the sea

Only about one-third of Britain's 2,700 miles of coastline are now worth fighting for, according to the National Trust. The rest is deemed to be too sick to recover, having been desecrated by various kinds of development, inundated with cara- vans, shacks and shanties or barred to the public by the Services. The English- man's ration of coast amounts, in fact, to no more than four inches.

With two-thirds of us still having to take our holidays in July and August, it is hardly surprising, therefore, that the popular resorts, especially those in the West Country, are deluged with cars and people, that peace and quiet is at a premium and that recreational resources are overstrained, with speedboats interfering with anglers and swimmers, water ski-iers with surfers, and sand yachters with those who just want to build sandcastles or sit on the beach. And there are likely to be 20 million more people taking holidays at home in ten years' time, making 50 million in all.

Cars are such a problem in the smaller resorts that one or two have stopped them from entering the town centre, and more will probably have to follow suit. Some measure of the problem is contained in the fact that on a fine summer's day 2½ miles of front at Barry, in Glamorgan, has to accommodate 10,000 cars! And it is forecast that there will be twice as many cars on the road by 1980.

If only we had had the foresight to stop so much coastal development taking place! This has either barred the public from the foreshore or made it so un- attractive that nobody would choose to go there. The proportion of built-up area along the coast is, in fact, twice as great as for the country as a whole. On the other hand, it may not be generally realised that there is no general right for the public to use the beaches. These are mostly owned by the Crown, but some are in the hands of local authorities and private individuals. People are only per- mitted to bathe, sunbathe and build sandcastles by the forbearance of the owners; except for sea fishermen, who have been granted a right under Magna Carta to fish from the shore, a right they share only with those engaged in navigation.

However, the harm which has been done to the two-thirds makes it all the more essential to preserve what remains. About 10 per cent lies within the area of our ten national parks and is thereby subject to development restrictions. Nearly a quarter (about 900 miles) have been designated as areas of outstanding natural beauty, which means that they are protected, though less stringently. The National Trust and Nature Conservancy own much beautiful coastal land, and the Trust will doubtless be adding to its acquisitions considerably as a result of the funds received from 'Enterprise Neptune'.

Development should as far as possible be confined to areas already built up, and even here should be strictly controlled. The borough of Crosby, in Lan- cashire, has shown the way. Faced with plans by Mersey Docks and Harbour Board to extend the dock system further north, which it was felt would ruin the foreshore and seafront and cause pollution, the borough council at first opposed the project and, when this failed, made a condition that proper landscaping be carried out. Under the agreed scheme, the council is constructing a sea wall and enclosing 166 acres of the shore, 100 of which will be grassed and the remainder turned into a boating lake. The project (estimated cost £400,000) received an award in the conservation awards scheme for 1971 sponsored jointly by *The Times* and the Royal Institution of Chartered Surveyors, and the judges commended the council on its 'vision and imagination'.

All kinds of studies have been made or are in progress – by the Nature Conservancy, British Tourist Authority and the Countryside Commission. In its publication, *The Planning of the Coastline*, the commission recommends that regional coastal parks be created and that the coast should be cleared of disfigurement caused by derelict military structures or other unsightly works, and argues strongly that special attention must be given to those coasts where the scenery is judged to be equal in merit to that found in national parks. This argument is amplified in a separate document, *The Coastal Heritage*, in which 34 areas are recommended for designation as Heritage Coasts.

Many studies of future needs and how they might be met are being carried out by planning authorities. All this concern, though belated, is welcome, but it should not stop there. Any progress in this respect will be nullified unless we can stop the seas themselves becoming polluted by oil, untreated sewage and the huge quantities of industrial waste and other junk now being dumped in it. Primitive practices like the dumping of three million tons of spoil a year into the sea from the collieries near Blackhall in Co. Durham, which makes miles of coastline unusable, represents a criminal disregard for amenity which should not be tolerated.

Legislation:

Town and Country Planning Acts 1947, 1968
National Parks and Access to the Countryside Act 1949
Countryside Act 1968.

Mainly responsible:

Local authorities, National park authorities, National Trust.

20. Where does all the water go ?

Nothing is more calculated to unite farmers, villagers, anglers and country lovers generally than the proposed siting of a new reservoir in some beautiful upland valley. Should the beneficiaries be British and the victims Welsh, the rumpus will be bolstered by nationalistic fervour stretching all the way from Cardiff to Llandudno.

The opposition has chalked up a number of successes in recent years – the Dulas Valley in mid-Wales, the Hebden Valley of West Yorkshire, and parts of the North York Moors and Dartmoor National Parks have been reprieved. In the 18 months up to May, 1971, Parliament approved only one private Bill for a major reservoir – Empingham, in Rutland (4,000 acres). Three others are under construction – in the Upper Towy Valley in Wales, and at Wraysbury and Datchet near London. The Wraysbury Reservoir was virtually complete at the time of writing.

This hostility to reservoirs has aroused much concern in official quarters and no little heart-searching as to the reasons. The Central Advisory Water Committee apparently feels the causes lie in poor public relations and failure to provide adequate compensation for the loss of land and livelihood, and for the disturbance involved. If only the issues had been properly explained, said the committee in a report published towards the end of 1971, a more favourable public attitude would have resulted.

I can't help feeling the committee is being somewhat over-optimistic. The public have become aware in recent times that valid alternatives do exist in the form of barrage schemes for the Dee, Morecambe Bay and The Wash, increased re-use of water, tapping underground supplies, tackling pollution so that river water can be more widely used and, most important perhaps, obtaining water from the sea.

It is true, as the committee said, that all these alternatives would be open to objection on amenity grounds – large desalination plants along unspoilt coast, for instance – but need the price be so high as with upland reservoirs which may not only flood villages and farmland, but may upset the whole regime of a river? Many a sparkling stream has been virtually dried up by ill-conceived abstraction. This serves nobody's interest, not even the abstractor's.

The committee is on stronger ground in pointing out that reservoirs can provide valuable recreation facilities and are often an asset to the landscape. But the same might be said of the large lakes formed by barrage schemes. Only a small proportion of reservoirs have been turned over to recreation anyway – though here there are signs of a change.

Even if all the alternatives were proceeded with, states the committee, there would still be a need for some reservoirs (it is estimated that about 20 major new ones will be needed by the year 2000). In this case the public will almost certainly insist that they be sited along the lower reaches of rivers or that they should be of the regulatory type, impounding flood water in winter and feeding some back in summer to boost the reduced flows. If this type of reservoir were more often constructed and its benefits to a river – in alleviating flooding and evening out the flow – more carefully explained, reservoirs might not arouse as much hostility as they do.

Much can also be done to meet public objections to unsightly buildings, noisy machinery and so on. The example of Ullswater, where £250,000 out of £1·6 million was spent on amenity safeguards, is an object lesson in tackling a large reservoir scheme in a beautiful landscape – yet these safeguards were only embarked upon as a result of fierce public protests.

One aspect which does need explaining is why we should be short of water anyway in a country so bountifully sprinkled with rain; an average, we are told, of 5,000 tons falls on every square mile every day. If this rainfall were evenly spread, the problem would be nothing like so great. Unfortunately, perverse nature has decided that around 200 inches a year should fall on the sparsely populated region of North-West Scotland and only about 20 inches on the densely-peopled and very thirsty South-East England.

Losses are inevitable in this kind of situation. They are magnified by evaporation and transpiration from plants. From an average annual rainfall of 30 inches, no less than 20 inches vanishes into thin air as it were and, of the remainder, we only manage to conserve about 3 inches at most, or roughly 5,500 million gallons a day.

Various man-made changes to the environment have exacerbated the situation. More buildings and roads, and better drainage means that instead of percolating slowly through the soil into underground reservoirs which help to replenish the rivers in dry weather, surface water is rushed into rivers and down to the sea much more quickly than it used to be. This is one reason for the widespread flooding of the Severn Valley and parts of the West Country which occurs most winters, and provides another big argument for planting more trees and water-holding foliage plants.

Down the drain – literally

Further large amounts of water are just wasted by industry and domestic consumers, either by forgetting to switch off the tap or tolerating leaks, or by using water of higher quality than really necessary for the job in hand. Should we, for instance, use the same tap for drinking, washing and cleaning the car?

Ways will have to be found of cutting these losses in the coming years if demands are to be met. The two biggest consumers at present are industry (4,200 m.g.d.) and the domestic user (1,900 m.g.d.). Water for agriculture is currently assessed at 500 m.g.d. Huge amounts of cooling water are also required by power stations. The Central Electricity Generating Board used about 7,000 m.g.d. in 1967, although it was all returned after use.

Higher living standards – including piped supplies in 96 per cent of dwellings and fixed bath or shower in 73 per cent – have pushed up the amount each of us uses in our homes in England and Wales to 35 gallons a day. And one can appreciate why industry's water demands are so great from the fact that it takes 800 gallons to produce one ton of cement and 60,000 gallons to produce a ton of paper. Estimates of the amount required to make a gallon of beer vary from 120 gallons of water to 350 – depending, perhaps, on the strength of the brew?

All these users will be needing more in future. The most widely quoted statistic in this respect is that the present abstraction rate of 14,000 m.g.d. is likely to be doubled by the end of the century. In the report already referred to, the Central Advisory Water Committee said that meeting this increasing demand constituted a major problem. 'Exploitable' water in England and Wales was scarcer than was often thought; the average amount available per head of population, about 850 gallons a day, was among the lowest in Europe – only Belgium, East Germany and Malta having less. The Proudman Committee had considered that our rainfall was sufficient to provide adequate supplies, but conservation methods would have to be further developed. 'And since in all districts', stated the CAWC, 'the relatively inexpensive local sources of supply have already been intensively developed, it is inevitable that in future increasing quantities of water must be moved over long distances and radically new plans examined.'

Demands are already heavy enough to cause concern. At least 50 schemes for new housing are reported to have been shelved because of imminent water shortages, and the Water Resources Board has warned local authorities that difficulties will arise 'in the next few years' in supplying even existing homes. In dry summers the flow of the Thames over Teddington Lock has to be reduced below its statutory minimum to supplement resources

Can the sea really help?

The large-scale re-use of water and reclaiming it from the sea are two possibilities being examined. So far as re-use is concerned, purification processes are now so good that it is perfectly feasible to use water several times in its journey down-river without causing pollution. A scheme to employ treated effluent for textile processing at a Pudsey woollen mill – announced as I write – illustrates the kind of operation required.

What has ruled out desalination so far has been the cost. Yet Professor Silver, of Glasgow University, who invented the multi-stage flash distillation process now being used by many countries, claims that in some parts of England the cost lines of desalination and conventional methods have already crossed. However, at an estimated 30p per thousand gallons, desalination is still generally more than twice the average cost of water from more conventional sources. But reservoirs will in future have to be built lower down-river. They are liable to be more expensive as much of the river water will be polluted – this is why we haven't yet been able to make use of the resources of a great river like the Trent, where feasibility studies are now under way to assess the cost of a clean-up.

Joint research on desalination has been in progress by the Water Resources Board and Atomic Energy Authority for some time, and in March, 1971, it was announced that the Government was to spend £4 million on two experimental projects – a £2 million desalination plant near Ipswich, the biggest of its type in the world and a £2 million feasibility study into building big freshwater reservoirs in The Wash, about a mile offshore. The Ipswich plant will produce about a million gallons of fresh water a day by freezing sea water.

Mr Leonard Millis, director of the British Waterworks Association, has sounded a note of caution, however. In a letter to *The Times* (May 19, 1971) he suggested that desalination could not influence the situation very much for 10–20 years. Meanwhile, there were urgent needs to be met.

So far as large-scale barrages are concerned, the prospects are decidedly long-term. And for more modest estuarial barrages along the lines of the Dutch delta projects to become feasible, we would have to promote much more vigorous action to clean up the estuaries.

Some of the acute problems of the south-east might be solved through pumping from the vast natural reservoir which lies in the chalk hills surrounding the London basin. Successful experiments in the Lambourn Valley produced 1–2 m.g.d. and it is estimated that up to 100 m.g.d. might be produced by this means. Doubts hang over the potential of this project, however, and fears have been expressed that it might have serious effects in time on tributaries of our most famous chalk stream, the Test. However, here again, technology might have the answer in a scheme for pumping water back into the reservoirs in times of high river flows.

Future management system

Much attention has been given recently to the future management of water – this was the subject of the Central Advisory Committee report already referred to. Those most closely concerned at present are some 200 water undertakings, which are responsible for supply, over 1,300 sewage disposal authorities, which treat water after it has been used, and the 29 river authorities established under the 1963 Water Resources Act which are responsible for land drainage, fisheries, and pollution control, and which control abstraction under a licensing system.

Then there is the Water Resources Board, set up under the same Act, to advise the Government on the proper use of water, and the British Waterways Board, which owns most of the canals.

Although the Central Advisory Water Committee made no firm proposals on management – merely setting out the alternatives – the Water Resources Board said in its 1970 report that it was 'becoming more widely recognised that the resources of each river basin need to be put under a single management, that water quantity and water quality are inseparable aspects of looking after water, that planning for all aspects of the water cycle must be integrated, and that administrative, financial and legal arrangements to suit these requirements must be provided'.

One of the objects of establishing the Water Resources Board was to facilitate transfers of supplies between areas with a surplus to others with a shortage. In evidence to the Central Advisory Water Committee,* however, the Board pointed out that the 1963 Water Resources Act gave it no power to borrow money or issue precepts. This had prevented much being done under this head and the one major inter-authority transfer at present being developed – the Ely Ouse – Essex scheme – was being financed almost entirely by the importing authority; a 'vigorous and forward looking authority (Essex) very conscious of the difficulties of its own water situation'.

If the 29 river authorities were to continue to exercise powers in areas substantially similar to those existing, or indeed, in any areas short of regional size, it was stated, consideration should be given to the part which might usefully be played by a national authority for the conservation and bulk movement of water, able to promote and acquire both storage and transmission works of regional or national significance and to run an appropriate equalisation account.

The Central Advisory Water Committee took up this suggestion of a national authority. In the report previously referred to, the committee proposed that the WRB should be enlarged to form such a body and that some 6 to 15 regional authorities should be set up to be responsible for one or all of the four major functions – water supply, sewage disposal, river management and planning and co-ordinating. The committee also advocated a reduction in the number of water undertakings to a number significantly lower than 100.

Whatever the pattern of administration† and however future supplies are obtained, the days of cheap water are surely numbered. As with every other commodity, if the demand tends to outstrip the supply and the costs of production go up, the consumer will have to pay more. Mr Eric Gilliland, Thames Conservancy treasurer, forecast 'massive increases' when he addressed the annual conference of the Institute of Municipal Treasurers and Accountants in June, 1971.

Probably supplies will have to be metered. This will at least focus attention on the amount of wastage. One section of the community for whom a bright future might be predicted are the plumbers, repairing all those leaky taps and cisterns.

* See appendix to Seventh Annual Report, Water Resources Board (HMSO 70p).

† See footnote, p. 77.

Legislation:

Water Acts 1945, 1948
Water Resources Act 1963, 1968
Public Health Act 1936

Mainly responsible:

Water undertakings, county boroughs, boroughs, district councils, Water Resources Board, Department of the Environment.

Wildlife

21. The killing has to stop

People in the Home Counties heaved a big sigh of relief when it was announced that the third London airport was to be sited at Foulness. Their relief was not tempered by any great regret for the waders and Brent geese whose habitat was thereby threatened.

Most people seemed prepared to accept that in a small and crowded island like Britain, with so many competing demands on land and water, the protection of wildlife should not come very high on the list of priorities. When animals die from pesticides, when they are killed on the roads as thousands are, when they are frightened away by the excavator digging out a new reservoir or when they have to be rescued from the sea with their feathers clotted by oil, it is deemed a regrettable consequence of modern life.

Attitudes of this kind have led to the liquidation of about 100 species of higher animals in the last 400 years or so; species which took at least 2½ million years to develop wiped out forever – by us. And 250 more are in danger of extermination today. They even include that symbol of America, the bald eagle, reported to be making its last stand in Florida and Alaska.

This killing is not inevitable. It arises from our actions, from our indifference, from our indiscriminate hunting, from our vanity and the greed of those who exploit it. The demand for sealskins results in the disgustingly cruel slaughter of baby seals at the mouth of the St. Lawrence River by beating them to death with clubs, which will presumably continue until there are few seals left, as the order books are full. The desire to wear hats adorned with decorative plumage has meant the decimation of tropical bird and osprey populations.

How much do we, or should we, really care? With so many human problems, can we afford to concern ourselves too much with the 'lower' animals?

I think we can and should, and for their own sake, not because of any benefit to ourselves – although there are such benefits and they are probably greater than we realise. All living things, of which man is but a part, are inter-dependent and the balance which nature has contrived is a most intricate and delicate one. We upset it at our peril. When we farm with no thought for it we produce dust bowls. When we shower the land indiscriminately with poisons, we can produce worse plagues than ever of the pests we are trying to eradicate; not to mention the plants and wild creatures we destroy in the process. When we kill off the rabbits with myxamotosis we induce the foxes to raid our chicken runs, and the scrub and

123

gorse which rabbits help to keep down begin to imperil lovely chalk downlands within a few years, choking the life from some of the rarer plants. And the rabbits, immune to the disease, are coming back. There is also reported to be a breed of 'super-rats' which the usual rat poisons are failing to deter.

Being part of nature, we humans cannot dispense with natural things just like that, especially in the limited state of our present knowledge. Nature will hit back in some way or other. If we behave in an arrogant or superior fashion towards wild creatures, we do not have to take a very big step to look upon other human beings as belonging to the lower orders – perhaps the roots of racial intolerance are buried in a contempt for the natural world. Those who regard the Vietnamese as 'gooks' also defoliate the jungle.

This, surely, is the real reason why we should protect and cherish all wildlife, not because we find them beautiful, need them for food or enjoy hunting them. It does not mean that we cannot have our third airport at Foulness and that we must stop building reservoirs. It does mean that we must see to it, when we carry out such developments, that wildlife come to as little harm as possible. If their habitats are ruined, we must provide others.

Conservation agencies

Although the idea of setting aside protected areas for wild creatures is not new – it dates back, in fact, to Saxon Britain – what is relatively new is our reason for doing so. In Saxon times the royal forests were for kings who wished to preserve beasts for the chase; today we are conserving wildlife because we feel they have as much right to live in this world as we do.

The movement began in this country in August, 1945, when the Government set up a committee to look into nature conservation. In its report, published in 1947, it listed proposed nature reserves in England and Wales where wildlife could be studied and protected. Another committee reported similarly on Scotland. These committees recommended that an official 'biological service' be set up to establish and maintain the reserves, do the required research and advise on nature conservation generally.

This was the role given to the Nature Conservancy when it was established by royal charter as a new research council in May, 1949. The Conservancy proceeded to acquire the proposed reserves and has added to them later, so that today it owns over 125 covering more than a quarter of a million acres. The largest of these is the 64,000 acres of mountain, moorland and pine forests in the Cairngorms, where you may still see wild cats, red deer and ptarmigan and even the golden eagle.

Another statutory duty imposed on the Conservancy was to notify Sites of Special Scientific Interest to planning authorities for places which could not be established as reserves. This ensures that the Conservancy has to be informed about any planning proposals affecting a site. There are more than 2,000 such sites at the present time.

But it soon became apparent that such measures were not sufficient to contain the pressures on habitats and that the Conservancy would have to widen its scope. Accordingly it welcomed the opportunity to become closely involved in the preparatory work for both 'Countryside in 1970' conferences in 1963 and 1965, under the presidency of Prince Philip.

In June, 1965 the Conservancy became part of the Natural Environment Research Council, set up by royal charter to co-ordinate the work of several bodies engaged on environmental studies.

Other bodies are prominent in wildlife protection too. The National Trust has one of our finest sea-bird colonies in the Farne Islands, also the haunt of seals, and magnificent work has been done by the Royal Society for the Protection of Birds, which owns several reserves and is perhaps best known by the public for its work with the famous ospreys of Loch Garten. The association has also, however, protected snowy owls in Shetland, red kites in Wales, Dartford warblers in Dorset and the delicate avocets at Havergate and Minsmere on the Suffolk coast. Incidentally, the red squirrel is also protected at Minsmere.

The most representative assembly in the world of ducks, geese and swans in captivity has since 1946 been gathered together by the Wildfowl Trust at Slimbridge. Between 2,000 and 3,000 birds may be seen in as near-natural conditions as possible. It is also the only place in Britain where flamingoes have bred. The Trust is especially renowned, however, for rescuing the Hawaiian Goose. In 1950 there were only 42 in the world. Three birds, a male and two females, were sent to Slimbridge and bred freely. Since then 619 have been reared by the Trust and 200 returned to Hawaii to be released in a wild reserve. In recent years there has also been a spectacular build-up of Bewick's Swans at Slimbridge.

Positive steps are being taken to conserve our butterfly stocks and in 1970 I was able to see the remarkable amount of public support for this when I attended the 10th anniversary open day of Worldwide Butterflies Ltd., of Sherborne, Dorset. This is one of only two butterfly farms in the world and is by far the largest. It breeds species threatened with extinction and so helps to maintain stocks. But it also encourages individual butterfly breeders too and carries out research.

One not unimportant way in which we can all help in our gardens is to grow butterfly-attracting plants like buddleia, valerian, ice plant, lavender and so on. Or we can join the British Butterfly Conservation Society (*see* section 24, 'Conservation Directory').

Much more attention is now being given to fishery conservation. Most fishing clubs impose strict limits on the number of game fish which may be retained by their members and it is the usual practice for coarse fishermen to return all their catch to the water. So far as stocks in the seas are concerned, it is generally accepted that these are being depleted – some seas, in fact, are virtually fished out. While restrictions on inshore fishing have limited these effects around our own coasts, there seems little doubt that the large-scale farming of both fresh- and salt-water species will have to be adopted here, as it already is elsewhere.

Is it feasible for all wildlife in Britain to be protected under one comprehensive Act? This is the question being considered by the Society for the Promotion of Nature Reserves. In its publication, *Conservation Review*, the society points out that there are at present separate protection Acts for birds, deer and seals, and a new Bill has been drafted to give much-needed protection to about 20 rare plants threatened with extinction and to curtail commercial exploitation of attractive species like wild orchids, gentians and primroses. Legislation has also been urged to protect the badger.

The society points out that there are many other species in need of protection, such as the much rarer pine marten, and many attractive butterflies and amphibians like the sand lizard. It might be simpler and more flexible, therefore, to draft comprehensive legislation rather than a series of separate Acts.

Indeed it might and in this and other aspects of their work the society and the other agencies concerned with wildlife protection deserve every possible support. Thor Heyerdahl, the Norwegian explorer, said recently that man hadn't basically changed over the years and that his primitive instincts still lay very close to the surface. There is much evidence to suggest that he is right, which surely makes it all the more important for governments and societies to stimulate the development of the more positive features in mankind, of which this growing movement to protect wildlife is one of the most inspiring.

Legislation:

Game Act 1831
Game Licences Act 1860
Grey Seals Protection Act 1932
Protection of Birds Act 1954
Deer Act 1963
Countryside Act 1968

Mainly responsible:

Nature Conservancy, Countryside Commission, planning authorities (nature reserves), all local authorities except parishes (wild birds protection).
Ministry of Agriculture
Department of the Environment

ACTION

22. Guarding what remains

One of the main tasks of recreational planners in future will be to avoid conflict, not only between different users but between townsfolk seeking to enjoy themselves in the countryside and farmers and landowners who have to make their living off the land.

It is not surprising that feelings run high when rubbish is strewn around, gates left open, fences and crops damaged, and when visitors generally behave in the thoughtless manner now all too familiar. People who would not dream of throwing a matchstick on the floor of their own homes will blithely cast cigarette packets out of car windows to litter the verges and laybys, and will leave all kinds of junk around when they have a picnic.

Many a fishing club has lost a stretch of water because of the bad behaviour of some of its members – usually a small minority spoiling things for the rest. Some anglers take their dogs with them, and they can not only be a general nuisance on the river bank but a positive menace to sheep. Irate farmers have been known to shoot dogs that worry sheep, so if you want to risk losing your pet, take it with you on your next fishing trip or picnic.

Farmers and landowners may also react to bad behaviour by refusing to allow visitors on their land and so perpetuating the divisions between town and country which a host of 'Keep Out' and 'Trespassers will be Prosecuted' signs have helped to foster.

One body which is well aware of all this is the Countryside Commission. The commission which, as the National Parks Commission, drew up the country code, tries to distribute it as widely as possible. But it will clearly be a long time before the message gets home. Exhortations have little effect on children taught in 'slum' schools or adults living in squalid surroundings, for instance.

Meanwhile, the commission has a difficult task in trying to determine the right degree of public accessibility for the ten national parks it has chosen and designated. These cover 5258 square miles and contain nearly one-tenth of the whole area of England and Wales. Shortly another park is expected to be added to the list – the Cambrian Highlands in Central Wales.

In formulating its policies the commission works closely with the planning boards and county council committees responsible for administering the parks. There may be changes here in future – the Maud Commission on Local Government recommended that the parks should have their own planning authorities; at present this only applies to the Peak and Lake Districts.

Another way in which the Countryside Commission seeks to safeguard fine

127

country is through areas of outstanding natural beauty. At September 30, 1970, there were 27 such areas covering 14,248 miles of England and 216 square miles in Wales; nearly 8 per cent of the total area of England and Wales.

A new form of protection was provided under the 1969 Act, whereby the commission may recommend Exchequer grants for country parks of up to 75 per cent, and there are similar arrangements in respect of picnic sites. (At the time of writing 71 such parks and picnic sites had been declared and 250 similar proposals are under review.) Through their information services, the commission also aims to create a fuller understanding and enjoyment of the countryside.

With the green belts and nature reserves, this means that something like 30 per cent of England and Wales are under some form of protection (there are no national parks in Scotland, though their establishment is being considered). But how valuable is this protection?

First, planning officers are legally obliged to take note of the existence of such designations when considering development applications. There is also the 'pious clause' in the 1968 Act which compels every Ministry, government and local government agency to take into account the amenity value and conservation of the countryside when considering any scheme. This applies to such bodies as the Gas Council, Central Electricity Generating Board, National Coal Board and so on.

However, there have been disturbing signs in recent years that the Commission and park authorities cannot resist the really powerful industrial interests, and power stations, oil refineries and mineral operations have been allowed in national parks. A large mining concern is threatening to invade Snowdonia in the area of the beautiful Mawddach Valley. It has only been given permission to carry out tests so far but no Government which sanctions testing can logically refuse to permit development if such tests prove favourable.

In its 1969 report, the Countryside Commission concluded that 'it is all too plain that amenity considerations in the national parks do not enjoy the priority in public policy that the (1949) Act intended that they should.'

Areas of outstanding natural beauty enjoy even less protection. Giant pylons stride the Sussex Downs and a power station and the M.40 will mutilate the Chilterns. John Barr wrote: 'Practically every AONB is now pockmarked, or soon will be, by active mineral workings: clay deposits in Dorset, gravel pits in the Mendips, sand workings on the Sussex Downs and countless other examples.'

Even if some of these developments were inevitable, he declared, at least the clearance of derelict land and disused military sites should have been expedited.

Evidence of the low priority given to the Countryside Commission's role is the cost – it comes to around 2p per head per year, about the price of a cigarette; poor support indeed for a very able and enthusiastic staff under its first-rate chairman, Mr John Cripps.

Towards viable villages

The best guarantee that there will still be any real countryside left for townsfolk to enjoy by the year 2000 is the provision of a satisfying and reasonably prosperous life for those who depend upon it for their livelihood. A flourishing agriculture is obviously a first requirement, but with mechanisation reducing the demand for human labour, it becomes more and more important to see that other industries are encouraged to establish themselves in the countryside.

If this is not done, many villages will decline. Rural depopulation is already serious in some areas, notably mid-Wales, parts of the West and North-west and East Anglia, and the Pennine region. Losses of over 10 per cent are not infrequent. Agencies like the Rural Industries Bureau are doing immensely valuable work in trying to reverse this trend.

The purchase of second homes in the country by town dwellers is also an important factor in off-setting population losses. It has led to the regeneration of thousands of cottages which would otherwise have crumbled away, but the contribution to village life which can be made by those who only live there at week-ends and holiday times is clearly limited.

Much more needs to be done to bring employment to country districts. If the 'country' aspects of town and country planning were given more weight, standards of living in the countryside, in the widest sense of the term, might be raised appreciably. Counties like Hampshire, Kent, Buckinghamshire and Cambridgeshire are among the few who have given any real thought to village planning.

One aspect which causes a great deal of discontent in the villages is the decline in public transport. Between 1957 and 1967 the British Rail passenger network slumped from 14,622 miles to just under 10,000 miles and country areas were among the hardest hit.

When closures occurred, angry villagers were promised that bus services would be introduced to replace them. This has not happened on anything like the scale required. Where services have been started they are often grossly inadequate, and many more have been stopped altogether as being uneconomic. The result has been a vicious spiral of poor services and more cars on the roads.

The Rural District Councils Association forecast that by the end of 1971 over one-fifth of Britain's country bus services would disappear. Whole counties could be deprived of all bus services. Nor are rail cuts at an end, it seems. Government spokesmen have been uttering ominous warnings about the cost of subsidies, although it has been pointed out that these only amount to about 0·1 per cent of the national income. It is absurd to suggest this nation cannot afford £40 million a year, when it can spend at least £800 million on a transport project of much more doubtful value like the Concorde and when road spending is barely questioned.

There are thousands of villagers who do not own cars and for whom local buses and trains are the only link with the social life of the town where they do their shopping, go to the cinema and so on. Many of them are elderly people who cannot walk long distances or ride bicycles. There is a need here which is not being met. Furthermore, in assessing the viability of rail or road services, no attempt is made to take into account the cost to the community in terms of increased road congestion, accidents and the decline in the quality of country life which follows from the failure to provide reasonable public transport facilities.

Apart from reviving the railways, which we shall probably be forced to do eventually, the chief hope for improvement would seem to lie in new bus licensing proposals announced by Mr John Peyton, Minister for Transport Industries, in

129

July 1971. He said the changes were prompted by 'a crisis in public transport caused by the tremendous and engulfing wave of private cars'. Under the proposals, cars and mini-buses would be exempt from road service licensing, as would tours, excursions and school buses. No public service vehicle seating fewer than eight people would require a licence.

This would mean that car owners would be able to give lifts for payment and mini-bus services could be started without arguments over the route with the main companies. The proposals were described by the Rural District Councils Association as 'a charter and a glimmer of hope for all country folk without cars'.

Early legislation to give effect to these changes will be appreciated in the villages, though it remains to be seen how far they will go to meet the situation. It has certainly been shown that running down public transport is just as much of a mistake in the countryside as in the towns. Village life has been harmed and it has led to the senseless destruction of lovely places by motor cars.

Beware the Maginot mentality

Britain has devised over the decades a pattern of good management of the countryside which is highly regarded throughout the world and which explains, perhaps, why visitors are pleasantly surprised that there is so much greenery left to admire. However, it is plain that this 'mosaic defence', as James Fisher called it, will have to be enormously strengthened if the situation is to be contained in the years to come.

It is not enough just to designate areas under this or that heading. We need positive management policies, backed by the resources to carry them out. At best, designation is no more than a valuable safeguard. At worst, like the Maginot line, which was easily turned by the Germans during the last war, it represents a trap for the unwary. It effectively disarms the defenders by creating the illusion of protection.

There is just no substitute for good husbandry, coupled with eternal public vigilance.

Further reading

Countryside – General

Bracey, H. E., *People and the Countryside*, Routledge and Kegan Paul, 1970.

Christian, Garth, *Tomorrow's Countryside*, John Murray, 1966.

Best and Coppock, *The Changing Use of Land in Britain*, Faber and Faber, 1962.

Crowe, Sylvia, *Tomorrow's Landscape*, Architectural Press, 1956.

Crowe, Sylvia, *The Landscape of Roads*, Architectural Press, 1960.

Blenkinsop, Arthur, *Enjoying the Countryside*, Fabian Society, 1968.

Stamp, Sir Dudley, *Nature Conservation in Britain*, Collins, 1969.

Rubinstein and Speakman, *Leisure, Transport and the Countryside*, Fabian Society, 1969.

Dower, Michael, *Fourth Wave – The Challenge of Leisure*, Civic Trust, 1965.

Leisure in the Countryside – England and Wales, HMSO, Cmnd 2928, 1966.

H. M. Abrahams (ed), *Britain's National Parks, Country Life*, 1959.

The Case for Forestry, Forestry Committee of Great Britain, National Agricultural Centre, Kenilworth, Warwickshire.

National Forest Parks, Forestry Commission, HMSO, 1961.
Britain's Forests, ten booklets, HMSO, 1948-65.
Countryside in 1970, second conference 1965: reports of study groups, Royal Society of Arts and Nature Conservancy.
Nature Conservation at the Coast, Nature Conservancy, 1970.
The Coastal Heritage, HMSO, 1971.
Planning of the Coastline, HMSO, 1971.
Hedgerow and Farm Timber, Report of Committee on, HMSO, 1955.
Rural Transport in Devon and *Rural Transport in West Suffolk*, (D o E Passenger Transport Division).

Water

Growing Demand for Water, Central Advisory Water Committee Report, HMSO, 1962.
The Future Management of Water in England and Wales, Central Advisory Water Committee, HMSO, 1971.
Morecambe Bay and Solway Barrages: Report on Desk Studies, HMSO, 1966.
Amenity Use of Reservoirs, study tour of the USA (British Waterworks Assn).
Water Resources Board annual reports, HMSO.

Canals

British Waterways: Recreation and Amenity, HMSO, Cmnd 3401, 1967.
Leisure and the Waterways, HMSO, 1967.
British Waterways Board annual reports, HMSO.

Footpaths

Campbell, Ian, *A Practical Guide to the Law on Footpaths*.

Wildlife

Fisher, James, and Prince Philip, *Wildlife Crisis*, Hamish Hamilton, 1970.
Fitter, R. S. R., *Wildlife in Britain*, Penguin, 1963.
Wildlife Conservation Special Committee (England and Wales) Report, HMSO, Cmnd 7122, 1947.
Simon and Geroudet, *Last Survivors. Animals and birds in danger of extinction*, World Wildlife Fund.
Fitzgerald, Brian Vesey, *Britain's Vanishing Wildlife*, Mayflower Paperback.
Hickling, C. F., *The Farming of Fish*, Pergamon, 1968.
Netby, Anthony, *The Atlantic Salmon, A Vanishing Species*, 1968.

23. A job for us all

Britain's greatness has been largely built up on the willingness of governments of all political persuasions to listen to those lay voices who have, in a sense, expressed the nation's conscience in so many ways.

The movements inspired by such men and women as Wilberforce, Chadwick, Shaftesbury and Elizabeth Fry provide a rich inheritance for those who are involved in the battle for conservation today.

Those modern campaigns which have been successful have cast their net widely, drawing liberally upon the wealth of talent existing within that ever-growing section of concerned people who are prepared to act on matters of principle whatever their political views. The net gathers up the architects and engineers, the barristers and solicitors, the public relations officers and journalists, the trade union leaders and the high-powered executives.

Programmes appear on radio and television, letters by eminent people are printed in *The Times* and the pros and cons are argued in the columns of the local and specialist press. Ultimately, of course, Members of Parliament and councillors must carry the issue into the places where decisions are taken; to ask questions, initiate debates and perhaps to promote Bills.

There have been many notable campaigns of this kind within the field we are concerned with in this book. Outstanding was the movement against the siting of the third London airport at Stansted. Not only did the opposition force Authority to change its mind, but it induced a new animal to leap on to the public stage – the wide-ranging inquiry – in what was essentially an anti-noise protest. And when that inquiry produced an unpopular verdict, the campaigners went into action again until public opinion was finally satisfied with the selection of Foulness.

The consequences of this campaign have yet to be fully appreciated. Certainly much of the apathy created by disillusionment with party politics has disappeared. There is a new spirit in the air, a renewed interest in democracy, a feeling that no matter what the politicians decide, the voice of the people can make itself heard.

This was, perhaps, the real value of Stansted. But it was not, of course, the only important victory for the pressure groups. There was the remarkably successful campaign by the advocates of abortion law reform, for instance, which resulted in an Act that could reduce the number of unwanted births. And there have been countless local battles over reservoirs and firing ranges, pylons and motorway routes which have been fought and won. There has also been the Campaign for Nuclear Disarmament.

One may argue about the part played by this remarkable post-war movement in bringing about the agreement to stop nuclear testing in the atmosphere. Certainly it was internationally known and respected, and there were attempts to emulate it abroad. It had a long list of aims, but what seemed to matter to most of its supporters were the risks to health, and especially to the unborn, by the release of strontium 90 into the atmosphere through nuclear explosions. Evidence that this *was* the major preoccupation is contained in the fact that after the test-ban agreement was signed, CND's supporters melted away and the movement has never been the same since.

It may therefore be regarded as the first mass anti-pollution campaign we have seen in this country. At the peak of its activities, its support was immense, especially among the young.

Thus two of the biggest post-war movements this country has seen were concerned with environmental matters – air pollution and noise. It is quite a thought for those who have always claimed – to put the argument in its crudest form – that there are no votes in sewage.

The post-war successes of pressure groups and the remarkable national and international awakening to environmental issues must surely give heart to those who might otherwise be inclined to feel that there is very little ordinary folk can do in face of such mighty problems.

Much has been achieved already and, with the new awakening, this can only be the beginning. Governments are now paying more than lip-service to conservation. Local authority officers and members have been working on these problems through the apathetic years. They know what needs to be done. Now they are more hopeful of getting the tools to do it.

Join a society – or form one

If the politicians fail to act, there is an astonishing number of organisations (many of them listed in the directory at the end of this book) covering every environmental interest, waiting in the wings and ready to join issue with them in the most determined fashion.

There is a multitude of jobs to be done and these organisations will welcome help. Through them you can work to save wildlife; to preserve and increase our stock of trees, especially traditional hardwoods; to clean up, and clean out, rivers, lakes and canals; to safeguard our heritage of fine buildings; to produce a quieter Britain; to reduce the amount of litter and rubbish of all kinds fouling our towns and countryside, and to carry on the fight for clean air.

The Ramblers' Association is appealing for volunteers to clear and mark thousands of miles of Britain's footpaths. By merely walking these tracks you help to ensure their survival. So those charitable bodies who are looking for safer walking country could do more than one useful job in this way. The Conservation Corps seeks the aid of young people in managing nature reserves and maintaining countryside amenities. Older folk can support the activities of the Council for the Protection of Rural England, which has branches throughout the countryside. For children there are field studies through the schools and the Countryside Commission. And we should all join the National Trust and help it to further its invaluable work of preserving great houses and fine scenery.

Good town and country planning can make life more civilised all round. The Town and Country Planning Association is an energetic and resourceful advocate of sane policies and will welcome the support of those interested and concerned in the wider issues. And let us not forget that housing is for millions of people the number-one environmental problem. 'Shelter', the National Campaign for the Homeless, has plenty of urgent jobs to be done.

If there should arise in your area a particular local issue of some moment about which you and your neighbours feel strongly – a motorway scheme perhaps – why not form a society to fight it? Why not form a society anyway, if there isn't one in your area, to take a continuing look at your neighbourhood and to see what can be done to make it a more pleasant place to live in.

Could your district do with more trees? Are you short of play facilities for children? Is the shopping area a disgrace and could you persuade retailers to get together for a general clean-up? What about the local railway station – could that do with a coat of paint? – and is there a lake or pond which needs cleaning out and which might be made into a sailing area or fishery? Do your local schools have environmental studies in their curricula? Does the river smell and, if so, what is your river authority doing about it? Can the streets be made safer for children and shoppers?

The Civic Trust, which has more than 700 such societies affiliated to it, will advise you on how to go about forming one.

What the individual can do

Perhaps you are not a joiner, however, but would like to do something on your own account to help the fight for a better Britain. Well, you could start a one-man anti-pollution war like a character in Kane County, west of Chicago, who calls himself 'The Fox'. Among the novel ideas thought out by this highly inventive individual in his campaign against a steel company polluting Lake Michigan was to spread 50 pounds of dead fish and sewage in the company's plush reception room, to block the company's drainage system and to attempt to seal off the plant chimney pouring acrid smoke into the air. He also left ripe skunks on the suburban doorsteps of company executives.

He is reported to have told a correspondent of the American magazine, *Time*, that he was an enthusiastic fisherman and hunter who remembered when Kane County was unspoiled. 'I got tired of watching the smoke and the filth, and the little streams dying one by one. A man ought to be able to drink from a stream when he's thirsty and take his son out fishing. Finally, I decided to do something.'

While one may have a sneaking regard for the daring of this latter-day Pimpernel, one will probably not feel obliged to adopt tactics of this kind; especially when there are countless, and possibly more effective, alternatives.

Women, with their immense purchasing power, can play a key role in conservation by demanding that manufacturers stop producing goods which cause pollution. In particular, they could campaign against excessive and undesirable packaging. Our countryside and coast are littered with plastic cups and cartons, and non-returnable bottles, most of which will be around for decades because they are not broken down by ordinary biological processes.

You pay twice for packaging. First, when you buy the product. According to *Modern Packaging*, a trade journal, the wrapping or container accounts for an average of 18 per cent of the price. You also pay for the disposal of the packaging by the local authority.

And there could be an added cost to the community in terms of litter and pollution.

There has been a good deal of talk recently about 'soft' and 'hard' detergents, and it is true that the 'soft' variety causes fewer problems at the sewage works. But make no mistake, all detergents are potential pollutants. We may be able to avoid the obvious signs, like foaming on our rivers, but phosphates and other chemicals are getting into our lakes and streams in alarming quantities. In

America, hitherto fresh and fish-full waters like Lake Erie have been rendered lifeless by such agents, and the wholesale use of detergents is one of the causes.

Enormous sums of money are spent on 'whiter than white' claims which are misleading in the sense that what is produced is an optical effect rather than increased cleanliness. These advertising costs are also reflected in the price of the product. So you are paying more for a very doubtful advantage.

The same can be said of the so-called 'enzyme detergents'. As the consumer magazine *Which?* pointed out, the benefits are marginal. There have also been complaints of skin troubles through their use, but the manufacturers have agreed to print a warning on the packet.

A switch back to soap flakes would be the best way of avoiding these dangers. Alternatively, using no more than the recommended amounts of detergents would help – most women use far too much.

Big savings could be made if packaging could be re-used, perhaps as drinking glasses or preserving jars, or sent to merchants for re-processing. The yellow pages of the telephone directory give details of waste-paper merchants, scrap dealers and so on. What you throw away may be valuable, if not to yourself then to charities, hospitals and schools, even to local tradesmen.

You can sell newspaper for about £5 a ton to the local agent or, in quantities of 5–8 tons, direct to the mills for £10 a ton.

If women deluged manufacturers with their packaging complaints and combined this with selective buying and campaigns against non-returnables (e.g. returning them to source), things would start to happen.

Consumer campaigns in America have already notched up important successes. The Coca-Cola firm, for instance, has been forced to change its policy on non-returnables and to set up glass collection centres.

Badger your local authority, too, if necessary about such matters as these . . .

Does the council have a separate waste-paper collection; if not, why not? To what extent is it reclaiming valuable material you put in your dustbin? Does it compost the autumn leaves or burn them?

And while we're on the subject, do *you* have a compost heap for kitchen waste? Do *you* leave taps dripping or use more water than you really need? If so, you are bringing nearer the day when water will be metered.

If women refused to buy clothing made from the fur or skins of wild animals or hats adorned with bird plumage, they would be helping to end the slaughter of wildlife (see 'The killing has to stop'). There are plenty of adequate synthetic materials available.

If the nation as a whole had a carefully considered population policy, environmental prospects would be infinitely brighter. Women (and men, too, of course) must demand adequate family planning facilities for all, coupled with more sex education at all levels and less commercial exploitation of sex. And why not adopt that third child if you want more than two?

What the motor car means to the individual male especially has been the subject of much social research, from which it is clear that the situation is changing. No longer does the 'get-up-and-go' status symbol portrayed by the advertisers have the same appeal. The car is also becoming more closely linked with jams and pollution, and a terrifying toll of injury and death.

This is not so much the fault of the car itself (although much could be done to make it safer and less of a polluter) as of the way we have used it. The common reaction of the motorist and those who speak for him to the difficulties of getting about, especially in towns, has been to demand more roads, but the experience here and elsewhere shows this to be self-defeating. More roads attract more cars and you are ultimately no better off.

The motorist, in his own interest, must be prepared to accept restrictions on his movement in towns. He can help to ease congestion and make these restrictions less severe by buying a small car, using it for journeys to town as little as possible and, if he really must commute, taking a few passengers along. Car pools have been very successful in reducing congestion in America.

At the same time, the motorist should lend his voice to demands that public transport be made cheaper and more convenient. A properly planned transport system would see that interchange links were provided to enable drivers to transfer to buses and trains, or vice versa. With the car used mainly as a means of getting to the nearest bus or railway station, would there really be any need for that second one?

The motorist is probably a gardener too, and there is a great deal which he, or she, can do to minimise pollution and increase soil fertility. Composting is one, avoiding the use of too many toxic sprays and weed-killers is another, cutting down the number of bonfires a third (this not only creates smoke nuisance but the smoke contains a cancer-producing agent).

There is some most useful advice on the safer insecticides and weed-killers in *Consumers' Guide to the Protection of the Environment* (Ballantine Books, 40p) compiled, I understand, with the aid of the Henry Doubleday Research Association (*see directory*).

A cleaner, fairer land

This small selection of ideas might start some trains of thought moving in a constructive direction. What is really important is to develop an attitude of mind towards the environment which will produce the right reaction to a given situation.

Every citizen of these islands must be prepared to take part in the long, slow haul to ensure not only survival, for that would be meaningless in an arid world, but a better life for all human beings everywhere. This implies not only more economic growth but a fairer distribution of the fruits thereof to aid the under-privileged and to improve the quality of life for us all. The well-being of a nation cannot be measured by the growth index alone; indeed, a lower growth rate may well mean that a higher proportion of the nation's wealth is being devoted to making it a more civilized place to live in.

World supplies of food and raw materials are running out. We are rapidly using up the land and poisoning the seas. Millions of people are dying slow deaths from polluted air and who knows what the long-term effects will be of all the chemicals we so liberally sprinkle on our soil?

Britain's cities are becoming uglier, noisier and more crowded, and it is harder for citizens to find peace and solace in the countryside or along the coast. Our rural landscape, still incomparable, is threatened as never before by economic pressures on farmers and by a growing population with ever-rising recreational demands.

There is no sense in being unduly alarmist; equally it would be foolish to play down the problems we face. We *can* win a better tomorrow if we match our own individual efforts, and see to it that governments match theirs, to the scale of the issues confronting us.

But individual efforts should as far as possible be co-ordinated. Isolated actions are useful as pace-setters, but there is really no substitute for vigorous, properly conducted campaigns. The decade ahead should see such campaigns mushrooming in every town and parish in the country; to fight pollution of all kinds, to avoid waste and conserve natural resources, to protect the countryside and to bring grace and beauty to our towns.

We have no time to lose. The new battle of Britain must begin here and now.

THE NEW BATTLE OF BRITAIN

Stop press information about societies:
There have been one or two changes since the Directory was compiled-

The Environmental Consortium is now at
14 William IV Street, London WC2N 4DW
(01-836 0908/9)

The Food and Research Educational Trust
(sec. Philip Dawes) has changed its name to
Food-watch. Address as printed,
telephone 0734-475605.

Friends of the Earth have moved to 9 Poland Street,
London W.1 (01-437 6121)

The Geographical Association, 343 Fulwood Road,
Sheffield S10 3BP issues useful lists of field study
centres and local authority field centres.

List of General Periodicals should include
"Your Environment" (quarterly), 10 Roderick Road,
London NW3.

ANIMALS IN DANGER CORPS. (AID)
Marston Court, Manor Road, Wallington, Surrey
Tel. 01-669 4995
Project of Wildlife Youth Service formed to raise money to save wildlife. Open to any young person of school age in UK, either as individual member or through

organised groups in schools, youth organisations, youth clubs, etc. AID is allocated to ten conservation projects per annum by World Wildlife Fund. No membership fee, badge available 12½p.

ANTI-CONCORDE PROJECT
70 Lytton Avenue, Letchworth, Hertfordshire
Tel. 046-26-2081
Secretary: Richard Wiggs
Campaigns against development and operation of supersonic airliners. Various publications thereon. Supported by voluntary contributions.

ARBORICULTURAL ASSOCIATION
59 Blythwood Gardens, Stansted, Essex
Tel. 027-971 3160
Secretary: D. R. Honour
Aims to encourage higher standards of tree care and education in tree matters, including setting-up of working party on arboricultural education. Meetings held twice a year in South-East and Midlands. Publications include newsletter and advisory booklets. Membership: 50p to £4 (depending on occupation).

ASSOCIATION FOR NEIGHBOURHOOD COUNCILS
18 Victoria Park Square, London, E2 9PF
Tel. 01-980 6263
Chairman: Michael Young
Pressing the Government to introduce 'neighbourhood' or 'urban' parish councils in new local government pattern.

ASSOCIATION FOR THE PRESERVATION OF RURAL SCOTLAND
39 Castle Street, Edinburgh, EH2 3BH
Tel. 031-225 8391
Secretary: Kenneth Macrae, WS
Seeks to arouse and educate public opinion for protection of rural scenery and amenities of country towns and villages. Membership: £1.

ASSOCIATION OF BRITISH TREE SURGEONS AND ARBORISTS
11 Wings Road, Upper Hale, Farnham, Surrey
Tel. 0251-3-5924
Secretary: Mrs E. Deller
Tree surgery work carried out to British Standard specifications.

ASSOCIATION OF RIVER AUTHORITIES
Grosvenor Gardens House, Grosvenor Gardens, London, S.W.1
Tel. 01-834 1866
Secretary: D. J. Kinnersley
Representative association for officers and members of river authorities – statutory bodies covering England and Wales responsible for water conservation, pollution prevention, fisheries, land drainage, flood protection and sea defences and in some cases navigation. Publishes *Year Book*.

ASSOCIATION OF TREE TRANSPLANTERS
31 London Road, Camberley, Surrey
Tel. 0276-21152
Advocates the improvement of transplanting techniques and high standards of workmanship.

BIRTH CONTROL CAMPAIGN
233 Tottenham Court Road, London, W1P 9AE
Tel. 01-580 9360
General Secretary: Mrs D. Cossey
Founded on initiative of Abortion Law Reform Association and workers in planned parenthood field to urge on Government comprehensive provision of birth control as integral part of National Health Service. Birth control defined as contraception, voluntary sterilisation and, as last resort, therapeutic abortion. Lobbies politicians at national and local levels, and collects and publicises information on availability of birth control. Presses for more family planning education at all levels and more medical and sociological research. Founded April, 1971. Membership: £2 p.a. (individual) and £3 p.a. (joint husband/wife).

BRITISH ASSOCIATION FOR THE CONTROL OF AIRCRAFT NOISE (BACAN)
30 Fleet Street, London, E.C.4
Tel. Smallfield (Surrey) 2382; Evenings/Weekends Horley (Surrey) 4200
Secretary: M. N. Jackson
National organisation with international links to co-ordinate efforts of all concerned about air noise. Deals with proper siting of airports, quieter engines, introduction and strict enforcement of noise abatement procedures, soundproofing without rating increases and adequate representation on all developments which affect people's interests and control of supersonic flights. Publications include newsletter and survey into effect of aircraft noise on education at Royal Holloway College. Membership: minimum 50p.

BRITISH BUTTERFLY CONSERVATION SOCIETY
Over Compton, Sherborne, Dorset
Tel. Yeovil (0935) 4608-9
Information Officer: Mrs Margaret Empedocles
7 The Drive, Kingston Hill, Surrey
Fights decline of butterfly stocks by campaigning against pesticides and other agents of destruction. Promotes breeding of rare species, cultivation of butterfly attracting plants and scientific study.

BRITISH ECOLOGICAL SOCIETY
c/o Department of Botany, University College of North Wales, Bangor, North Wales

BRITISH NATURALISTS' ASSOCIATION
10 St. Catherine's Drive, Bridport, Dorset

BRITISH ORNITHOLOGISTS' UNION
c/o Bird Room, British Museum (Natural History), London, S.W.7

BRITISH SCRAP FEDERATION
33–34 Chancery Lane, London, WC2A 1ER
Tel. 01-405 0514/5
Secretary: D. N. Willmott
Represents interests of scrap iron and steel, and metal merchants. Membership: Scrap merchants through regional association.

BRITISH SOCIETY FOR SOCIAL RESPONSIBILITY IN SCIENCE
70 Great Russell Street, London, W.C.1
Secretary: David Dickson
Strives to create awareness of scientists' social responsibilities through meetings, working and local groups, and summer school at Dartington Hall in August, 1971. Publishes *News-sheets* and *The Social Impact of Modern Biology*. Membership: £1 p.a.

BRITISH TRUST FOR CONSERVATION VOLUNTEERS
see CONSERVATION CORPS

BRITISH TRUST FOR ENTOMOLOGY
41 Queen's Gate, London, S.W.7

BRITISH TRUST FOR ORNITHOLOGY
Beech Grove, Tring, Hertfordshire

CAMPAIGN FOR BIOLOGICAL SANITY
24 Abercorn Place, London, N.W.8
Tel. 01-286 4366

CAMPING CLUB OF GREAT BRITAIN AND IRELAND
11 Lower Grosvenor Place, London, S.W.1
Tel. 01-828 9232
Secretary: G. A. Cubitt
Promotes and protects interests of campers and caravanners. Winners of Civic Trust Award for design of camp site buildings in Dorset and joint winners of Duke of Edinburgh Countryside Award for ECY 70. Publishes monthly magazine, *Camping and Outdoor Life*, *Year Book* and *Sites List* (annually), *International Camping* (annually).

CENTRAL COMMITTEE FOR THE ARCHITECTURAL ADVISORY PANELS
4 Hobart Place, London, S.W.1
Tel. 01-235 4771
Co-ordinates work of panels set up to assist local planning authorities. Panels offer expert technical advice with aim of improving design standards.

CENTRAL COUNCIL FOR RIVERS PROTECTION
Fishmongers' Hall, London, E.C.4
Tel. 01-626 8591
Representative of national bodies interested in maintaining purity of rivers.

CENTRAL COUNCIL OF PHYSICAL RECREATION
26 Park Crescent, London, W1N 4AJ
Tel. 01-580 6822
Secretary: Walter Winterbottom
Seeks to improve physical and mental health of community, and especially schoolchildren, through physical recreation. Services of qualified staff offered to wide range of appropriate agencies. Runs six fully established national sports centres. Publishes quarterly journal, *Sport and Recreation*, books, pamphlets and annual report. Membership: 50p.

CENTRE FOR ENVIRONMENTAL STUDIES
5 Cambridge Terrace, Regent's Park, London, N.W.1
Tel. 01-486 3956
Secretary: Miss Christine Adnitt
Independent research body looking into problems of urban and regional planning. Financed by Government and Ford Foundation. Publishes *Working Papers* (over 100) and book, *Developing Patterns of Urbanisation* (ed. Peter Cowan).

CENTRAL RIGHTS OF WAY COMMITTEE
166 Shaftesbury Avenue, London, W.C.2
Tel. 01-836 7220
Secretary: I. S. Campbell
Co-ordinating committee serviced by Commons, Open Spaces and Footpaths Preservation Society for rights of way survey and to examine all proposals for closure and diversion of public paths.

CIVIC TRUST
17 Carlton House Terrace, London, S.W.1
Tel. 01-930 0914
Director: Michael Middleton
Founded 1957. Independent body supported by voluntary contributions. Works for higher standards of city planning and design, for removal of ugliness and for greater public awareness of the environment. Encourages formation of civic and amenity societies, and publicises their activities. Demonstrates economical improvements through pilot projects. Campaigned for Civic Amenities Act 1967, against heavy lorries, closely involved in Lea Valley Regional Park. Operates awards schemes. Publishes bi-monthly *Newsletter* and numerous books and pamphlets on conservation. 750 local amenity societies registered.

CIVIC TRUST FOR NORTH-WEST
56 Oxford Street, Manchester, M1 6EU
Tel. 061-236 7464
Director: Graham Ashworth
Aims as Civic Trust. Projects include Tame Valley Improvement Scheme (cleaning up river and dereliction); scheme for conserving Bronte village of Haworth (1,000 inhabitants and influx of over half a million tourists a year); advice on study of Blackburn recreational facilities; environmental vocabulary for village development; pioneer study of rehabilitation in Rochdale (preceded both Ministry of Housing report on similar area in that town and Halliwell Report on Bolton district); pilot scheme for recovery of Skelmersdale old town; points system for measuring condition and environmental quality of small housing area of Liverpool. Publications on above projects and others. No individual membership, but individuals may subscribe to Trust finances alongside industry, commerce and local authorities. Individuals may also join 100 or so civic and amenity societies registered in North-West. Full-time professional staff.

CIVIC TRUST FOR THE NORTH EAST
34–35 Saddler Street, Durham
Tel. Durham 61182
Director: N. Whittaker
Regional body of Civic Trust. Campaign for increased tree planting culminated in Jarrow Trees Conference in 1966. Achievements also include setting up of

Youth Enterprise, voluntary work arm of Trust, and formation of over 40 civic and amenity societies in region. Publications include bulletin. Membership by subscription.

CIVIC TRUST FOR WALES
6 Park Place, Cardiff
Tel. Cardiff 26006
Director: George Yeomans
Mainly engaged in promoting civic societies in Wales. Publishes six-monthly magazine 'Network'.

CLEAN AIR COUNCIL FOR ENGLAND AND WALES
Queen Anne Chambers, 28 Broadway, London, SW1 H9NA
Tel. 01-930 4300 ext. 345
Secretary: G. I. Fuller
Keeps under review progress made in abating air pollution in England and Wales, and advises Secretary of State for the Environment.

CLEAN AIR COUNCIL FOR SCOTLAND
c/o Scottish Development Department, 21 Hill Street, Edinburgh, EH2 3JY
Tel. 031-226 5208
Secretary: W. M. Robertson

COASTAL ANTI-POLLUTION LEAGUE LTD
Alverstoke, Greenway Lane, Bath, Somerset, BA2 4LN
Tel. Bath 64094
General Secretary: J. Amey
Fights contamination of tidal waters and pleasure beaches, and promotes advancement of education in science of sewage disposal so far as such objects are charitable. Seeks co-operation of public and other institutions and authorities. Publications: *Golden List of Beaches* and *Water Pollution in Coastal Areas – the layman's point of view*. Membership: £1.

COMMITTEE FOR ENVIRONMENTAL CO-ORDINATION (Co En Co)
4 Hobart Place, London, S.W.1
Tel. 01-235 4771
Secretaries: A. F. Holford Walker, Peter Conder
Information Officer: John Yeoman
An alliance of 14 national amenity bodies formed in 1969 to promote a forum for the discussion of problems of common concern and to promote concerted action thereon.

COMMONS, OPEN SPACES AND FOOTPATHS PRESERVATION SOCIETY
166 Shaftesbury Avenue, London, W.C.2
Tel. 01-836 7220
Secretary: I. S. Campbell
Seeks preservation of commons, public open spaces and greens for public use in town and country, and retention and extension of footpaths and bridleways to aid fullest public enjoyment of countryside. Also campaigns for widest public access to open country and advises and assists local authorities, commoners and interested laymen. Publications include journal and campaign pamphlets. Membership: £1·50 minimum for individual or local society.

CONSERVATION CORPS
Zoological Gardens, Regent's Park, London, N.W.1
Tel. 01-722 7112
Chairman: John Coleman-Cooke
Assists with maintaining character and amenity of countryside where such work is compatible with scientific and conservation interests. Trains and educates members in principles and practice of nature conservation. Assists in maintenance and management of nature reserves and other scientifically important sites. All members unpaid volunteers.

CONSERVATION SOCIETY
21 Hanyards Lane, Cuffley, Potters Bar, Hertfordshire
Tel. Cuffley 2517
Secretary: S. G. Lawrence
Seeks survival of race through stabilisation and reduction of population and wise use of earth's finite resources. Pressing British Government to draw up population policy. Aims to make society's attitude central to the teaching of most school subjects. Seeks conservation of natural resources. Publications: *Why Britain Needs a Population Policy*. *Why Britain Needs a Conservation Policy for the Environment*. *The World's Too Small*. Membership: Individual £2, joint (husband and wife) £3 and student 50p.

COUNCIL FOR BRITISH ARCHAEOLOGY
8 St. Andrew's Place, Regent's Park, London, N.W.1
Tel. 01-486 1527
Secretary: Miss Beatrice de Cardi, BA, FSA
Works for improved legislation on protection of ancient monuments and recognition of early industrial monuments meriting protection. Conducting national survey of industrial monuments and mesolithic sites, and promoting research into urban development. Co-ordinates activities of archeological societies. Publishes periodicals and occasional papers. Membership Institutional, archaeological societies, museums and universities with archaeological departments – various subscription rates.

COUNCIL FOR ENVIRONMENTAL EDUCATION
26 Bedford Square, London, W.C.1
Tel. 01-636 4066
Secretary: C. L. Mellowes
Established 1968 by Duke of Edinburgh's standing committee for 'Countryside in 1970', to bring together local authorities, teachers and others concerned with environmental management in advancing education in environmental subjects. Publishes *Outdoor Studies Code* and *Directory of Centres for Outdoors Studies in England and Wales*. Membership through nomination.

COUNCIL FOR THE CARE OF CHURCHES
83 London Wall, London, EC2M 5NA
Tel. 01-638 0971/2
Secretary: Judith G. Scott
Central body formed to co-ordinate and assist work of diocesan committees; reconstituted in 1958 as council with 25 members appointed by Church Assembly. Diocesan committees control changes to church fabrics and furnishings, and

143

offer advice on design of new parish churches. Council has conservation committee of experts in various fields. Publishes news letter, *The Churchyards Handbook, Church Planning and Arrangement, Building New Churches, The Disposal of Cremated Remains, The Care of the Churches,* etc.

COUNCIL FOR NATURE

Zoological Gardens, Regent's Park, London, NW1 4RY
Tel. 01-722 7111
Information Officer: Timothy S. Sands
Representative body of British natural history movement; has 450 member natural history and conservation societies and represents their interest on national level. Active in supporting (or opposing where necessary) legislation affecting wildlife and its conservation. Advised on Deer Bill, Countryside Bill and Wild Plant Protection Bill, and vehemently opposed Tees Valley and Cleveland Water Bill. Sponsored Countryside in 1970 Conference, and represented on standing committee. Also works closely with national amenity bodies and young people. Numerous publications. Membership: £1, associates £5, affiliated £2–£5 (depending on size).

COUNCIL FOR THE PROTECTION OF RURAL ENGLAND

4 Hobart Place, London, S.W.1
Tel. 01-235 4771
Joint Secretaries: M. V. Osmond and A. F. Holford-Walker
Guards beauty of English countryside, villages and country towns. Collects and dispenses information on threats to rural scenery. Seeks to arouse public opinion to understand need for action. Not opposed to all change but aims to guide it. Has taken part in many successful campaigns, including those to save Windermere and Ullswater, Rainbow Wood, Swincombe, Ferndale and Hebden Valleys, Levens Park and Great Chishill; to prevent raising of weight limits for lorries; and for siting of third London airport at Foulness. Currently engaged on proper siting of motorways, speed-up of derelict land clearance, release of land by Services, better public transport in countryside, limitations on development in national parks, especially mineral extraction, etc. Fifty-one constituent bodies. Publishes monthly bulletin. Also available: *Notes for the Guidance of (Architectural) Panels* and *The Houses We Build.* Membership: £2·50 (individuals and affiliates).

COUNCIL FOR THE PROTECTION OF RURAL WALES

Meifod, Montgomeryshire, SY 22 6DA
Tel. Meifod 383
Secretary: S. R. J. Meade
Organises combined action to secure improvement, protection and preservation of countryside and towns and villages. Also information and advisory centre.

COUNTRYSIDE COMMISSION

1 Cambridge Gate, Regent's Park, London, NW1 4JY
Tel. 01-935 0366 and 01-935 5533
Secretary: M. F. B. Bell
Statutory national body concerned with conserving and enhancing landscape, beauty and amenity in England and Wales. Provides and improves facilities for countryside enjoyment, including need to secure public access for open-air recreation. Chooses and designates national parks and areas of outstanding natural beauty. Allocates grants to local authorities for country parks and picnic

sites. Draws up proposals for long-distance footpaths such as Pennine Way, Cleveland Way and Pembrokeshire Coast Path. Distributes Country Code and organises research, experiment and information services. Members appointed by Secretary of State for the Environment. Many publications; available at Government bookshops.

DARTMOOR PRESERVATION ASSOCIATION
23 Wellpark Close, Exeter, EX4 1TS
Tel. Exeter 59095 (evenings only)
Secretary: Brian le Messurier
Energetic campaigners for protection, preservation and enhancement of characteristic wilderness and natural beauty of Dartmoor landscape, who seek to maintain for public its traditional privileges and rights of access. Prominent in successful campaign against proposal to build reservoir on central Dartmoor. Publishes *Newsletter*. Also *Misuse of a National Park – Military Training on Dartmoor and The Dartmoor Bibliography*. Membership: 50p.

ENVIRONMENTAL CONSORTIUM
27 Nassau Street, London, W1N 8EQ
Tel. 01-636 0726
Press Officer: George Hay
Promotes creation of safe and happy environment through publicity and research projects. Formed Environmental Improvements Ltd to carry through projects on business basis. Publications: Series of reports on historic London, water use, etc. Membership: Group £5 p.a. and Individual £1·50.

FARM BUILDINGS ASSOCIATION
Coombe Farm, Twineham, Bolney, Nr Haywards Heath, Sussex
Tel. Bolney 227
Secretary: Guy J. Caren
Provides opportunities for those interested in farm buildings to meet and exchange information, ideas and experience on design and construction. Responsible for establishment of the Farm Buildings Centre at the National Agricultural Centre, Stoneleigh, working in co-operation with Royal Agricultural Society of England. Publishes quarterly *Farm Buildings Centre Digest*. Membership: £3·15 p.a.

FAUNA PRESERVATION SOCIETY
c/o Zoological Society of London, Regent's Park, London, N.W.1
Tel. 01-586 0872
Secretary: Richard Fitter
Conservation of wildlife throughout the world. Publication: *Oryx*, three times a year. Membership: £3 p.a.

FIELD STUDIES COUNCIL
9 Devereux Court, Strand, London, WC2R 3JR
Tel. 01-583 7471
Secretary: R. S. Chapman
Functions as teaching and research body on environmental matters. Aims to promote appreciation of countryside through field studies in schools, higher education centres and among adults. Runs residential courses at nine centres and centre for day visits in Epping Forest. Publishes *Field Studies* annually. Membership: Individual £2 with journal (50p without); corporate (schools, colleges, etc.) £2·50 with journal (£1 without).

FOODS RESEARCH AND EDUCATIONAL TRUST
10 Derby Road, Caversham, Reading
Covers entire field of human nutrition, including effect of air pollution, water pollution, use of insecticides, pesticides and chemical fertilisers, unnatural rearing of animals for food and the foods they are fed on. Results published in monthly magazine.

FRESHWATER BIOLOGICAL ASSOCIATION
The Ferry House, Far Sawrey, Ambleside

FRIENDS OF FRIENDLESS CHURCHES
12 Edwards Square, London, W.8
Tel. 01-937 1414
Hon. Director: Ivor Bulmer-Thomas

FRIENDS OF THE EARTH
8 King Street, London, WC2 8HS
Tel. 01-836 0718
Secretary: Miss Lynda Hillyer
International non-profit-making body prepared to take aggressive legal and political action to ensure better life, by bringing pressure to bear locally and nationally on authorities and industries blind to ecological effect of their activities. Provides legal and technical assistance. Publications include *The Environmental Handbook, The Population Bomb, Concorde – the Case Against Supersonic Transport* and *Consumer's Guide to the Protection of the Environment.* All published in conjunction with Pan/Ballantine. Membership: Free, but friend and supporter £3, full supporting member £100.

GEORGIAN GROUP
2 Chester Street, London, S.W.1
Tel. 01-235 3081
Secretary: Miss Eleanor V. de B. Murray
Founded in 1937 to awaken and direct public opinion to urgent need to protect nation's diminishing Georgian heritage, and through Parliament and Press to rescue from demolition squares, terraces and individual buildings. Title was adopted for convenience only, as all buildings designed in classical manner come within its scope. Advises owners and public authorities on preservation and repair. Membership: Individual £2·10 and Junior 50p. Corporate membership: Details on application.

GOOD GARDENERS' ASSOCIATION
Arkley Manor, Arkley, Nr Barnet, Hertfordshire
Tel. 449-2177
Secretary: Mrs Irene R. Shewell-Cooper
Advocates correct composting and conservation of all vegetable waste. Help and advice on organic gardening. Open days at Arkley Manor for demonstrations. Publications: *The A.B.C. of Soils, Humus and Health* and *The Compost Gardening Book.* Membership: £2 p.a.

HENRY DOUBLEDAY RESEARCH ASSOCIATION
20 Convent Lane, Bocking, Braintree, Essex
Tel. Braintree 1483
Director-Secretary: Lawrence D. Hills
Research into improved methods of farming and gardening without chemical

fertilisers or persistent pesticides. 470,000 copies of *Give Up Smoking Bonfires* – making compost and leafmould instead of causing air pollution by bonfires – sent out in rate demands by local authorities. Sponsors voluntary research by amateurs in methods of poisonless pest control, especially ladybirds, hoverflies and cultivation methods, and weed control by plants with killer root secretions. Undertakes laboratory work on trace elements and plant nutrition, and provides compost advisory service for organic gardeners. Publications include *Pest Control Without Poisons, Fertility without Fertilisers, Fertility Finder* (guide to councils selling municipal compost and sludge-selling councils), *Biological Pest Control Report No. 3* (on British predators), *Operation Tiggywinkle* (hedgehogs as pest controllers). Subscription: £2.

HISTORIC BUILDINGS BUREAU
2, Marsham Street, London, SW1P 3EB
Tel. 01-212 5008
Director: T. W. R. Bridson
Seeks new uses for historic buildings.

HISTORIC BUILDINGS COUNCIL FOR ENGLAND
25, Savile Row, London, W.1
Tel. 01-734 6010
Makes recommendations to Government about grants for repair and maintenance of historic buildings.

HISTORIC BUILDINGS COUNCIL FOR SCOTLAND
122 George Street, Edinburgh 2
Tel. 031-225 2533

HISTORIC BUILDINGS COUNCIL FOR WALES
Gabalfa, Cardiff
Tel. 0222-62131

HISTORIC CHURCHES PRESERVATION TRUST
Fulham Palace, London, S.W.6
Tel. 01-736 3054
Director: Mr H. Llewellyn Jones
Assists parishioners and others with preservation of churches and chapels which are of historic or architectural value.

HOLIDAY FELLOWSHIP LTD
142 Great North Way, Hendon, London, NW4 1EG
Tel. 01-203 3381
Secretary: J. S. Edbrooke
Encourages healthy enjoyment of leisure and love of open air; furthers interest of education, culture and physical recreation; promotes social and international friendships, and organises holidays and other activities. Publishes *Holidays That Are Different, Holiday for Parties of Young People*, etc. Membership through £1 shareholdings; interest not less than 5 per cent annually on holding of £8 and upwards.

HOMES BEFORE ROADS
28 Grove Park Gardens, London, W.4
Tel. 01-994 0296
Director: Derrick Beecham

Founded in 1970 to publicise road proposals in Greater London Development Plan. Contested GLC elections with 85 candidates on anti-motorway ticket. Now national movement.

HOUSING CENTRE TRUST
13 Suffolk Street, London, S.W.1
Tel. 01-930 2881
Secretary: Mrs M. C. Baker
Works for improvement of housing conditions. Clearing house for information and ideas on housing policy, slum clearance, urban renewal, better standards of house design and layout, and planned environment for better living. Organises meetings and exhibitions, conferences and tours, initiates research and publishes monthly periodical *Housing Review*. Membership: Individual £3, group from £5·25 and local authorities from £5·25 according to population.

INLAND WATERWAYS ASSOCIATION LTD
114 Regent's Park Road, London, NW1 8UQ
Tel. 01-586 2556 and 2510
Secretary: R. W. Shopland
Founded in 1946 to advocate fullest use, maintenance and development of inland waterways of British Isles; in particular to restore navigable ones so that they may be used by commercial and pleasure traffic. Conducted vigorous campaign which was largely responsible for safeguarding of canals under 1968 Transport Act. Publishes bulletin six times a year and *Waterways Holiday Guide*. Membership from £2·50 to £5.

INTERNATIONAL COUNCIL FOR BIRD PRESERVATION
c/o British Museum (Natural History), Cromwell Road, London, S.W.7
Secretary: Miss P. Barclay-Smith, CBE
Stimulates interest in all countries for more adequate protection of wild bird-life. Sixty national sections, of which British section is one.

INTERNATIONAL YOUTH FEDERATION FOR ENVIRONMENTAL STUDIES AND CONSERVATION
40 Pensford Avenue, Kew, Surrey
Permanent address: c/o IUCN 1110 Morges, Switzerland
Tel. 01-876 6051
Secretary-General: David Withrington
Organises international projects, study camps, conferences, etc. for young people. Provides advice and information to youth conservation programmes and produces information bulletin for Europe. List of projects and camps available. Also various international working groups of young people. Establishing permanent centre in London for development of youth and student environmental action on world-wide basis, which is supported by Unesco to become nerve-centre of international network of young environmental activists.

KEEP BRITAIN TIDY GROUP
76 Strand, London, W.C.2
Tel. 01-836 6463
Director-General: David J. Lewis
Campaigns against litter in co-operation with local authorities, schools and other organisations. Publishes annual report, campaign guide and pamphlets. Membership: Individual £1, charitable organisation £2, and local authorities from £5 according to population.

LOCATION OF OFFICES BUREAU
27 Chancery Lane, London, WC2A 1NS
Tel. 01-405 2921
Secretary: L. W. Aldous
Appointed by Minister of Housing and Local Government in 1963 for purpose of encouraging decentralisation of office employment from congested London to suitable centres elsewhere. Promotes publicity, research and information.

LONDON ANTI-FLUORIDATION CAMPAIGN
36 Station Road, Thames Ditton, Surrey
Exists to preserve right of every individual to look after his own health and health of his children in ways he thinks best. Opposes addition of fluorides and other additives to public water for purpose of influencing development or functioning or human body (or mind). Membership: 12½p.

LONDON ENVIRONMENTAL ORGANISATION (LEO)
c/o Civic Trust, 18 Carlton House Terrace, London, S.W.1
Secretary: Mrs J. Kennish, 47 Thornhill Road, London, N.1
Tel. 01-607 1904
Promotes concept of London as a city for people to live in as well as work in and a higher standard of planning and architecture in the area of the Greater London Council. Instigates and co-ordinates action on common problems facing amenity societies within the area.

LONDON SOCIETY
3 Dean's Yard, London, S.W.1
Tel. 01-222 1562
Hon. Secretary: Miss E. Bright Ashford
Founded in 1912 to stimulate wider concern for beauty of capital city, for preservation of its charms and careful consideration of its development. Membership: £1·05.

MEN OF THE STONES
The Rutlands, Tinwell, Stamford, Lincolnshire, PE9 3VD
Tel. Stamford 3372
Secretary: A. S. Ireson
Stimulates public interest in architecture and good buildings. Advocates wider use of stone and other natural and local materials. Advises on preservation, repair, and use of period buildings and re-use of good stone and other materials; co-operates with government departments, local authorities and others. Membership: 50p.

MEN OF THE TREES
Crawley Down, Crawley, Sussex
Secretary: Mrs M. A. Blackburn
Campaigns for planting and preservation of trees, and stimulation of arboriculture through lectures and bi-annual conferences. Publishes journal *Trees* three times a year. Membership: Single or corporate £2·10p, married couple £3·15, student 50p.

NATIONAL ANGLERS' COUNCIL
17 Queen Street, Peterborough, PE1 1PJ
Tel. Peterborough 4084
Representative body for anglers. Seeks to improve status of anglers in negotiations with Government, to increase supply of water for angling and to protect
angling interests generally. Campaigns for conservation and against pollution.
Publishes quarterly *Newsletter*. Membership: Regional organisation £10 p.a.,
angling club £5 p.a., individual £1 p.a.

NATIONAL COAL BOARD OPENCAST EXECUTIVE
Coal House, Lyon Road, Harrow, Middlesex
Tel. 01-427 4333
Large-scale reclamation projects completed and planned. Undertakes trans-
planting of semi-mature trees for local and public authorities in certain circum-
stances.

NATIONAL FEDERATION OF COMMUNITY ASSOCIATIONS
26 Bedford Square, London, W.C.1
Tel: 01-636 4066
Central body for local community and residents' associations.

NATIONAL FEDERATION OF HOUSING SOCIETIES
12 Suffolk Street, Pall Mall, London, S.W.1
Tel. 01-930 1693

NATIONAL HOUSE-BUILDERS REGISTRATION COUNCIL
58 Portland Place, London, W.1
Tel. 01-387 7201
Seeks gradual improvement in housing standards and better understanding
between house-builders and purchasers. Issues certificates for houses built to
approved specifications.

NATIONAL HOUSING AND TOWN PLANNING COUNCIL
11, Green Street, London, W1Y 4ES
Tel. 01-629 7107
Secretary: A. H. Small
Campaigning for the general improvement and amelioration of the housing
conditions of the poorest classes of the public of the UK and to secure by all
possible means the abolition of unhealthly and undesirable housing conditions.
Publications: *Housing and Planning Review*, bi-monthly. Membership: Individual
minimum £2·10p and local authorities according to population, £2·10p minimum.

NATIONAL INDUSTRIAL MATERIALS RECOVERY ASSOCIATION
P.O. Box 8, 9 Sea Road, Bexhill-on-Sea, Sussex
Tel. Bexhill 5018/9
Secretary: A. W. V. Holden
Non-profit-making body run by industrialists to stimulate maximum recovery
and economical use of redundant or waste materials and by-products, to help
members find new uses for waste and surplus materials, and to provide an advisory service on recovery problems. Responsible for establishment of new
industries, such as waste oil recovery and re-use of rubber scrap, etc. Membership
for companies: £5.

NATIONAL MONUMENTS RECORD (ENGLAND)
Fielden House, 10 Great College Street, London, S.W.1
Tel. 01-930 6554
Compiles and maintains for public reference a complete record of English architecture.

NATIONAL MONUMENTS RECORD OF SCOTLAND
52/54 Melville Street, Edinburgh 3
Tel. 031-225 5994/5

NATIONAL MONUMENTS RECORD OF WALES
Summit House, Windsor Place, Cardiff

NATIONAL PLAYING FIELDS ASSOCIATION
57B Catherine Place, London, SW1E 6EY
Tel. 01-834 9274 and 8151
Secretary: Major-General Sir John Nelson
Encourages provision of recreational facilities for all age groups, with particular attention to needs of village communities. Provides technical advice and information, and carries out research on planning, design and construction of indoor and outdoor sporting facilities. Specialises in recreation for children and young people, and seeks provision of playgrounds for all from 2½ to 20 years and appointment of playleaders. Raises funds and makes grants and loans. Publishes pamphlets; list on application.

NATIONAL RURAL AND ENVIRONMENTAL STUDIES ASSOCIATION
County Hall, Cauldwell Street, Bedford
Tel. 0234-63222
General Secretary: D. G. Alexander
Professional body for teachers and others interested in rural environmental studies in schools. Co-ordinates work of county associations. Holds annual conference, conducts research, prepares syllabuses, provides information. Publishes annual journal and series of information leaflets. Membership: Individual 52½p or through country associations at 30p per member.

NATIONAL SOCIETY FOR CLEAN AIR
134–137 North Street, Brighton, BN1 1RG
Tel. Brighton 26313
Director: Rear-Admiral P. G. Sharp
Promotes recognition of importance of clean air and informed public opinion. Pioneered systematic study and measurement of air pollution, from which has developed national survey under Government auspices. Initiated testing of domestic fuel appliances and sponsored first classes for boilerhouse operators. Conceived idea of smokeless zone (now smoke control areas). Publications: *Clean Air Year Book, Smokeless Air* (quarterly), annual conference proceedings and other booklets. Membership: Individual £3, local authorities according to population (minimum £10).

NATIONAL TRUST
42 Queen Anne's Gate, London, S.W.1
Tel. 01-930 0211
Secretary: J. D. Boles
Two separate independent charities covering England, Wales and Northern

Ireland (founded 1895) and Scotland (1931). Preserves and protects historic buildings and open countryside of natural beauty through ownership or protective covenants; nearly 500,000 acres in all, including more than 100 miles of coastline, to much of which public has access (publishes lists of properties). Promoted 'Enterprise Neptune'. Publications include: *The Continuing Purpose*, *The What to See Atlas* and *The National Trust*. Dependent on voluntary support – donations, legacies and members' subscriptions. Membership: Individual £2, family £3 (two members).

NATIONAL TRUST FOR SCOTLAND

5 Charlotte Square, Edinburgh, EH2 4DU
Tel. 031-225 2184
Secretary: J. C. Stormonth Darling
Founded in 1931 to protect and care for fine buildings and beautiful scenery. Has some 60 properties and over 80,000 acres in its care. Publishes *Newsletter*. Membership: Individual £2, family £3, junior 50p, corporate £5·25.

NATURE CONSERVANCY

19/20 Belgrave Square, London, SW1X 8PY
Tel. 01-235 3241
Director: Dr M. E. D. Poore
Official body established by Royal Charter in 1965 to advise on nature conservation, to establish and manage nature reserves and to carry out research under the aegis of the Natural Environment Research Council. From 1949–65 Conservancy was separate research council. Publishes scientific monographs, reports and leaflets. Not open to public.

NOISE ABATEMENT SOCIETY

6 Old Bond Street, London, W.1
Tel. 01-493 5877
Hon. Secretary: Miss T. Adler
Aims at elimination of excessive and unnecessary noise. Contributed to Noise Abatement Act, Wilson Committee on Problems of Noise, Vehicle Noise Regulations, Noise Advisory Council, Foulness Airport campaign; advocates noise torch and garage noise testing stations. Publications: *Law on Noise*, *Feasibility Study on Third London Airport*, monthly *Noise News Digest* and periodical *Quiet Please*. Membership: Organisations £5·25, individuals £1·05.

PEDESTRIANS' ASSOCIATION FOR ROAD SAFETY

4 College Hill, Cannon Street, London, EC4R 2RQ
Tel. 01-248 5116
Secretary: Mrs Marjorie Gray
Promotes safety of walking public; protects and preserves their rights and amenities, and seeks to make roads safe for all users. Spearheaded campaign to have driving tests made obligatory, for speed limits in urban areas and for pedestrian crossings. Initiated public opposition to proposal for 44- and 56-ton lorries. Studying measures to protect environment from effects of road traffic. Publications: Journal, *Arrive*, three times a year, *A Pedestrians' Bill of Rights* and *The Lorry and the Community*. Membership £2.

RAMBLERS' ASSOCIATION
1/4 Crawford Mews, York Street, London, W1H 1PT
Tel. 01-262-1477
Secretary: Christopher Hall
Aims to protect interests of ramblers and maintain their rights and privileges. Fosters greater knowledge, love and care of countryside and works for preservation of natural beauty. Publications: *Rucksack*, quarterly, and other booklets.

REDUNDANT CHURCHES FUND
St. Andrew by the Wardrobe, Queen Victoria Street, London, E.C.4
Tel. 01-248-3420
Secretary: John H. Bowles
Established in 1969 by Parliament and Church Assembly to own and maintain churches of architectural or historic interest no longer required for worship.

REGIONAL STUDIES ASSOCIATION
Newcombe House, 45 Notting Hill Gate, London, W.11
Tel. 01-727-8252
Hon. Secretary: Miss Irene Foster
Provides forum for exchange of ideas and information on regional problems. Stimulates studies and research in Great Britain in regional planning and related fields. Organises seminars, study groups and conferences. Publishes *Regional Studies*, quarterly, and *News Letter*. Membership: Individual £5 p.a., student £2·50, corporate £30.

RIVER THAMES SOCIETY
2 Ruskin Avenue, Kew, Surrey
Tel. 01-876-1520
General Secretary: J. Watson Parton
Dedicated to safeguarding interests of those who boat on Thames, drive to it, fish in it, walk along it, camp near it or live close to it, and to preserving all that is beautiful, desirable and unique in the river. Publishes *The Thamesman* (five times a year), and *The Thames Book*. Membership: £1 p.a.

ROYAL COMMISSION ON ENVIRONMENTAL POLLUTION
Great George Street, London, S.W.1
Tel. 01-930-3324/6
Secretary: Miss D. M. Wilde, MA
Advises on national and international pollution problems; on the adequacy of research in this field and future possibilities of danger to environment. Currently investigating pollution of tidal waters, estuaries and coastal waters. First report (Cmnd 4585) published by HMSO in February, 1971. Members appointed by Royal Warrant.

ROYAL COMMISSION ON ANCIENT MONUMENTS IN WALES AND MONMOUTHSHIRE
Edleston House, Queen's Road, Aberystwyth
Tel. 0970-2256

ROYAL COMMISSION ON ANCIENT AND HISTORICAL MONUMENTS OF SCOTLAND
54 Melville Street, Edinburgh, EH3 7HF
Tel. 031-225-5994
Secretary: Dr K. A. Steer

Responsible for compiling and publishing detailed records of ancient and historical monuments in Scotland. National Monuments Record of Scotland, branch of Commission and housed in same premises, contains extensive collection of photographs, drawings, printed books, etc., which may be consulted by public. Publishes county inventories of ancient and historical monuments.

ROYAL FINE ART COMMISSION
2 Carlton Gardens, London, S.W.1
Tel. 01-930-3935
Consultative body with responsibility for advising Government departments on matters of public amenity or artistic importance, and drawing attention to projects likely to affect amenities.

ROYAL FINE ART COMMISSION FOR SCOTLAND
22 Melville Street, Edinburgh 3
Tel. 031-225-5434

ROYAL COMMISSION ON HISTORICAL MONUMENTS (ENGLAND)
Fielden House, Great College Street, London, S.W.1
Tel. 01-930-6554
Records all buildings and earthworks from before 1850 and publishes results, area by area.

ROYAL FORESTRY SOCIETY OF ENGLAND, WALES AND NORTHERN IRELAND
102 High Street, Tring, Hertfordshire
Tel. 0442-82-2028
Secretary: P. S. Leathart
Encourages good management of private woodlands and enlightened conservation of country's tree heritage. Holds outdoor meetings in woodlands and arboreta at home and abroad, and indoor meetings in winter. Publishes quarterly *Journal of Forestry*. Membership open to all, from 75p to £5·25.

ROYAL SCOTTISH FORESTRY SOCIETY
26 Rutland Square, Edinburgh, EH1 2BU
Tel. 031-229-3651
Secretary: W. B. C. Walker
Oldest constituted society in English-speaking world for the advancement of forestry. Played important role in formation of national forest policy. Encourages planting of trees by private landowners and public bodies alike, and brings together all engaged in expanding forest industry and lovers of Scottish countryside. Publishes quarterly journal, *Scottish Forestry*. Membership: From 75p to £5.

ROYAL SOCIETY FOR THE PROTECTION OF BIRDS
The Lodge, Sandy, Bedfordshire
Tel. Sandy 551
Director: P. J. Conder
Seeks to protect Britain's wild birds in changing environment. Maintains 40 reserves, helps enforce bird protection laws and collects information to fight pollution on land and sea at national and international level. Opening nature centres where trained staff can introduce urban children to nature conservation. Publications: Journal, *Birds*, six times a year, and *Farming and Wildlife*. Membership: Fellow £4, member £2, junior £1.

RURAL INDUSTRIES BUREAU
35 Camp Road, Wimbledon Common, London, S.W.19
Tel. 01-946-5101
Aims to develop economic prosperity of small firms in rural areas.

SALTIRE SOCIETY
Gladstone's Land, 483 Lawnmarket, Edinburgh 1
Tel. 031-225-7780
Seeks to preserve best in Scottish cultural traditions and to encourage new developments.

SCOTTISH CIVIC TRUST
24 George Square, Glasgow, C.2
Tel. 041-221-1466/7
Director: Maurice Lindsay
Aims as Civic Trust. Arranged survey and international conference resulting in setting up of Edinburgh New Town Conservation Committee. Campaigns: Biggar Street Improvement Scheme; Highland Village Project 1970 (with Crofters Commission): Survey of Park Circus Area, Glasgow (with Glasgow Institute of Architects). Currently engaged in 'Facelift Glasgow', aimed at involving every firm and individual in city improvement drive. Publishes journal *Environment Scotland* and *Environment a Basic Human Right*. Membership through local civic or amenity society.

SCOTTISH COUNCIL OF PHYSICAL RECREATION
4 Queensferry Street, Edinburgh 2
Tel. 031-225-3117

SCOTTISH FIELD STUDIES ASSOCIATION
141 Bath Street, Glasgow, C.2
Tel. 041-248-3889

SCOTTISH GEORGIAN SOCIETY
41 Castle Street, Edinburgh, EH2 3BH
Tel. 031-225-8391
Secretary: Mrs Margaret Gilfillan
Founded in 1956 for study and protection of Scottish architecture after 1600. Submits evidence to planning inquiries but aims at catching cases at earlier stage. Provided source materials for *Scottish Architectural History* by John Dunbar, 1969. Membership: Individual £2, family £3, patron £4, student 50p.

SCOTTISH NATIONAL HOUSING AND TOWN PLANNING COUNCIL
Town Clerk's Office, Monkdyke, Alexandra Drive, Renfrew, Renfrewshire
Tel. 041-886-2387
Hon. Secretary: Hugh D. M. McCutchem
Seeks support of local authorities and others in securing adequate provision of houses and good standards of design and layout in Scotland. Represents Scottish opinion to governments on housing and town planning questions. Arranges conferences. Membership: Individuals £2, organisations £3 and local authorities from £4.

SCOTTISH RIGHTS OF WAY SOCIETY LTD
Registered Office: 32 Rutland Square, Edinburgh 1
Hon. Secretary's address: 6 Abercromby Place, Edinburgh 3
Tel. 031-556-3942
Hon. Secretary: D. H. McPherson
Campaigns for preservation, defence, and acquisition of public rights of way in
Scotland by recording on maps and signposting. Publications: *A Walker's Guide
to the Law of Right of Way in Scotland* and *The Cairngorm Passes*. Membership:
Ordinary 50p, corporate £1.

SCOTTISH SOCIETY FOR INDUSTRIAL ARCHAEOLOGY
c/o Department of Economic History, University of Strathclyde, Glasgow, C.1
Secretary: Dr J. Butt
Studies and records industrial buildings. Arranges field excursions and conferences. Publishes *Newsletter*. Membership: 50p.

SCOTTISH WILDLIFE TRUST
8 Dublin Street, Edinburgh, EM1 3PP
Tel. 031-556-4199
Secretary: Bernard Gilchrist
Seeks conservation of wildlife – plants, animals and birds – together with habitats. Ten regional branches. Creates reserves, provides advice and promotes
better understanding of countryside problems. Publishes booklets on reserves,
nature trail pamphlets and list of films. Membership: £1, juniors 50p.

SCOTTISH YOUTH HOSTELS ASSOCIATION
7 Glebe Crescent, Stirling
Tel. 0786-2821

SHELTER
86 The Strand, London, WC2R 0EQ
Tel. 01-836-2051
Director: John Willis
National Campaign for the Homeless. Launched in December, 1966, when it
brought together five major national bodies in voluntary housing movement.
Highly successful in publicising plight of families living in distressing housing
conditions and in raising money for relief of such conditions. Has concentrated
on 'rescue operation' for homeless in blackspot cities of London, Birmingham,
Liverpool and Glasgow. More than £2 million raised and over 3,000 families
rehoused throughout country. Has organised neighbourhood action project in
Liverpool and runs housing aid centre jointly with Catholic Housing Aid
Society. Publishes bulletin, campaign pamphlets, leaflets, etc. Membership by
donation.

SOCIETY FOR ENVIRONMENTAL EDUCATION
16 Trinity Road, Enderby, Leicester, LE9 5BU
Tel. 053-729-4396
Secretary: G. C. Martin
Provides opportunities for discussion and interchange of ideas on role of environment in education. Arranges conferences, courses and meetings, and distributes bulletin, newsletter and occasional papers. Membership: Individual £1,
corporate £2, student 50p.

SOCIETY FOR THE PROMOTION OF NATURE RESERVES
The Manor House, Alford, Lincolnshire
Tel. Alford 2444
Hon. Secretary: A. E. Smith
Collates information on areas in UK or elsewhere in Commonwealth suitable for development as nature reserves and prepares schemes. Represents 60,000 members of county trusts for nature conservation at national level. Publications: *Conservation Review, Conservation Code Handbook* and technical booklets. Donation or subscription of not less than £1 entitles member to free copy of annual handbook.

SOCIETY FOR THE PROTECTION OF ANCIENT BUILDINGS
55 Great Ormond Street, London, WC1N 3JA
Tel. 01-405-2646 and 01-405-4541
Secretary: Mrs Monica Dance
Founded in 1877 by William Morris to preserve irreplaceable ancient buildings, ecclesiastical and secular. Advises on repair and treatment of old buildings. Prepares surveys and reports on historic areas of cities, towns and villages and gives advice. Publishes information on history and care of old buildings, their features and fittings. Membership: £2·10p, junior 52½p.

SOCIETY OF ARCHITECTURAL HISTORIANS OF GREAT BRITAIN
Deneholme, Clayton Road, Newcastle upon Tyne 2

SOIL ASSOCIATION
Walnut Tree Manor, Haughley, Stowmarket, Suffolk, IP14 3RS
Tel. Haughley 235
Secretary: Brig. A. W. Vickers
Explores vital relationship between soil, plant, animal and man. Undertakes and assists relevant research, keeps public informed of developments. Maintains experimental farms. Publishes *Journal of the Soil Association* (quarterly) and *SPAN* (monthly). Membership: £3 and £1 for retired people and students under 25.

SPORTS COUNCIL
4 Richmond Terrace, London, S.W.1
Tel. 01-839-6371
Consultative body advising Government on development of amateur sport and physical recreation services and fostering co-operation among statutory authorities and voluntary organisations.

SURVIVAL
19 Carleton Road, London, N.7
Tel. 01-609-1819
Secretary: Mrs D. Hayward
Formed in January, 1971, to campaign for most urgently needed legislation which would substantially contribute to solution of over-population and pollution through meetings and study groups. Assesses policies of conservation societies and political parties with view to establishing merit and priority. Full membership: £1, associate 25p.

TOWN AND COUNTRY PLANNING ASSOCIATION
17 Carlton House Terrace, London, SW1Y 5AS
Tel. 01-930-8903/4/5
Director and Secretary: David Hall
Advocates and promotes understanding of national and regional planning policies to improve living and working conditions, safeguard best countryside and farmland, enhance natural, architectural and cultural amenities, and advance economic efficiency. Provides environmental education service for schools and colleges. Publishes *Town and Country Planning, A Planning Bulletin, Bulletin of Environmental Education,* and many other books and pamphlets, especially on new towns. Membership: Personal £5, corporate £7·50, local authority from £8.

ULSTER SOCIETY FOR THE PRESERVATION OF THE COUNTRYSIDE
West Winds, Carney Hill, Holywood, Co. Down
Tel. Holywood 2300
Hon. Secretary: Wilfrid M. Capper
Aims to safeguard the amenities of Northern Ireland and to do everything possible to preserve and enhance its beauty for our own and future generations.

UNIVERSITIES FEDERATION FOR ANIMAL WELFARE
230 High Street, Potters Bar, Hertfordshire
Tel. Potters Bar 58202
Secretary: Mrs C. Brockhurst
Investigates conditions under which animals may suffer. Research has been carried out on problems associated with seals. laying hens, sheep, goats and monkeys. The welfare of farm livestock, the transport of animals and the slaughter of food animals have all been studied and recommendations have been made. Publishes *Handbook on the Care and Management of Laboratory Animals* and *The Care and Management of Farm Animals.* Membership: University graduates and Associate members £1 p.a.

VICTORIAN SOCIETY
12 Magnolia Wharf, Strand on the Green, London, W.4
Tel. 01-994-1510
Secretary: Mrs Edward Fawcett
Seeks to improve understanding of, and preserve, the best of Victorian and Edwardian architecture, design, crafts and decoration.

WATER POLLUTION RESEARCH LABORATORY
Elder Way, Stevenage, Hertfordshire, SG1 1TH
Tel: Stevenage 2444
Director: Dr A. L. Downing
Investigates effects of pollution of natural waters and methods for its control. Currently studying effects of pollution on freshwater streams and estuaries; dispersion of sewage from sea outfalls; toxicity of substances to fish; methods of treatment of sewage and industrial waste waters; disposal of sludges; polishing of sewage effluents and reclamation of water; development of monitoring instruments. Controlled by Department of the Environment. Publishes annual report, technical papers and *Notes on Water Pollution.*

WEST WALES NATURALISTS' TRUST LTD
4 Victoria Place, Haverfordwest
Tel. Haverfordwest 2341
Secretary: Dillwyn Miles
Aims to secure and protect places of natural beauty and special interest as habitats of animals and plants; to protect wild plant and animal life; to promote and encourage research in all aspects of nature study and in natural sciences. Administers nature reserves. Publishes journal, *Nature in Wales*, and various handbooks.
Membership: Fellow £2, member £1·05, associate 50p.

WILDLIFE YOUTH SERVICE
Marston Court, Manor Road, Wallington, Surrey
Tel. 01-669-4995
Director Cyril Littlewood, MBE
The education service of the World Wildlife Fund. Encourages children and young people of school age (up to 18), to take a more active interest in conservation. Publications: *Animals Magazine* and *WYS Newsletter*. Membership: Individual £1.25, Associate (for Panda Club members 5-11) 15p., Wildlife Rangers 11-18, 25p.

WORLD WILDLIFE FUND
7/8 Plumtree Court, London, E.C.4
Tel. 01-353-2615
Administrator: Arnold Thorne
Launched in 1961 to assist in conservation of wildlife and wild places in Britain and throughout the world. Over 500 projects for conservation approved by Fund and over £2 million raised. Publications: *World Wildlife News* (UK), *Annual Yearbook* (international). Membership through AID (Animals in Danger), Wildlife Rangers (11–18), Panda Club (5–10) and Field Rangers.

YOUTH HOSTELS ASSOCIATION (ENGLAND AND WALES)
Trevelyan House, St Albans, Hertfordshire
Tel. 56-55215

YOUTH HOSTELS ASSOCIATION OF NORTHERN IRELAND
Bryson House, 28 Bedford Street, Belfast 2
Tel. 0232-24733

25. Journals and Films

GENERAL PERIODICALS

Environment, monthly, 17 Ridgmont Road, Bramhall. Cheshire.
Ecologist, monthly, 73 Kew Green, Richmond, Surrey.
Environment and Industry, monthly, Current Publications, Longwood, Maidenhead Court Park, Maidenhead, Berks.

Pollution Control, monthly, controlled circulation, Factory Publication Ltd., Hermes House, Blackfriars Road, London, S.E.1.

Pollution Monitor, bi-monthly, Terminus Publications Ltd., Speedway House, Quarry Hill, Parade, Tonbridge, Kent.

SPECIAL PERIODICALS

Smokeless Air, National Society for Clean Air.
Quiet Please, Noise Abatement Society.
Arrive, Pedestrians Association for Road Safety.
Rucksack, Ramblers' Association.
Regional Studies, Regional Studies Association.
Town and Country Planning, Town and Country Planning Association.
Bulletin of Environmental Education, Town and Country Planning Association.
Journal of Forestry, Royal Forestry Society of England.
Scottish Forestry, Royal Scottish Forestry Society.
Birds, Royal Society for the Protection of Birds.
Conservation Review, Society for the Promotion of Nature Reserves.
Journal of the Soil Association and *Span*, Soil Association.
Water Pollution Control, Institute of Water Pollution Control, 49-55 Victoria Street, London, SW1.
Water and Water Treatment, DR Publications Ltd, 103 Brigstock Road, Thornton Heath, Surrey.
World Wildlife News (*UK*), World Wildlife Fund.

FILMS

Compiled with the assistance of Michael Kendall, of the BBC Natural History Unit. The following bodies have films available on conservation and pollution . . .

Anglers' Co-operative Association; Beehive Films; British Antarctic Survey; British Film Institute; British Transport Films; Czechoslovak Embassy, London; Cedok, London; Centrala Wynajmu Filmow, c/o Polish Cultural Institute, London; The Civic Trust, London; Columbia Pictures; Commonwealth Scientific Research Organisation; Concord Films; Contemporary Films Ltd; Countryman Films Ltd; Council for Nature; Countryside Commission; Danish Embassy, London; Educational and Television Films Ltd; Fauna Preservation Society; Forestry Commission; Gateway Films; Global Television Services Ltd; Golden Era Film Distributors; Granada Television; High Commission of India, London; Hungarofilm, Hungary; Icelandic Embassy, London; Independent Artists; Information Service of India, London; Institut Francais du Royaume-Uni, London; Institute of Animal Genetics; Institute of Oceanography; International Society for the Protection of Animals; Irish Tourist Board; Japan National Tourist Organisation; Kenya High Commission, London; McGraw-Hill Publishing Co. Ltd; MacQueen Film Organisation Ltd; Ministry of Agriculture, Fisheries and Food; National Film Board of Canada; National Film Library, Dublin; National Trust; Nature Conservancy; New Zealand National Film Unit; Norwegian State Railways; Plymouth Films Ltd; H. J. Pollock, c/o

Global TV Services Ltd; Royal Society for the Protection of Birds; R.S.P.C.A. Film Library; Saffron Films; Sand and Gravel Association; Union of South Africa State Information Office; Scottish National Trust; Sovexportfilm, Russia; Swedish Institute for Cultural Relations, London; Time/Life TV Features; Town and Country Productions Ltd; Universities Federation for Animal Welfare; Unilever Film Library; United States Atomic Energy Commission; United States Information Service; U.S. Navy; Visnews; Walt Disney Productions Ltd., London; Western Australian Government Office, London; Whitbread & Co. Ltd; Yugoslavija-Film, Yugoslavia.

Index

167

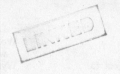